# Social Interaction in Second Language Chat Rooms

# Social Interaction in Second Language Chat Rooms

Christopher J. Jenks

EDINBURGH
University Press

Edinburgh University Press Ltd
The Tun – Holyrood Road
12 (2f) Jackson's Entry
Edinburgh EH8 8PJ
www.euppublishing.com

Typeset in 10/12 Minion by
Servis Filmsetting Ltd, Stockport, Cheshire,
printed and bound in Great Britain by
CPI Group (UK) Ltd, Croydon CR0 4YY

A CIP record for this book is available from the British Library

ISBN 978 0 7486 4949 5 (hardback)
ISBN 978 0 7486 4948 8 (paperback)
ISBN 978 0 7486 4950 1 (webready PDF)
ISBN 978 0 7486 9349 8 (epub)

# CONTENTS

Acknowledgements      viii

1    Introduction to the Book      1
    1.1   Introduction      1
    1.2   Book Contents      2

SURVEY

2    Social Interaction and Chat Rooms      7
    2.1   Introduction      7
    2.2   Social Interaction      7
       2.2.1   Conversation Analysis      10
    2.3   Chat Rooms      12
       2.3.1   Online Communication      14
          2.3.1.1   Computer Networks      14
          2.3.1.2   Computer-mediated Spoken Interaction      16

3    CMC and Applied Linguistics      17
    3.1   Introduction      17
    3.2   CMC and Applied Linguistics      18
       3.2.1   Teaching and Learning      19
       3.2.2   Language and Discourse      22
       3.2.3   Sociality and Culture      25
       3.2.4   CMSI Studies      28
    3.3   Conclusion      32

4    Introduction to CMSI      34
    4.1   Introduction      34
    4.2   CMSI Platforms      36
       4.2.1   Voice over Internet Protocol      37
          4.2.1.1   Skype      37
          4.2.1.2   Skypecasts      39
    4.3   Key Technological and Contextual Features of CMSI      42
    4.4   Transcription Conventions      45
    4.5   The Study and Data Set      47

ANALYSIS
5 Talking Online: CMSI Features   51
   5.1   Introduction   51
   5.2   Turn-taking   52
      5.2.1   Turn Construction and Transition   52
      5.2.2   Overlapping Utterances   55
      5.2.3   Turn Allocation   59
   5.3   Summons–answer Exchanges   64
   5.4   Identification Practices   67
   5.5   Discussion and Conclusion   73

6 Turn-taking in Chat Rooms: Texting versus Talking   76
   6.1   Introduction   76
   6.2   Turn-taking   78
      6.2.1   Turn Construction and Transition   78
      6.2.2   Overlapping Utterances   82
      6.2.3   Turn Allocation   89
   6.3   Discussion and Conclusion   93

7 Contextual Variables in CMSI   95
   7.1   Introduction   95
   7.2   Background Noises   96
   7.3   Online Presence   101
   7.4   Pauses   106
   7.5   Ongoing Talk   110
   7.6   Audibility   114
   7.7   Discussion and Conclusion   118

APPLICATION
8 Teaching and Learning   123
   8.1   Introduction   123
   8.2   Second Language Acquisition   124
      8.2.1   Interactional Competence   126
         8.2.1.1   CMSI-based Tasks   130
   8.3   Discussion and Conclusion   135

9 Social and Cultural Issues   136
   9.1   Introduction   136
   9.2   English as a Lingua Franca   137
      9.2.1   Norms and Conventions   138
      9.2.2   Language Identities   146
   9.3   Discussion and Conclusion   151

10 Discussion and Conclusion   154
   10.1   Introduction   154

10.2    Research Ethics                            157
10.3    Future Directions                          158

References                                         161
Index                                              175

# ACKNOWLEDGMENTS

I would like to thank my wife and daughter for their support and understanding during the writing of this book. I am indebted to Steve Walsh and Paul Seedhouse who have provided excellent editorial assistance throughout the entire process. Special thanks must also be given to the editors and reviewers of Edinburgh University Press.

# INTRODUCTION TO THE BOOK

## 1.1 INTRODUCTION

This book investigates second language chat rooms from a social-interaction perspective. More specifically, it examines how speakers of English as an additional language manage their voice-based interactions in chat rooms. As such, this book contributes to the body of work known as computer-mediated communication (CMC). The study of CMC is concerned with examining the social, interactional, and linguistic effects of technology (Herring 2004; Thurlow *et al.* 2004). The present study examines the interactional effects of technology (see Chapters 5–7), and later explores the social and linguistic implications of communicating in second language chat rooms (see Chapters 8–10).

Although second language chat rooms have been investigated somewhat extensively in the CMC literature, comparatively little work has adopted a social-interaction perspective (for a review of CMC studies, see Chapter 3). This is noteworthy, as a social-interaction perspective is able to provide an account of CMC which is detailed in its treatment of discourse and revelatory in the social actions accomplished in, and through, talk and interaction (for a discussion of what a social-interaction perspective is, see Chapter 2).

It should also be noted that this book does not examine what can be called the prototypical chat room (for a description of the data collected for this study, see Section 4.5). That is to say, nearly all of the chat rooms investigated in the CMC literature are text-based (e.g. Negretti 1999; Simpson 2005; Smith 2008). Conversely, the present study examines voice-based chat rooms. The interactions that take place in voice-based chat rooms are referred to in this book as online spoken communication (this term is used interchangeably with "computer-mediated spoken interaction"; see Section 2.3.1.2). Voice-based interactions represent a small, but growing area of study in the CMC literature (see Section 3.2.4). This book builds on this body of CMC work by using a social-interaction perspective to uncover the sequential, interactional, and social organization of online spoken communication.

Before discussing what a social-interaction perspective is, it is worth mentioning that a book on CMC, electronic-mediated communication (see Baron 2008a), computer-mediated discourse (see Herring 2004), or whatever term that is in current fashion or application, is both timely and outdated. A book on CMC is timely in that societies are increasingly reliant on hyper-connectivity and technology-driven communication. Immigration and migration has, in part, increased the need to communicate across many time zones and nation states (Taran and Geronimi 2003), while younger generations are effectively socialized into a world of digital communication and media (Buckingham and Willett 2006). Studying these societal trends is important to the development of the social sciences in general, and CMC in particular.

However, a book on CMC is, and will always be, outdated in that technologies advance at a much faster rate than the time it takes for a book to be written and put through the rigors of peer-review publication. An observation made in one year will likely be outdated, technologically speaking, the following year. While researchers can predict future trends and applications, CMC applications are constantly evolving and shifting. Yet this does not mean that technological changes and advancements make older CMC studies obsolete, nor do these changes and advancements take away from the empirical utility and validity of past and ongoing investigations of online communication. CMC researchers have a professional obligation to document and understand current communication trends, build on previous observations and findings, and identify and suggest ways to advance their area of study.

This book does precisely that: it begins with a literature review of CMC (see Chapter 3), provides data-driven, transcript-based observations of online spoken communication (see Chapters 5–7), applies these findings to issues related to language teaching and lingua franca encounters (see Chapters 8–9), and ends with suggestions for future research (see Chapter 10). The book has been written for applied linguists, but readers with an interest in CMC that come from education, communication, linguistic anthropology, and sociology will also find this book useful.

## 1.2  BOOK CONTENTS

The book is divided into three sections: survey, analysis, and application. Each section comprises three chapters. The survey section reviews key concepts, terminology, and the state of CMC research (Chapters 2–4). The analysis section provides data-driven observations of CMSI (Chapters 5–7). The application section applies an understanding of CMSI to language teaching, lingua franca interactions, and CMC research ethics and future directions (Chapters 8–10).

The chapters that make up the survey section are Chapters 2 to 4. Chapter 2 introduces the social-interaction approach used in this book and provides technical descriptions of chat room and online communication. Chapter 3 discusses the CMC literature as three overlapping empirical strands: teaching and learning, language and discourse, and sociality and culture. The aim of this chapter is to identify research themes and gaps. Chapter 4 introduces CMSI, the object of study in this book. The chapter begins with a general discussion of CMC, and then introduces the CMSI platform examined in the present study. This chapter provides important technological and contextual information regarding CMSI. Chapter 4 also identifies the transcription conventions adopted in the book and introduces the data set used to carry out the study.

The chapters that constitute the analysis section are Chapters 5 to 7. In Chapter 5, a conversation analytic account of CMSI is provided. Using detailed transcripts of

CMSI, readers are provided with an understanding of how interactants manage online spoken communication in the absence of physical co-presence. Topics include turn-taking, summons-answer exchanges, and identification practices. Chapter 6 identifies the interactional similarities and differences between text-based CMC and CMSI. In so doing, Chapter 6 builds on the analytic observations made in Chapter 5. Example topics include turn transition, overlapping utterances, and turn allocation.

Chapter 7 examines how several contextual variables shape the management of CMSI. The aim of this chapter is to show how CMSI participants deal with contextual issues and circumstances that are unique to speaking online. This chapter builds on the findings established in Chapters 5 and 6. The five contextual variables examined are background noise, online presence, ongoing talk, pauses, and audibility. As with the two previous analytic chapters, the analyses conducted in Chapter 7 are based on detailed transcripts of CMSI.

The chapters that make up the application section are Chapters 8 to 10. Chapters 8 and 9 apply an understanding of CMSI to key issues and themes in applied linguistics research. Chapter 8 contributes specifically to the teaching and learning strand of CMC research by applying an understanding of CMSI to second language acquisition and task-based learning. The issues that are examined in this chapter are interactional competence and task design. Chapter 9 builds on the sociality and culture strand of CMC research by applying an understanding of CMSI to lingua franca interactions. The issues that are examined in this chapter are communicative norms and conventions and language identities.

Chapter 10 closes the book by summarizing key findings and themes. This chapter also discusses research ethics as they pertain specifically to the study of CMSI. The chapter ends by examining the future of CMSI research.

# SURVEY

# SOCIAL INTERACTION AND CHAT ROOMS

## 2.1 INTRODUCTION

This chapter reviews two concepts that are fundamental to the investigation conducted in this book: social interaction and chat rooms. This is done by first identifying and explicating what is meant by, and included in, a social-interaction perspective. This section also introduces the conversation analytic methodology used in this book. The chapter then discusses the importance of chat rooms in relation to technology and society. This section also provides technical descriptions of chat room and online communication. The chapter ends with a brief discussion of the investigation's object of study.

## 2.2 SOCIAL INTERACTION

Social interaction, which often includes, but does not require, spoken words and utterances, is the primary means by which the process of socialization occurs. Social interaction makes it possible to inform, contest, create, ratify, refute, and ascribe, among other things, power, class, gender, ethnicity, and culture. Furthermore, social interaction is the means by which people perform a range social actions and activities, from learning a first language to managing a multinational company. In other words, social interaction is the primordial site of sociality (Schegloff 1986). Accordingly, social structures—for example, the communicative norms of a business negotiation, taking turns in a classroom, the cultural identity of a Korean, or power relations between employee and employer—exist because of social interaction. What this means is that social structures are not external to human interactions (for a classic, alternative view of how social structures shape human conduct, see Parsons 1937). Rather, social structures are derived from the contact that people have with others. To extend this observation further, the knowledge and commonsense practices that people have and use in order to, for example, understand who they are, what is right and wrong, and how to communicate in certain contexts, are shaped in, and through, social interaction. The idea that talk and interaction is central to the organization of social actions and structures is a central conversation analytic principle, the primary methodology adopted in this book.

The understanding of social interaction presented above contains several methodological implications for the study of human conduct (for a detailed account of these implications, see ten Have 2007; Hutchby and Wooffitt 2008), though only two are germane to the present introductory discussion: analyzing and transcribing data. First, studies that investigate human conduct according to the definition of social interaction outlined above do not formulate exogenous theories and hypotheses. That is, analytic observations and findings are based on the social practices and actions that interactants carry out and perform *in situ*. This approach is commonly referred to as data-driven, inductive, or bottom-up. Theories, hypotheses, and generalizations, if needed at all, are based on, and situated within, talk and interaction.

Consequently, examining online communication through a social-interaction lens requires researchers to show how their analytic descriptions are relevant for the interactants under investigation (for an account of how conversation analysts address the issue of relevance, see Schegloff 1991: 49). The aim is to formulate analytic observations according to what is relevant for the interactants under investigation, rather than to seek out episodes of social interactions that best suit a particular theory or hypothesis. The methodological issue of relevance stems from the understanding that contexts are shaped and reshaped as social interaction unfolds. An observation based on a researcher's *a priori* understanding of a context, however similar to the object of study, is potentially alien to the social practices and actions that take place during the turn-by-turn moments of communication.

Second, social-interaction studies, and especially those informed by conversation analytic principles, approach the task of transcribing communication data according to the belief that no detail of talk and interaction should be taken for granted. All aspects of talk and interaction—however ostensibly mundane—are potentially relevant to an understanding of how people manage social interactions. In methodological terms, this means that recordings of communication data are meticulously transcribed and given the same amount of attention in their representation as the analysis of social interaction (Jenks 2011). The importance placed on transcription detail comes from belief that social interactions, as captured in data recordings and presented in written form, provide an empirical window into how interactants co-construct an understanding of the world around them. Transcripts devoid of such detail provide a smaller empirical window to examine social interaction.

The notion that researchers should abandon their preconceptions of what is and what is not important in data recordings is referred to as unmotivated looking (Hutchby and Wooffitt 2008). Unmotivated looking is associated with inductive, bottom-up approaches to social interaction. For example, transcripts that are based on unmotivated looking are used in conversation analytic and ethnomethodological studies (Garfinkel 1967; ten Have 2007). Liddicoat states that unmotivated looking is

> a process of listening to the data and/or reading through the transcribed text to obtain a feel for the data. This is a process of immersing oneself in the data in order to see what is happening in it. It is a way of letting the data speak to the researcher rather than having the researcher impose an interpretation on the data. (Liddicoat 2011: 70)

In theory, unmotivated looking is intuitively appealing. It promotes the idea that transcripts should be highly detailed and devoid of preconceptions and biases. In practice, however, all studies of social interaction are shaped by theoretical and methodological principles, and constrained by available time and resources. Paradoxical as unmotivated looking may seem, the true utility in this approach or idea lies in its understanding of, and importance placed on, social interaction as a site of investigation. Unmotivated looking, as the above quote suggests, is about embracing the complexities involved in, and the nuances associated with, social interaction. Unmotivated looking requires subscribing to the belief that these complexities and nuances offer a rich understanding of human conduct.

For a study of second language chat rooms, this means capturing and representing online spoken communication so that little interactional detail is lost during data collection and transcription (for a discussion of the practicalities of producing highly detailed transcripts, see Jenks 2011). Again, the underpinning belief is that all aspects of social interaction are potentially relevant to an understanding of online communication.

Conversely, for text-based communication, very little, if any at all, transcription work is needed, as most programs store written records of interactions that are ready for analysis and dissemination—that is, data collected in text-based CMC settings are "research ready." The ease with which data are collected in text-based CMC settings allows researchers to quickly disseminate research based on discussion boards, emails, and blogs.

For online spoken communication, however, the task of capturing, transcribing, and disseminating recordings of social interaction is much more complex and onerous. The time it takes to collect and transcribe online spoken communication data is indeed one reason why few researchers have explored how voice-based interactions in online settings are organized (for a review of research on online spoken communication, see Section 3.2.4).

The theoretical and methodological principles outlined above have been used to examine a range of issues and phenomena. For example, examinations have developed a deeper understanding of how social structures are constructed in, and through, social interaction: studies have examined how interactants construct cultural identities (Brandt and Jenks 2011), mediate opposing views (Goodwin and Goodwin 1990), shape gender and sexuality (Stokoe and Smithson 2001), and elicit responses from students (Lee 2008), to name a few. Furthermore, studies have identified and explicated the sequential and organizational structures of many social activities, from opening a talk radio show (e.g. Hutchby 1999) to structuring pedagogical lessons (e.g. Seedhouse 2010).

In addition to investigating social structures and structures of social activities, studies have treated talk as an investigation in its own right; studies have expanded the discourse analytic literature on, for instance, topic transitions (Holt and Drew 2005), repair initiators (Drew 1997), turn-taking (Schegloff 2000), and preference organization (Boyle 2000). As demonstrated by these different investigatory foci, studies of social interaction have contributed much to an understanding of communication.

These studies provide a rich and diverse set of observations and findings that can be used for investigating online communication, but they also have practical relevance for the professionals, non-academics, and practitioners that take part in investigations of social interaction. For example, an understanding of social inter-action has been used to inform language teaching practices (Wong 2002), equip medical "experts" with the knowledge to better communicate with "non-expert" patients (Gülich 2003), train call handlers with a set of best practices for dealing with customers in need of technical support (Baker *et al.* 2005), and advise mediators on how to deal with disagreements (Trinder *et al.* 2010). Therefore, a social-interaction approach to CMC can offer practical guidance for professionals and non-academics that use technology in the workplace.

Social interaction, as defined previously and discussed in terms of its practical implications for carrying out research, is the overarching theoretical stance taken in this book on second language chat rooms. The methodology that is used to investigate second language chat rooms is conversation analysis.

## 2.2.1 CONVERSATION ANALYSIS

The main methodological approach adopted in this book is conversation analysis (CA). While many other approaches to spoken discourse analysis exist (for a review of different approaches, see Schiffrin *et al.* 2003), including some that have been used to investigate online platforms that are similar to the type of second language chat rooms examined in the present study (e.g. Freiermuth 2001; Herring 2004), CA is well equipped to examine the organization of online spoken communication because the methodology is centrally concerned with understanding talk and interaction in its own right.

This is an important observation to make, as there is a tendency in the CMC literature to investigate online spoken communication with little regard to how the unique interactional and prosodic features of talk are used and organized for social-interaction purposes. For example, statistical measures are often used in the literature when examining online spoken communication (see Table 3.1).

Investigating online spoken communication "in its own right" requires researchers to abandon theories that are based on oversimplified and decontextualized notions of language and communication (e.g. the assumption that CMC is a hybrid language system that consists of elements of written and spoken discourse). Furthermore, this principle requires researchers to discard approaches that strip away the subtle but complex ways spoken conversations are conducted (e.g. coding and quantifying fea-tures of repair sequences in order to test language learning theories).

Because there is a tendency in the CMC literature to investigate online spoken com-munication with little regard to how the unique interactional and prosodic features of talk are used and organized for social-interaction purposes, using conversation ana-lytic principles to study second language chat rooms seems prudent and timely. Put differently, CA, with its rigorous procedures for detailed representations and analytic descriptions of spoken communication, is the most suitable methodology for a study that examines how speakers of English as an additional language manage their voice-based interactions in chat rooms. The following discussion identifies and explicates the conversation analytic principles that are adopted in the present investigation.

Central to a CA-informed investigation of online spoken communication is the belief that there is a reflexive relationship between talk and interaction on the one hand, and social structures and organization on the other hand (for a detailed discussion of CA, see ten Have 2007; Hutchby and Wooffitt 2008). In simple terms, this means discussions of human social behavior, or any contextual variable deemed important to an investigation—say, how interactants jointly deal with the absence of physical co-presence in online spoken communication encounters, or the technological affordances and constraints of dealing with overlapping utterances in online, voice-based settings—must be underpinned by an examination of talk and interaction:

> For the target of its [CA] inquiries stands where talk amounts to action, where action projects consequences in a structure and texture of interaction which the talk is itself progressively embodying and realizing, and where the particulars of the talk inform what actions are being done and what sort of social scene is being constituted. (Schegloff 1991: 46)

The idea that talk and interaction is progressively embodying action also highlights CA's understanding of context. For conversation analysts, context is a temporally unfolding event that is situated in the exigencies of communication. That is, talk and interaction is both context-dependent and context-shaping: Communication is dependent on the context in which interactants find themselves interacting, but it can also shape and re-shape context. The methodological upshot is that CA observations of talk and interaction are firmly grounded in communication data. While this approach to talk and interaction is not particularly unique (cf. grounded theory), CA's inductive, bottom-up methodology is different in that it requires researchers to adopt an emic perspective to data analysis. An emic perspective means observations of talk and interaction are made from the standpoint of the participants/interactants/social actors. However, for CA, this does not mean asking participants to provide their understanding of past communicative events, but rather examining how the interactants themselves participate on a turn-by-turn basis. An emic perspective to online spoken communication requires making analytic observations that are demonstrably relevant to the participants of online communication. Take, for example, the issue of anonymity: A conversation analytic study would approach this issue by showing how interactants demonstrably make relevant, in and through their talk and interaction, the issue of anonymity—whether, for example, anonymity affords interactants the freedom to interact in a particular way (rather than asking them how they deal with anonymity during online communication). Providing emic descriptions that address the issue of relevancy, for both the interactants and interaction under investigation, is a central conversation analytic principle:

> It is a problem of analysis to be worked at: how to examine the data so as to be able to show that the parties were, with and for one another, demonstrably oriented to those aspects of who they are, and those aspects of their context, which are respectively implicated in the "social structures" which we may wish to relate to the talk. If we treat this as a problem of analytic craft, we can use it as

leverage to enhance the possibility of learning something about how talk-in-interaction is done, for it requires us to return again to the details of the talk to make the demonstration. (Schegloff 1991: 51–2)

As articulated in this quote, talk and interaction is the site of investigation for CA. However, this does not mean that conversation analysts are limited to examining, for example, turn-taking, adjacency pairs, repair types and sequences, and preference organization. Issues that are commonly understood as so-called macro social issues—for example, national identity and power—can be examined using, and have indeed been investigated with, CA (for a conversation analytic study of identities in online encounters, see Brandt and Jenks 2011; see also Chapter 9). For online spoken communication research, this means conversation analytic observations of CMC need not be limited to sequence organization (e.g. turn-taking and adjacency pairs). Though not mutually exclusive, conversation analysts are also interested in showing how people create intersubjectivity and orderliness in, and through, talk and interaction, as well as understanding the production of social actions as they are locally situated and occasioned in the "here-and-now" (see Hutchby and Wooffitt 2008).

These objects of study require conversation analytic studies to pay special attention to the representation of communication data. In other words, the task of transcribing communication data is central to carrying out conversation analytic studies, including those that are concerned with online spoken communication (for a list of transcription conventions used in the present study, see Section 4.4).

## 2.3  CHAT ROOMS

Technology is ubiquitous and has been so for millennia. The invention of the wheel in Mesopotamia and its subsequent applications is an example of early society benefiting from technological advancements. Although societies have benefited from scientific knowledge for thousands of years, technology-enabled devices have only recently shaped communicative practices in profound ways. A somewhat recent example is telephone communication. The telephone was invented a little over a century back, and has since changed the ways in which communication is conducted. The telephone represents a meaningful development with regard to the application of technology for communication purposes for several reasons. Telephones enable transnational communication, facilitate international business transactions, and connect geographically displaced family members, to name a few. More importantly, the telephone has spawned new communication technologies that are still in current use (Hutchby 2001).

A second, more recent example of technology interfacing with social interaction is email communication. Although the telephone represents a significant technological advancement, it could be argued that real societal change on a global scale started several decades ago when the first email message was sent on a computer network (some figures show that approximately 200 billion emails are sent every day; see Radicati Group 2012). Like the telephone, email technology quickly moved from serving the sole purpose of governments and institutions to being a part of everyday life in developed countries.

The pervasiveness of telephone conversations and email communication, as well as the widespread use of other CMC types (e.g. blogs, instant messaging, video conferencing), represents a growing dependency on technology. As this dependency grows and spreads wider, so too does the need to provide social-interaction descriptions of technology-driven communication. This book addresses this need by examining second language chat rooms. While chat rooms have not experienced the same type of popularity as telephones and email communication, chatting online is integral to the communicative lives of many.

Chat rooms are used by interactants to discuss topics of common interest, form communities with likeminded people, locate life partners or short-term relationships, and simply chat for the sake of chatting. Chat rooms are sometimes used to converse with friends and family members, conduct classroom lessons, and carry out business negotiations. Chat rooms played an important role in the popularity of the Internet in the 1990s when texting was the only way communication was conducted in these online spaces. Although chat rooms are less popular now than they were two decades ago, people continue to chat online but now have the option of using voice and/or video in addition to text. Chat rooms have recently experienced a resurgence of interest because they are now used in multiplayer computer games and virtual online worlds (e.g. Second Life).

This book is chiefly interested in voice-based chat rooms and the online spoken communication that takes place within them (Section 4.5 provides detailed information regarding the study and data set used to carry out the analysis). Despite great efforts to examine text-based chat rooms, many questions regarding voice-based chat rooms (and online spoken communication) remain unanswered. For example, how do participants of voice-based chat rooms establish mutual orientation in the absence of physical co-presence (see Chapter 5)? What are the turn-taking differences and similarities in text- and voice-based chat rooms (see Chapter 6)? How do pauses shape the management of online spoken communication (see Chapter 7)? How can an understanding of online spoken communication inform language teaching and learning theories and practices (see Chapter 8)? How do second language chat rooms shape lingua franca interactions (see Chapter 9)? These and other questions will be answered in the present study.

With these questions in mind, what technologies should be used as a point of reference in a book on second language chat rooms? A book on second language chat rooms should include some discussion of telephone communication. Telephone communication has been the object of study for many decades (e.g. Sacks 1995), and because of this, a wealth of observations that are relevant to audio-only communication exists. For instance, the findings established in studies of telephone openings have been used to better understand newer technologies, including mobile phones (see Hutchby and Barnett 2005). Indeed, telephone studies have been useful for recent studies of online spoken communication (see Jenks 2009a; Jenks and Brandt 2013; Jenks and Firth 2013). Similarly, studies that have examined two-way radios (Szymanski et al. 2006), audioconferencing tools (Ackerman et al. 1997), and mobile phones (see Arminen 2005), are potentially useful in a discussion of second language chat rooms and online spoken communication (see Section 3.2.4).

Therefore, it could be said that a book on second language chat rooms should be underpinned by a deeper understanding of how technologies shape communication. In other words, a study of second language chat rooms should not preclude a discussion of telephones, mobile phones, other "non-computer" related devices, and even face-to-face interactions. The latter setting is particularly germane to online spoken communication, as face-to-face interactions have been a point of comparison for many CMC studies (see, for example, Herring 1999; Jenks 2009a). While it is clear that there are technologies relevant to the study conducted in this book, what is online spoken communication and how is it managed from a technical perspective?

## 2.3.1  ONLINE COMMUNICATION

Online spoken communication is a type of CMC, but not all CMC types are the same. To complicate matters further, CMC is often used as an umbrella term that covers all forms of communication mediated by electronic devices, including mobile telephones (for an extended discussion of CMC as a terminological construct, see Chapter 4). Furthermore, CMC covers an array of participatory structures (e.g. dyadic talk, multiparty interactions, human–human conversations, computer–human communication) and communication technologies (e.g. cellular networks and the Internet). Although CMC is not limited to any single communication technology, the present study is only concerned with second language chat rooms conducted on computer networks. Therefore, it is necessary to discuss what computer networks are, provide an overview of how communication is conducted on these networks, and identify the type of CMC examined in this book (see also Chapter 4 for a detailed discussion of the online platform examined in the present study).

### 2.3.1.1  Computer networks
Computers are networked locally (e.g. within the same room or building) or area wide (e.g. in different national regions or countries); communication in both network types relies on data communication protocols. A protocol is a system of rules that computers use to send and receive information. The protocols that are commonly used for communication on computer networks are transmission control protocol (TCP) and Internet Protocol (IP). These protocols define Internet-based communication. In other words, when researchers use the term Internet-based communication, they are referring specifically to the type of communication that relies on TCP and IP to send and receive information. The term online communication simply refers to the fact that computer users are "on" the network as opposed to "off" it.

On a descriptive level, the transmission of information from one computer to another is ostensibly simple: online communication comprises three stages of information transmission. First, a computer (or computing/electronic device) sends information to the Internet. The raw form of this information is what the computer user sees on the screen (e.g. an email message). During this first stage, the TCP converts the email message into smaller bits of information for the Internet.

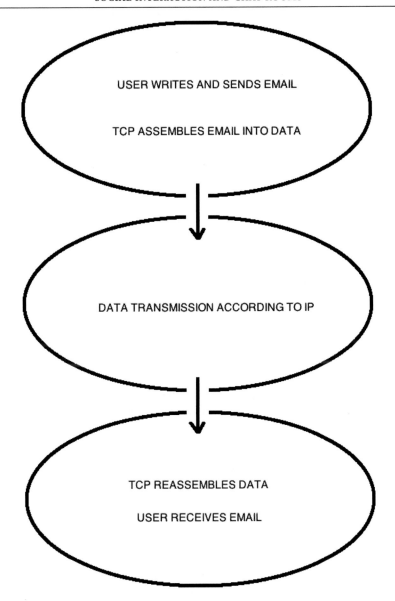

*Figure 2.1    Internet-based communication*

Second, the smaller bits of information are sent over or through the network using, and according to, the IP. Third, the recipient's computer receives the bits of information. During this final stage, the recipient's computer reassembles the bits of information back into the email message. As with the first stage of data transmission, the TCP is responsible for the assembly process. Figure 2.1 illustrates the three basic stages of Internet-based communication.

Although the description in Figure 2.1 uses two computers for the information transmission example, Internet-based communication is not restricted to computers (i.e. desktops and laptops). For example, mobile phones can gain "entry," and thus send information, onto the Internet using a different set of rules than those outlined in the TCP protocol. Similarly, a computer can use TCP/IP to send information to a mobile phone connected to a cellular network. Thus, the term Internet-based communication is a slight misnomer, as the TCP protocol is not the only way information is transmitted onto, and through, the Internet. It is for this reason that the term online communication is used throughout this book (as opposed to Internet-based communication). Though slightly more ambiguous than Internet-based communication, the term online communication includes all networks and cross-network possibilities.

### 2.3.1.2 Computer-mediated spoken interaction

The type of online communication examined in this book is referred to as computer-mediated spoken interaction (CMSI). Although Chapter 4 provides an extended definition of CMSI, it is important to briefly outline here what is meant by this term. CMSI refers to any synchronous or asynchronous online spoken communication (for stylistic purposes, CMSI and online spoken communication are used synonymously), though this book is only concerned with synchronous CMSI. Again, online communication involves at least two computing devices that send and receive information over one network or across two or more networks (e.g. Internet, intranet, or cellular). Computing devices refer to traditional desktops and laptops, as well as mobile and tablet devices (i.e. any portable electronic device that has the capability of connecting to a network), though the present study deals primarily with communication conducted on computers. CMSI includes communication that is conducted entirely in the spoken medium or in combination or conjunction with text and/or video. The observations made in the analytic chapters are based almost entirely on the spoken medium.

# CMC AND APPLIED LINGUISTICS

## 3.1 INTRODUCTION

In three decades, access to, and applications of, computers have quickly changed from being almost exclusively available to, and serving the function of, governments and institutions, to being at the disposal of many people and serving varied functions from the mundane to the professional. This technological shift has resulted in substantive changes in the way people go about conducting their social lives. Perhaps the most substantive change relates to how people maintain social and professional relations. For example, numerous studies have demonstrated how notions of interpersonal contact have changed as a result of social networking websites and other forms of online communication (e.g. Baym *et al.* 2004). Extant observations and findings point to a growing trend in using online communication technologies to establish and maintain personal and occupational networks (e.g. Tillema *et al.* 2010).

CMC is a significant form of social interaction in today's world, in part, because of the communicative needs of people involved in international workforces and global migration. Not only has technology allowed geographically displaced friends, family, and colleagues to maintain open channels of communication across many time zones and great distances, but rapid global connectivity has also made it easier for people to migrate from, and immigrate to, various places around the world. The need to use computers and the Internet is strong for these reasons, and even stronger for younger generations born into a world of online media (Buckingham and Willett 2006). For these younger members of society especially, the Internet is an indispensable form of communication and tool for life management (Rosen 2010).

As a result of the burgeoning growth in online media and communication, many investigatory issues and questions pertaining to the social and linguistic characteristics of CMC have been identified and asked. For instance, what are the communicative norms of social networking websites? How is access to the Internet changing the cultural values of developing countries? What are the pedagogical consequences of using computers in classrooms? Is chat room communication different than face-to-face interaction?

CMC has also been investigated extensively in applied linguistics. For several decades, applied linguists have examined the social, linguistic, and pedagogical implications of CMC (Crystal 2006; Danet and Herring 2007). Despite growing interest in, and awareness of, CMC, there are still many unanswered questions, especially with regard to CMSI. For instance, how can an understanding of second language chat rooms be used to inform teaching practices (see Chapter 8)? What aspects of technology mediate CMSI (see Chapter 5)? Are voice-based chat rooms different than text-based chat rooms (see Chapter 6)? What are the communicative affordances and constraints of multiparty voice-based chat rooms (see Chapter 7)? Although many research gaps exist with regard to a social-interaction understanding of CMSI, the CMC literature represents a large body of empirical work. This chapter reviews the CMC literature from a mostly applied linguistics perspective, and identifies research gaps as they pertain to the study of CMSI. This literature review will help readers understand the importance of examining CMSI and appreciate the contributions made in this book.

## 3.2 CMC AND APPLIED LINGUISTICS

Applied linguistics is a discipline that is concerned with the way language is used in real-life situations: applied linguistics is "the theoretical and empirical investigation of real-world problems in which language is a central issue" (Brumfit 1995: 27). Applied linguistics research is a reflection of contemporary society; in other words, applied linguists investigate issues that possess social and linguistic relevance to people living and working in today's world. This focus has led to the research of many communicative settings and contexts, including anything from healthcare communication to dinner conversations. As a discipline, applied linguistics is also concerned with new and emerging societal trends and technological advancements. Therefore, it should come as no surprise that CMC is an important area of study in applied linguistics.

With access to the Internet reaching approximately 1.6 billion people (International Telecommunication Union 2010), the social and interactional applications of CMC are rich and empirically sustainable areas of investigation. While this observation is truer today than three decades ago, applied linguists have a long-standing interest in the study of CMC. For example, the first publication of the Annual Review of Applied Linguistics includes a discussion piece on the pedagogical value of computers in language teaching and learning (see Otto 1980). Although teaching and learning issues were the main topics of investigation in early applied linguistics research, the study of CMC is now varied and interdisciplinary (e.g. Myers 2006; Thorne and Black 2007).

The study of CMC in applied linguistics comprises three distinct, yet sometimes overlapping, empirical strands: teaching and learning, language and discourse, and sociality and culture.

Issues pertaining to teaching and learning are by far the most commonly investigated. This is demonstrated in the many international journals dedicated to the study of computers in the language classroom (e.g. *Language Learning and Technology, Computer Assisted Language Learning, ReCALL,* and *CALICO Journal*). This strand is commonly known as computer assisted language learning (CALL). The second empirical strand is language and discourse. This empirical strand has received a great deal of attention in the literature. Topics that have been investigated include interactional coherence, text shorthand, floor management, as well as CMSI. The third and final empirical strand is sociality and culture. The study of social and cultural issues—which

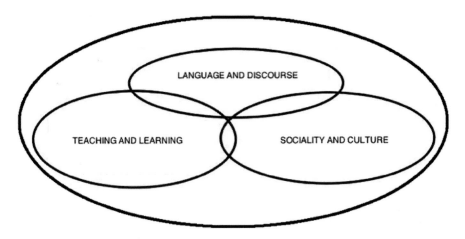

*Figure 3.1   Three empirical strands*

includes, but is not limited to, gender, identity, and intercultural communication—often overlaps with the teaching and learning and/or language and discourse empirical strands (e.g. the learning of intercultural awareness in pedagogical settings; see O'Dowd 2007). Although sociality and culture is a growing domain of inquiry, it is a much smaller enterprise than the teaching and learning empirical strand.

In the subsections that follow, key themes in each empirical strand will be identified and explicated. Teaching and learning will be discussed first, as it represents the largest empirical strand. This section will be followed by a discussion of language and discourse, and then sociality and culture. The final subsection deals with the literature on CMSI.

### 3.2.1  TEACHING AND LEARNING

Discussions concerning the benefits of using computers for language teaching and learning occurred as early as the 1960s (Marty 1981), though CALL research was largely stagnant until the 1970s and 1980s (see, for example, Chapelle 2001: 1, who anecdotally recalls her CALL presentation at the annual TESOL convention in 1980). The 1970s and 1980s marked the beginning of personal computers, though few teachers at the time were utilizing, and indeed thinking about, computers for instructional purposes. In fact, CALL research was at the time in the earliest stages of development, and many applied linguists were unaware of the full potential of computers. The state of technology and development of CALL research at the time is perhaps best represented by the fact that state-of-the-art reviews would begin with, or include, a definition of a computer (see Otto 1980: 58). While few researchers and teachers today require a definition of a computer, it would not be unfair to say that the full pedagogical potential of current technologies has yet to be realized. This is partly because technological advancements occur at a much faster rate than the time it takes to disseminate and publish research. In this sense, not much has changed in five decades of CALL research and application. Conceptual gaps existed in CALL research in the 1960s, and will continue to exist in the decades to come (e.g. Hubbard and Levy 2006). Yet despite rapid developments in technology and changes in online media consumption, the CALL literature covers a broad range of teaching and learning issues.

Example topics of investigation include language development, second language pedagogy, memory, materials design, reading, and motivation (for a description of CALL as an area of study, see Debski 2003). Extensive research has also been carried out on the design and implementation of CALL materials—this topic of investigation addresses a number of pedagogical issues, including, but not limited to, task-based learning, pronunciation, independent learning, online collaboration, assessment, and project-based activities (for collections that represent the diversity of CALL research, see Arnold and Ducate 2006; Stickler and Hauck 2006). The CALL literature is thus varied and extensive (for comprehensive reviews of the CALL literature, see Fotos and Browne 2004; Hubbard 2009). Despite this wealth of knowledge, there is only one subarea of CALL research that is relevant to the study of CMSI: computer-mediated communication (CMC). This area of CALL research is typically referred to as CALL-CMC (cf. CMCL; see Lamy and Hampel 2007).

CALL-CMC research investigates interactions in formal and informal second language settings with the aim of developing and assessing tasks and activities that promote learning (for a detailed explanation and historical overview of CALL-CMC research, see Chapelle 2001). CALL-CMC research has been investigated from a number of different theoretical and methodological perspectives (e.g. sociocultural theory, language socialization, and CA). However, social-interaction perspectives are arguably the most underrepresented. The bulk of CALL-CMC research published over the past two decades has adopted the interactionist perspective (for an overview of the interactionist perspective, see Long 1996). The review of CALL-CMC research below will focus on this perspective, though references to other approaches will be made.

CALL-CMC research that adopts the interactionist perspective "strives to document how synchronous CMC (SCMC) stimulates negotiations of meaning with similar benefits to those documented in face-to-face exchanges" (Blake 2007: 77). While the underlying theoretical assumptions of the interactionist perspective are related largely to cognition, this quote highlights three investigatory issues that all CALL-CMC research strives to examine, including the study of CMSI: synchronicity, learner language, and modality.

First, all CALL-CMC research investigates at least one synchronicity type (i.e. synchronous and/or asynchronous). CALL-CMC research informed by the interactionist perspective is concerned primarily with synchronous CMC (see Blake 2007; Smith 2008; Blake 2009). Synchronous CMC is the main communication type investigated in studies that adopt the interactionist perspective because second language acquisition (SLA) theories and hypotheses are based largely on the learning that takes place during spoken communication (e.g. negotiating for meaning and noticing gaps in linguistic knowledge while speaking; for a review of SLA theories, see Mitchell and Myles 2004). It is believed that CMC settings, which mimic face-to-face spoken communication and promote interactions that lead to the negotiation of language forms, provide the best opportunities for learning. Despite the importance placed on spoken communication, CMSI has only recently been investigated within the interactionist perspective (for a review of CMSI studies, see Section 3.2.4 below). The bulk of work done from an interactionist perspective is based on text-based CMC (e.g. text chatting). Interactionists do not examine social interaction as conceptualized in Chapter 2, because they are concerned with what happens inside the brain as a result of communication. Consequently, language learning is not investigated as a phenomenon that is situated in, and achieved through, social interaction (for an example of how language learning can be discussed from a social-interaction perspective, see Chapter 8). This leads to the second investigatory issue.

Second, all CALL-CMC research investigates learner language (for examples of learner language, see Ellis and Barkhuizen 2005). The interactionist perspective examines learner language that is related to meaning negotiation, which includes comprehension checks and clarification requests (see Bower and Kawaguchi 2011). The reason for examining such language is motivated by a cognitive understanding of learning, and the works of Michael Long, Susan Gass, and Larry Selinker have been particularly influential in this way of thinking (see Gass and Selinker 2001). Like most CALL-CMC research (for linguistic complexity, see Sauro and Smith 2010; for oral proficiency, see Payne and Whitney 2002), the interactionist perspective relies heavily on the practice of coding and quantifying discrete linguistic items and/or discourse units.

This methodological approach partly stems from the belief that pedagogical tasks should maximize opportunities for students to resolve communication breakdowns and engage in comprehension checks. In other words, a task is deemed pedagogically useful when it can produce frequent communication breakdowns and comprehension checks (Chapelle 2007). The more-the-merrier approach naturally leads to analyses of learner language that are largely statistical in nature—coding and quantifying learner language allows interactionists to discuss the pedagogical value of CALL tasks in relation to SLA theories. From a social-interaction perspective, relying solely on statistical measures is inherently problematic because these mathematical tools do not adequately reveal how language learners use linguistic items and discourse units during their ongoing work to complete a pedagogical task or communicative activity (see Negretti 1999; see also Chapter 8).

Third, all CALL-CMC research is concerned, to some degree, with comparing the findings of one communicative setting with those of another. For example, text-based chatting is often compared with physical classrooms because such comparisons allow researchers to investigate whether online tasks and activities provide similar learning opportunities as those identified in face-to-face interaction (e.g. oral fluency; see Blake 2009). For the interactionist perspective, similar comparisons are made in order to see whether negotiated interactions are present in the language used in an online task (Chapelle 1997). Because physical classrooms are the dominant setting in which language teaching and learning occur, online tasks and activities are often evaluated according to existing understandings of what works well (or does not work well) in face-to-face encounters (e.g. Doughty and Long 2003).

Comparisons between different CMC modalities are made for similar reasons (e.g. to evaluate which CMC modality provides the most opportunities to negotiate for meaning). In addition, CMC modalities are compared to provide a better understanding of how technology influences teaching and learning (see Smith *et al.* 2003). That is, comparing different modalities allows researchers to identify technological affordances and constraints, which in turn assists in designing online tasks and activities according to specific teaching and learning needs (for an example of how an understanding of CMSI can be used to design second language tasks, see Section 8.2.1.1). Although many modality types have been compared in the CALL-CMC literature, few studies have compared text-based CMC with CMSI (see, however, Jepson 2005; see also Chapter 6).

The discussion of the interactionist perspective sheds some light on how a study of CMSI can contribute to the CALL-CMC literature. The CALL-CMC literature, including research informed by the interactionist perspective, is disproportionately made up of studies that examine synchronous text-based CMC. Comparatively few studies have explored what can be learned pedagogically as a result of examining online spoken communication. CMSI studies can contribute to the CALL-CMC literature by using an understanding of online spoken communication to make comparisons between pedagogical platforms. Such comparisons can be used to uncover the interactional similarities and differences that exist between text and voice chatting (see Chapter 6), which is in turn potentially useful in designing pedagogical activities according to technological affordances and constraints (see Section 8.2.1.1). Simply put, CMSI studies can assist language teachers and researchers in better understanding how online spoken communication uniquely shapes learning opportunities and challenges.

The discussion of synchronicity, learner language, and modality also demonstrates that a social-interaction perspective can contribute much to the CALL-CMC literature. This is because much of what is currently known about CALL-CMC is derived from statistical computations of linguistic items and discourse units (for a statistical analysis of CMSI, see Jepson 2005). A social-interaction perspective can, conversely, provide a context-sensitive understanding of how language is used as an interactional resource to engage in formal and informal learning activities. The importance placed on data transcripts in social-interaction research is also pedagogically useful (for a discussion of the transcription conventions used in this book, see Section 4.4). For example, transcribing and analyzing CMSI requires researchers to pay special attention to the micro details of online spoken communication (see Chapter 5), including fluctuations in stress and intonation. It is possible that these aspects of spoken communication are fundamental to the ways in which learners organize their talk in online activities (see Section 8.2.1). Despite these potential benefits, the study of CMSI presents many investigatory challenges, as discussed in the next section.

### 3.2.2 LANGUAGE AND DISCOURSE

Advances in technology, changes in media consumption, and increased dependency on the Internet have also spawned investigations of the language and discourse of

CMC. Studies that belong to the language and discourse empirical strand are broadly concerned with the way technology is used to communicate and how communication is shaped by technology. Investigations have examined a wide range of language and discourse features, though the literature is largely made up of studies that investigate interactional and lexical phenomena (e.g. for utterance-specific phenomena, see Provine *et al.* 2007; for interactional practices, see Rintel and Pittman 1997). Few studies have, conversely, examined syntactic structures in educational and non-educational contexts (see Abrams 2003; Williams and van Compernolle 2009; Cho 2010).

CMC researchers have a long-standing interest in the language and discourse of online communication (e.g. Hiltz and Turoff 1978), though research published in applied linguistics and related journals did not begin to appear until the late 1980s and early 1990s (e.g. Wilkins 1991). In earlier language and discourse research, CMC researchers were particularly interested in understanding the hybrid nature of text-based communication (e.g. Ferrara *et al.* 1991). For instance, studies investigated how CMC differs from, or is similar to, face-to-face communication (see, for example, Herring 1999, for a seminal investigation of interactional coherence in text-based chat rooms).

In more recent CMC studies, researchers have turned their attention to the level of interaction (see Herring 2004, for a discussion of different levels of analysis). For example, turn-taking is a popular area of investigation within the language and discourse empirical strand (e.g. Garcia and Jacobs 1999; Simpson 2005), as this feature of interaction is highly malleable with regard to technological affordances and constraints. Much of the work on turn-taking has adopted a social-interaction perspective.

For instance, Garcia and Jacobs (1999) examined the turn-taking system of a text-based computer conferencing program using conversation analytic principles (see also Anderson *et al.* 2010), and observed that the permanency of the text medium allowed for more flexibility in turn-taking practices than the prototypical one-speaker-at-a-time rule reported in dyadic, face-to-face spoken communication (see Sacks *et al.* 1974). Negretti (1999: 82) also uses a conversation analytic framework to study text-based CMC, and similarly observes that text chatting involves "no smooth sequential order," and therefore interactants "are forced to manage turn-taking and turn-giving in ways that are different from oral talk."

Although conversation analytic principles have proven useful in the study of text-based CMC, Simpson (2005) argues that a conversation analytic understanding of turns is not the most appropriate analytic unit for text chatting. Building on Edelsky's (1981) concept of the conversational floor, Simpson (2005) shows that turn adjacency and turn-taking rules are not consequential to co-constructing meaning in text-based CMC, and are thus less useful in understanding the overall interactional and sequential organization of text chatting. Similar observations regarding the turn-taking differences between text chatting and face-to-face communication have been made with regard to interactional coherence (Herring 1999) and overlapping topics (Markman 2009).

In addition to text chatting (see also Kitade 2000), many other types of CMC have been investigated at the level of interaction (for emails, see Condon and Cech 2001;

for discussion boards, see Wilkins 1991). However, few interaction studies have examined CMSI settings (see, however, see Jenks 2009a, for an investigation of overlapping talk in CMSI; for a review of CMSI studies, see Section 3.2.4 below).

At the lexical and utterance level, CMC researchers are primarily concerned with identifying and explicating the "language of the Internet." This aim is articulated in recent book-length publications that explicitly set out to examine netspeak or Internet shorthand, two terms that are used in the literature to represent the words and utterances of CMC (see Crystal 2004; 2006). A study of lexical and utterance level phenomena generally entails examining the way meaning is typographically and orthographically shaped in online settings. For example, Internet shorthand is a term that has come into being through observations of people using abbreviated language during text communication (e.g. "brb" for "be right back," and "lol" for "laughing out loud").

Although Internet shorthand is now a widely accepted form of communication, this was not always the case. When CMC was in its infancy, many people within and outside of the academic community feared that Internet shorthand would deteriorate so-called standard writing conventions and exacerbate spelling errors (see Li 2000). As a result of this widespread misconception, CMC researchers have made it their objective to demonstrate that Internet shorthand is not a degenerate form of communication. Researchers have done so by showing that interactants are required to use abbreviated language in order to, for example, manage a rapid turn-taking system and deal with multiple conversational topics; it has also been shown that Internet shorthand requires a high degree of creativity and linguistic awareness (Crystal 2006).

Similarly, researchers have argued that emoticons are a common (and necessary) form of communication because they allow interactants to quickly and accurately convey meaning in settings that are often devoid of verbal and non-verbal cues. For instance, Lotherington and Xu's (2004) identification of English and Chinese features of Internet shorthand demonstrates that text-based CMC constitutes a hybrid language system, comprising both written and spoken conventions that interactants use to maximize comprehensibility (see also Gao 2001; Lee 2002; Randall 2002).

As alluded to in the discussion above, studies that belong to the language and discourse empirical strand are varied in theory and investigate many different linguistic phenomena. Despite this diversity, the bulk of research done in the language and discourse empirical strand is based on text-based CMC. Two interdependent reasons exist for this disproportion. First, text-based CMC has "historical precedence" over other CMC media, and is still arguably the most widely used online communication medium (Herring 2010). Email is an almost indispensable form of CMC, and communication mediated by popular social networking services is largely text-based. Websites are generally read, and participation in discussion boards, blogs, and instant messaging programs minimally require, yet sometimes only allow, written contributions.

In fact, text-based CMC is so prevalent that it is sometimes used synonymously with CMC (i.e. all CMC modes and types). For example, in a recent review of sociolinguistic research conducted in online settings, Georgakopoulou (2006: 550) states of the CMC researcher, "[he/she] surely has to be the envy of the interactional analyst who faces the daunting task of transcribing . . . I have personally worked with both interactional and CMC data and can testify to the easy life that CMC data afford."

The quote also leads to the second reason why the literature is disproportionately made up of text-based CMC studies. That is, the data that are used to carry out investigations of text-based CMC require minimal time and effort to prepare for analysis. For both asynchronous (e.g. discussion boards) and synchronous (e.g. instant messaging) text-based CMC, records of written conversations are often stored within a software program and/or locally on a computer, allowing the researcher to bypass the time-consuming task of transcribing data recordings. Thus, text-based CMC data are not only widely available, but also automatically stored in a format that is "research ready."

Conversely, collecting CMSI data requires specialized knowledge of recording software, and the data must be transcribed into text-based documents before they can be used for the generation and dissemination of analytic observations. These methodological challenges may be one reason why there is a dearth of CMSI studies. Researchers must invest a substantial amount of time and resources into carrying out a study of CMSI, and the initial learning curve for dealing with the technical aspects of collecting and transcribing spoken data is indeed steep (Jenks 2011). Despite these challenges, CMSI represents a small, but growing area of investigation in the CMC literature (for a review of CMSI studies, see Section 3.2.4 below).

### 3.2.3 SOCIALITY AND CULTURE

The third empirical strand is sociality and culture. It is not uncommon for researchers working in this area of investigation to examine social and/or cultural issues in conjunction with a second or third empirical strand. Gender, for example, is a classic social issue: the study of gender is often investigated alongside issues that are associated with the language and discourse empirical strand (e.g. for a study looking at linguistic differences in blog entries between male and female authors, see Herring and Paolillo 2006; for a study examining gender differences in turn-taking practices in chat rooms, see Panyametheekul and Herring 2003). Social and cultural issues have investigated so-called micro (e.g. social identities) and macro issues (e.g. language policy), and many different methodologies have been adopted within this empirical strand (e.g. questionnaires, quantitative sociolinguistics), including social-interaction approaches (e.g. conversation analysis).

Social and cultural studies are not concerned with examining CMC in its own right, but rather how language and discourse are used to enact social identities (e.g. Rellstab 2007), form interpersonal relationships (e.g. Jenks 2009b), manage cultural differences (e.g. Tudini 2007), and ridicule co-interactants (e.g. Jenks 2012a). Sociality and culture is the newest empirical strand (Georgakopoulou 2006), though it is a growing area of investigation in the CMC literature (see Androutsopoulos 2006a).

Social and cultural issues are a new area of investigation because for the first two or three decades of scholarly inquiry, many researchers were predisposed to the idea that CMC should be investigated as a single mode of communication with unique interactional and linguistic features that required documentation (see Herring

1996; Crystal 2006). While few researchers today subscribe to the idea that CMC is a genre of communication, remnants of this idea exist in current research because the description of interactional and linguistic features is fundamentally what CMC research is about (Herring 2004; 2011).

A great deal of overlap and interconnectedness exists between sociality and culture (N.B. this overlap and interconnectedness is one reason why the word sociocultural is often used to characterize studies within this empirical strand), yet the two terms represent different subdomains of inquiry. This is not because researchers believe social and cultural issues should be investigated independent of each other. Sociality and culture simply represent different empirical interests. For example, phenomena that have been investigated within the sociality subdomain can be characterized as classic sociolinguistic topics (e.g. identities and language variation), though socio-linguistics is not the only approach that has been used to investigate such issues (see, for example, conversation analysis; see Hutchby and Tanna 2008). Culture studies are primarily concerned with how national and regional similarities and differences are managed and made relevant in CMC settings, and phenomena examined within this subdomain are often related to teaching and learning (see, however, Montero-Fleta *et al.* 2009). While social and cultural issues have been investigated concurrently, in the same study (e.g. Peterson 2009), each subdomain will be discussed independently below.

Within the sociality subdomain, many phenomena have been studied (e.g. code-switching, see Siebenhaar 2006; dominance and deception, see Zhou *et al.* 2004; diaspora, see Androutsopoulos 2006b; and ethnicities, see Parker and Song 2006), though social identities and communities are perhaps the two most prominent issues (for exemplary studies on social identities, see Herring and Martinson 2004; Rellstab 2007; for an exemplary study on online communities, see Stommel 2008). Aspects of technology that have been shown to influence the formation and management of social identities and communities include, but are not limited to, medium of com-munication (e.g. Kim *et al.* 2007), participatory structure (e.g. Postmes *et al.* 1998), geographic locations of interactants (e.g. Walther 1997), communicative goals (e.g. Stommel 2008), social presence (e.g. Herring and Martinson 2004), and anonymity (e.g. Rellstab 2007).

Despite this breadth of knowledge, the sociality subdomain is overwhelmingly made up of observations based on text-based chat, discussion boards, and emails. For example, all of the studies in a recent seminal special issue on the sociolinguistics of CMC were based on observations of text media (see Androutsopoulos 2006a). As a result, the sociality subdomain possesses few studies that examine—from a social-interaction perspective—how social identities and communities are enacted, contested, and co-constructed, in CMSI settings (for an exploration of how identi-ties and communities are constructed in CMSI-based lingua franca encounters, see Chapter 9).

The culture subdomain comprises mostly pedagogical investigations, and more specifically, the teaching and learning of second languages (e.g. Bower and Kawaguchi 2011). Although culture has been investigated in non-educational settings (e.g. Lewis and George 2008), this section will focus on pedagogical studies.

Teaching and learning studies do not examine the so-called culture of CMC (see Calefato 2004; Herring 2008), though many researchers believe that this is an important pedagogical issue (see Ware and Kramsch 2005). Rather, culture is used synonymously with nationality (see, for example, Bjorge 2007). As a result, studies often investigate the teaching and learning of national practices and values (e.g. O'Brien and Levy 2008). Research of this type is conducted by designing pedagogical tasks that require transnational online communication with geographically displaced students (e.g. O'Dowd 2003; 2005). For instance, studies regularly investigate second language learners interacting with speakers of a target language and culture (see Tudini 2007). These intercultural encounters are referred to as language exchanges or tandem learning (see also telecollaboration; Belz 2003).

Intercultural encounters are thought to be important for language teaching and learning. The underlying belief here is that language learning is inextricably tied to culture (Risager 2005). CMC settings are often used for culture learning because cultural similarities and differences do not have to be taught explicitly and/or didactically; rather, students acquire cultural knowledge interculturally (Levy 2007). That is, language exchanges are thought to provide opportunities for second language learners to develop intercultural awareness and competence through CMC (Gray and Stockwell 1998). Learners can also meaningfully interact with speakers that are considered ideal models of the target language and culture (Stockwell and Levy 2001; Toyoda and Harrison 2002).

A central pedagogical aim in investigating culture is to design, and subsequently examine, online courses that (1) facilitate language learning through intercultural communication, (2) promote multicultural awareness, and (3) celebrate cultural and linguistic diversity (Kinginger *et al.* 1999). However, asking two culturally and linguistically different groups of learners to communicate with the aim that their differences will result in learning opportunities has led to much criticism in the literature (e.g. Coleman 1998). Researchers have argued that the logic in designing and examining language exchanges reduces culture to a construct that is restricted to nationalities or regional identities, thus perpetuating stereotypical beliefs (Meager and Castanos 1996; Fischer 1998; for a study on how stereotypes are co-constructed in CMSI, see Brandt and Jenks 2011).

Furthermore, it has been argued that prearranged intercultural encounters overshadow the more important issue of how culture is constantly evolving and reflexively connected to context. For example, several CMC researchers have discovered that online interactions between geographically displaced students result in the creation of third cultures (O'Dowd 2003; Ware and Kramsch 2005). A third culture refers to the continuous process of enacting, negotiating, and sometimes contesting, culture. In other words, the potential problem with prearranged intercultural encounters is that they move researchers away from the notion that culture is not fixed, but rather organic and fluid (for an example of how cultural identities related to being an English speaker are negotiated in CMSI, see Section 9.2.2). Culture reflects an entire communicative context, and not just who the interactants are and where they come from.

Whether culture is equated to nationality or conceptualized as an organic manifestation of communication, all research within the culture subdomain is concerned with uncovering how facets of technology shape cultural knowledge. For instance, Ware and Kramsch (2005) observe that the absence of nonverbal and verbal cues in discussion boards exacerbated misunderstandings between American students of German and German students of English. Ware and Kramsch (2005: 201) argue, "the primary difficulty of online communication is that the speakers themselves are invisible; only their words appear on the screen, bearing the full weight of their historical, ideological, social, and cultural density." In other words, text-based communication in discussion boards acts as both an affordance and a constraint in intercultural learning encounters.

While language exchanges have been investigated in many pedagogical contexts and in different modes of online communication, the culture subdomain is predominately made up of studies that examine text-based CMC. In other words, the culture subdomain rarely investigates CMSI settings. If culture is investigated in a CMSI setting, then it is done so in passing and with no detailed observations pertaining to how online spoken communication shapes the formation of culture and cultural knowledge (see, for example, Volle 2005). This observation is, of course, not a criticism. By and large, culture is not the main analytic focus in many CMSI studies (see, however, Chapter 9).

This concise review of the sociality and culture empirical strand demonstrates that CMSI studies can contribute to the advancement of the CMC literature in several ways. For example, to what extent would the interactants in Ware and Kramsch's (2005) study experience intercultural problems had they been communicating verbally and/or with video? This would seem an important question to ask, as the absence of nonverbal and verbal cues in discussion boards was cited as a reason for cultural misunderstandings. Similarly, is gender an important mediating factor in CMC, as observed in blogs and text-based chat rooms (e.g. Panyametheekul and Herring 2003; Herring and Paolillo 2006), or is it possible that gender differences were reported because the interactants were communicating via text messages? That is to say, would similar gender differences occur in CMSI settings? This is, of course, an empirical question that deserves further investigation.

Although gender is not investigated in this book, the chapter on social and cultural issues provides a better understanding of how CMSI is used as an interactional resource to construct social identities, community norms, and cultural knowledge (see Chapter 9). Despite the effort made in previous research and later in this book, there is still a great deal of work to be done within the sociality and culture empirical strand. CMC researchers must continue to explore how social and cultural phenomena are shaped in online encounters, especially in and with platforms that support CMSI.

### 3.2.4 CMSI STUDIES

The review of literature as three overlapping empirical strands shows that CMSI has received far less attention than other CMC types, in particular text-based communication. However, there is a relatively small, but growing, body of work that examines CMSI and CMSI-based platforms. This section provides a concise overview of this body of work, identifies key themes and research gaps, and offers a methodological critique of existing CMSI studies based on the theoretical principles of social interaction outlined in Chapter 2.

The bulk of research done on CMSI has been carried out for one of three reasons. First, CMSI studies are conducted because of an underlying interest in teaching and learning. That is, CMSI settings are investigated in order to better understand how online spoken communication can be used in pedagogically useful ways (cf. CALL-CMC research). Second, CMSI is a site of investigation because CMC researchers seek to understand the systems and platforms that enable online spoken communication—often the primary reason for conducting this type of research is to design better online systems and platforms. Third, CMSI studies are carried out to understand online spoken communication in its own right. That is, researchers are concerned primarily with uncovering the interactional and sequential features of CMSI. Sometimes these three foci overlap. For example, a study can examine the turn-taking system of a CMSI platform (i.e. third reason; see also Chapter 5) in order to design pedagogical tasks that reflect an understanding of how technology shapes communication (i.e. first reason, see Section 8.2.1.1). The present study has been carried out for the first and third reasons. This section provides an overview of all three types of research.

First, the CMSI literature on teaching and learning spans two decades and includes studies that examine both voice- and video-enabled online platforms. The literature review conducted for teaching and learning includes twenty-seven journal publications from 1998–2012. While these journal publications do not represent the entire CMSI literature on teaching and learning (for a literature review of fourteen studies that examine teaching and learning issues in audio conferencing platforms, see Hassan *et al.* 2005), the papers included below provide a general picture of what has (and has not) been investigated.

Table 3.1 summarizes the twenty-seven empirical studies according to methodological approach. In the interest of simplicity, research that adopts a mixed methods approach is classified according to the primary methodology adopted in the study. For instance, many studies claim to use a mixed methods approach (e.g. statistics and qualitative discourse analysis), but the analysis of data is based largely on statistical measures. In this case, the study has been classified as quantitative.

More than half of the teaching and learning studies use some form of quantification in their treatment of CMSI. In many of these quantitative studies, CMSI is not examined at all (e.g. writing, perceptions, anxiety). While some quantitative studies adopt a mixed methods approach and therefore provide qualitative observations of CMSI (e.g. Vetter and Chanier 2006), these investigations are largely based on statistical analyses (see also Jepson 2005). Quantification of CMSI is not inherently problematic, but a great deal of meaning is carried in spoken communication. Pauses, stress, and intonation are just a few aspects of CMSI that are used to manage online encounters (see Chapters 5 and 7). With quantitative studies, it is often the case that many interactional and paralinguistic features are not transcribed and/or examined in any detail. Therefore, the CMSI literature on teaching and learning does not provide a clear and comprehensive picture of what makes online spoken communication unique. Furthermore, it is difficult to determine how technological affordances and constraints shape the ongoing, turn-by-turn management of CMSI.

Table 3.1   CMSI (teaching and learning) studies from 1998–2012

| Methodology | Study and analytic focus |
|---|---|
| Statistical analyses/quantification | Alastuey (2010), pronunciation; Ciekanski and Chanier quantification (2008), writing; Deutschmann *et al.* (2009), oral participation; Heins *et al.* (2007), spoken interaction; Jepson (2005), repair moves; LaRose *et al.* (1998), course design; Satar and Özdener (2008), speaking proficiency and anxiety; Sindoni (2011), students' perceptions; Vetter and Chanier (2006), student participation; Volle (2005), oral skills; Wright and Whitehead (1998), students' perceptions; Yamada and Akahori (2007), social presence; Yang and Chang (2008), oral proficiency; Yanguas (2010), negotiated interactions; Yanguas (2012), vocabulary acquisition |
| Case study | Hampel (2003), theory development; Hampel (2006), task design framework; Hampel and Hauck (2004), pedagogical framework; Jauregi *et al.* (2011), task design framework; Rosell-Aguilar (2005), task design; Wang (2004), pedagogical framework; Wang *et al.* (2010), teacher development |
| Social semiotics | Guichon (2010), teacher development; Lamy (2004), oral competence |
| Discourse analysis | Levy and Kennedy (2004), teaching methodology; Sykes (2005), pragmatic development; Wang (2006), negotiated interactions |

CMSI is not the focus of analysis in any of the case studies cited in Table 3.1. These investigations are concerned with testing a theory and/or applying a pedagogical framework, rather than examining the interactional features of CMSI. Social semiotics and discourse analysis studies are largely qualitative, and are thus potentially useful to a social-interaction study of second language chat rooms. These studies do not, however, adopt social-interaction perspectives. Consequently, detailed transcripts of CMSI, which from a social-interaction perspective should minimally include timed pauses and paralinguistic features, do not represent the empirical basis from which observations of online spoken communication are made (the same conclusion can be drawn from reading the literature review conducted in Hassan *et al.* 2005).

The overview of the teaching and learning literature demonstrates that although CMSI platforms, including second language chat rooms, have been investigated, online spoken communication has, as an object of qualitative inquiry, received far less attention. Therefore, a social-interaction perspective of CMSI can contribute much to the teaching and learning literature by, for example, showing how online spoken communication presents unique interactional opportunities and challenges (see, for example, Chapters 6 and 8).

Table 3.2 CMSI (HCI) studies from 1992–2009

| Transcript-based research | Study and research design |
| --- | --- |
| Yes | Ackerman *et al.* (1997), experimental; Aoki *et al.* (2002), experimental; Aoki *et al.* (2003), experimental; Hindus *et al.* (1996), experimental; Huang *et al.* (2009), experimental; O'Conaill *et al.* (1993), non-experimental |
| No | Dourish *et al.* (1996), experimental; France *et al.* (2001), non-experimental; Geerts (2006), experimental; Hindus and Schmandt (1992), experimental; Isaacs and Tang (1994), experimental; Rodenstein and Donath (2000), experimental; Schmandt *et al.* (2002), experimental; Sellen (1995), experimental; Singer *et al.* (1999),experimental; Wadley *et al.* (2007), non-experimental; Weisz and Kiesler (2008), experimental; Woodruff and Aoki (2004), experimental |

Second, most CMSI studies conducted outside of educational settings belong to the area of research known as human–computer interaction (HCI). HCI studies do not belong to applied linguistics, but are relevant to some of the issues investigated in this book (e.g. Chapter 6).

Although HCI is a flourishing area of investigation with varied interests and empirical foci, many studies are experimental in nature. That is, HCI studies generally take place in laboratories and/or investigate experimental CMSI platforms. This is not, in itself, problematic. However, from a social-interaction perspective, the social actions and practices that are performed and carried out are different in laboratories and mundane encounters (see Section 2.2), and thus caution must be taken when making connections between the findings established in HCI and naturally occurring online settings.

Of the eighteen HCI studies from 1992–2009 reviewed here, fifteen took place in a laboratory and/or examined an experimental CMSI platform. Although many of these studies claimed to use social-interaction approaches, only six were carried out using detailed transcripts of CMSI. Table 3.2 summarizes these observations.

Table 3.2 shows that although a fair amount of CMSI research has been conducted in HCI, only a small portion of these studies use transcripts of online spoken communication. Consequently, only a third of the HCI studies identified in the table above are directly relevant to this book. Although non-transcript-based studies are potentially relevant to a social-interaction investigation of CMSI, analytic observations made in HCI are often anecdotal and/or rely on intuition data (e.g. asking research participants how they communicate in an online platform as opposed to analyzing how talk is managed in a CMSI setting). In subsequent chapters, the HCI studies that are directly relevant to second language chat rooms will be discussed in greater detail, including some that are not based on transcripts.

The issue of experimental designs is important to the present literature review, as naturally occurring interactions are the preferred data type to analyze from a social-interaction perspective. Conversely, experimental designs are the preferred way of conducting CMSI investigations in HCI. This is because HCI researchers are concerned with providing technical descriptions of online platforms in order to, for example, design better communication systems. Furthermore, these researchers often come from disciplines that do not stress the importance of naturally occurring data, which is the case in computational linguistics and software engineering. While experimental studies provide useful observations vis-à-vis CMSI affordances and constraints, communication conducted in laboratories and/or with prototype online platforms is socially and interactionally different than "ordinary" talk. Again, caution must be taken when applying the findings made in experimental studies to naturally occurring CMSI settings.

Finally, six CMSI studies analyze online spoken communication in its own right (see Luff and Heath 2002; Arminen 2005; Hutchby 2005; Hutchby and Barnett 2005; Szymanski *et al.* 2006; Rintel 2013). All of these studies adopt the same social-interaction perspective taken in this book. However, only one study examines an online platform that is similar to the chat rooms investigated in the present study. That is, Rintel (2013) examines long-distance video interactions conducted on computers, whereas the five remaining studies investigate mobile telephones (Arminen 2005; Hutchby 2005; Hutchby and Barnett 2005), fixed or stationary radios (Luff and Heath 2002), and portable push-to-talk radios (Szymanski *et al.* 2006). Telephone communication, of which many conversation analytic observations have been made, is not classified as CMSI. However, the conversation analytic literature on telephone communication is particularly germane to the present study, and will be discussed in subsequent chapters when relevant to the analysis of second language chat rooms.

## 3.3 CONCLUSION

This chapter has discussed the study of CMC in applied linguistics as three distinct, yet sometimes overlapping, empirical strands: teaching and learning, language and discourse, and sociality and culture. Each empirical strand is made up of studies that examine a number of different online contexts and phenomena. Online contexts that have been examined include language teaching, business negotiations, informal chatting, personal dating services, podcast lectures, and social media interactions. Phenomena that have been investigated include, but are not limited to, interactional cohesion, code-switching, meaning negotiation, language acquisition, national identities, diaspora, and communities of practice.

Although these three empirical strands are composed of decades of research that examine a multitude of online settings and phenomena, this chapter has demonstrated that text chat, discussion boards, and other similar forms of text-based communication represent the bulk of work done in the CMC literature.

As highlighted in the review of CMSI studies, when online spoken communication is investigated, it is often done using statistical measures and/or with little regard to how stress, intonation, pitch, and other vocal aspects of talk are used to co-construct meaning (for a discussion of how these aspects of talk can be transcribed, see Jenks 2011). That is to say, few studies have examined CMSI from a social-interaction perspective. Notable exceptions include, but are not limited to, conversation analytic investigations of mobile telephone communication (e.g. Arminen 2005; Hutchby and Barnett 2005), push-to-talk radios (e.g. Szymanski *et al.* 2006), and audio conferencing (Ackerman *et al.* 1997).

Examining CMSI with transcripts that are devoid of interactional and paralinguistic features is especially problematic given the amount of meaning and social actions that are accomplished in, and through, spoken communication. This is why social-interaction perspectives, like the conversation analytic methodology adopted in this book, are needed in order to truly understand how technology interfaces with CMSI. That is to say, social-interaction perspectives possess the tools necessary to transcribe and analyze online spoken communication in full detail, as it unfolds in real time and is managed *in situ* by interactants (see Section 2.2).

The need to provide more social-interaction descriptions of CMSI presents many research opportunities and challenges. The description of CMSI features is needed in order to expand the current empirical database. However, CMSI researchers do not have the luxury of analyzing data that are research ready—examining CMSI from a social-interaction perspective requires many hours of transcription work.

Despite the time and effort required to transcribe spoken discourse, CMSI investigations are needed in order to advance current understanding of CMC in general (e.g. generating findings that can be used to make comparisons between different communicative settings and online platforms), and online spoken communication in particular (e.g. uncovering how turn-taking is managed in the absence of physical co-presence). Furthermore, CMSI investigations can contribute to the three empirical strands of research identified above by providing a more comprehensive understanding of what CMC types work best for specific language teaching and learning objectives (see Chapter 8), uncovering interactional features of online spoken communication (see Chapters 5–7), and examining how social identities, communities, and cultural knowledge are co-constructed in second language chat rooms (see Chapter 9).

# 4

# INTRODUCTION TO CMSI

## 4.1 INTRODUCTION

The aim of this chapter is to discuss CMSI, the object of study in this book. This is done by discussing CMSI in relation to CMC, introducing the online platform investigated in the present study, reviewing the transcription conventions used to transcribe and analyze the recordings of online spoken communication, and describing the data set that forms the basis of this investigation.

CMSI represents several CMC types. As such, it is necessary to first identify the different subcategories of communication that fall under the rubric of CMC. CMC is typically broken into two communication types: medium and temporality. Herring (2007) identifies other categories (e.g. "persistence," for the time that utterances/ messages remain on the screen), though most of the technological facets that are included in her classification system are, to a large extent, influenced by medium and/ or temporality. While this short discussion of CMC is limited to medium and temporality, Herring's (2007) technological facets are central to an understanding of how computers mediate communication. The observations made in subsequent chapters draw on other categories when germane to the analysis of CMSI (e.g. granularity, length, and identity).

The first category, medium, includes text, audio, and video. Although some CMC platforms are conducted primarily in one medium (e.g. communication conducted in discussion boards is largely text-based), it is useful to think of this category as three intersecting circles that form seven subcategories: (1) text, (2) text and audio, (3) audio, (4) text and video (5) text, audio, and video, (6) audio and video, and (7) video (see Figure 4.1).

The study of CMSI encompasses every communication type except for subcategory 1. Subcategory 7 is related to CMSI, as most video communication relies heavily on spoken interaction. The present study is concerned primarily with subcategory 3 (see, however, Chapter 6, for a discussion of the similarities and differences between CMSI and text-based CMC).

The second category, temporality, includes asynchronous and synchronous communication. Traditionally, asynchronous communication is understood as interaction with delay, whereas synchronous communication is defined as concurrent interaction. With regard to CMSI, synchronicity can be further broken down into two categories: full duplex and half duplex. Full duplex communication allows for over-

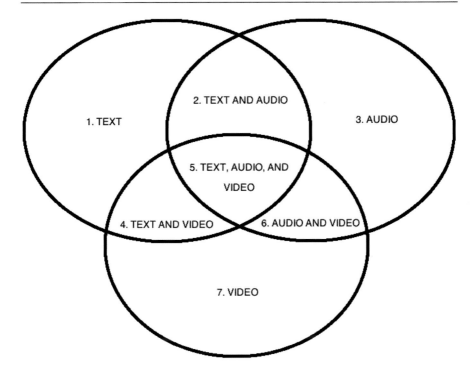

*Figure 4.1    CMC media*

lapping talk. Conversely, in half duplex communication, only one user can transmit a voice message at a time. The former type of communication is similar to the type of conversations that occur with telephones. The latter type of communication is similar to the conversations that take place with two-way radios (see Szymanski *et al.* 2006). Only full duplex communication is analyzed in this book.

Synchronicity is best conceptualized as a continuum, as even the most traditional asynchronous forms of CMC can occur with high rapidity. For example, an email exchange between two colleagues can occur in a matter of seconds, if both interactants are quickly sending, and attentively waiting to receive each other's, messages (Kalman and Rafaeli 2007). Conversely, communication conducted with synchronous CMSI can experience considerable delay if an interactant is communicating with a slow network connection. That is to say, the issue of synchronicity is shaped by how interactants make use of online communication technology, rather than, or in addition to, CMC shaping the speed with which interactants send and receive messages. The book is only concerned with synchronous CMSI.

The discussion above demonstrates that CMC takes many forms and is conducted in varied ways. As a terminological construct, CMC is adequate, and indeed effective, in covering the range of online communication that exists. Despite this, the area of study known as CMC requires more specific, context-sensitive constructs so that important communicative differences can be identified, studied, compared, and discussed. For instance, the term CMSI is particularly helpful in reminding researchers that online spoken communication is, in many ways, different than text-based CMC (e.g. ephemerality). More importantly, the term CMSI is needed because researchers often erroneously use CMC and text-based communication interchangeably (see, for example, Georgakopoulou 2006: 550; Blake 2009: 227). While attempts have been made to develop classification systems that capture different technological facets of online communication (see Herring 2007), the belief that CMC is primarily about texting and writing remains in the literature (e.g. Crystal 2006). This assumption will continue unless more effort is made in distinguishing, terminologically and empirically, between the different CMC types that exist. It is for these reasons that the term CMSI has been created and used for the present study.

The final terminological issue that is germane to the present discussion is related to the types of technology subsumed under CMC. For the first few decades of CMC inquiry, computers were the main focus of study. This is because most online communication at the time was conducted with a computer (e.g. emails, listservs, and instant messaging). With recent developments in technology and changes in online media consumption, however, researchers have started to question whether CMC is the best term to use for this area of study. Suggestions have been made to replace CMC with a term that is more encompassing—one that covers not only new technologies (e.g. tablets and mobile phones), but also more traditional forms of computing devices (e.g. laptops and desktops).

Baron (2008a), for example, uses the term electronically mediated communication (EMC) to cover the range of technologies used to interact online. While EMC and other similar terms (e.g. technology-mediated communication) cover a wider set of technologies than CMC, it is important to continue using more specific, context-sensitive terminological constructs, like CMSI. This is because substantive interactional and linguistic differences exist between CMC types (see Chapter 6).

In this book, the analysis of CMSI is restricted to computing devices that are generally used in a "single" space (i.e. desktops and laptops). However, observations and findings from (mobile) telephone and other electronic forms of communication will be discussed occasionally for cross-referencing purposes.

## 4.2 CMSI PLATFORMS

CMSI is a verbal dialogue between interactants conducted with computers connected to the Internet or a local area network (e.g. a local area network for a business that is used for internal communication). CMSI can be conducted entirely in the spoken medium, though many online platforms allow interactants to simultaneously communicate with text and/or video. CMSI can unfold synchronously or asynchronously between two or more interactants.

Asynchronous CMSI is sometimes referred to as asynchronous audio communication (other researchers use the term asynchronous voice; see Ross 2003). Asynchronous CMSI is a series of pre-recorded audio files that are uploaded online. Interactants create voice messages that are saved, and listened and responded to, at different time intervals. With asynchronous CMSI, interactants do not need to be online at the same time. Voice messages are a common way of communicating with telephones and mobile devices, though asynchronous CMSI is far less common in online settings. Many of the asynchronous CMSI platforms that are in current use have been designed for instructional purposes (e.g. VoiceThread and Wimba Voice Board).

Although asynchronous CMSI is an important area of investigation, this book is only concerned with synchronous CMSI. This section introduces the technical procedure that underpins synchronous CMSI (i.e. voice over Internet Protocol). This discussion is followed by a review of the synchronous CMSI program that is examined in the present study (i.e. Skype), and the chat room service that is associated with this platform (i.e. Skypecast). The aim of this discussion is twofold: (1) to provide a technical, but introductory, account of synchronous CMSI, and (2) to explain the basic communicative functionality of Skypecasts.

### 4.2.1 VOICE OVER INTERNET PROTOCOL

The communication technology that facilitates synchronous CMSI is voice over Internet Protocol, commonly referred to as VoIP (sometimes pronounced as /voyp/). VoIP is the transmission of voice using IP, which simply means that the Internet is used as a medium for online spoken communication (for a discussion of the functionality of IP in relation to online communication, see Chapter 2). VoIP technology can also be used to communicate between two or more VoIP-enabled devices connected to a local area network that does not rely on the Internet (e.g. intranet used at an institution) or a personal area network that is connected to the Internet (e.g. home wireless network). While VoIP is the so-called channel that transmits voice over networks, CMSI is conducted using online platforms that make use of this technology (e.g. Skype). Some services only allow communication between users of the same online platform, whereas other services can be used to interact across different online platforms.

VoIP communication is minimally conducted with two interactants using VoIP-enabled devices. Most CMSI platforms provide multiparty talk functionality. Many online platforms that use VoIP technology also allow interactants to communicate with text and/or video. Furthermore, VoIP is increasingly being used to communicate with devices connected to landlines (public switched telephone network—PSTN) and cellular networks, and mobile phone-to-mobile phone VoIP communication is rising in popularity. The discussion below begins with the CMSI platform that hosted the second language chat rooms investigated in this book.

#### 4.2.1.1 Skype

Skype is a popular CMSI platform that offers online spoken communication capabilities. Skype also allows interactants to engage in dyadic and multiparty synchronous text-based CMC. Furthermore, Skype users can conduct multiparty conference calls in audio and/or video, text asynchronously between two interactants, and transfer files (for a full list of features, see Skype Limited 2012). While current estimates vary, Skype has approximately 560 million registered users, and up to 23 million users are online in any given day during peak times (Rosenberg 2010). Skype first gained in

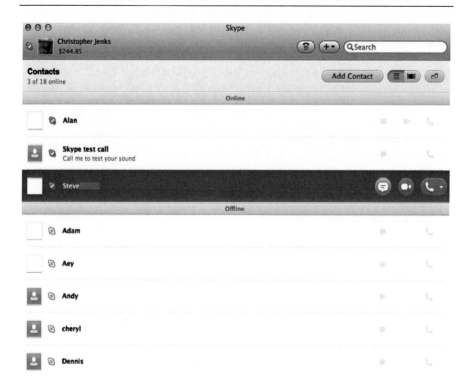

*Figure 4.2    Skype UI*

popularity as a computer-based VoIP provider, but now the online platform can be downloaded and used on mobile phones and tablet devices. Figure 4.2 is a screenshot of the user interface (UI) as seen on a computer.

Three channels of synchronous communication are displayed as buttons to the right of each highlighted user on the list of contacts (see "Steve" in Figure 4.2): a blue chat box button for text, a green video camera button for video, and a green telephone button for audio. The audio button allows users to make calls to a contact's Skype account or any landline or mobile phone number listed in a contact's profile. In other words, the audio button allows calls to be made via Skype-to-Skype, Skype-to-PSTN, or Skype-to-cellular network. In addition to communicating in one medium, Skype users can interact simultaneously with two or more media (e.g. text and audio), or chat with different media (e.g. one user with video and another with audio). The dial pad button located near the top right-hand corner of the window allows users to manually enter phone numbers and send asynchronous text messages to mobile phones using short message service (SMS). Thus, the main Skype UI has four primary buttons for communication, and each button varies in terms of what type of participation and communication is possible.

Figure 4.3 is an illustration of what a Skype user sees after pushing the green telephone button.

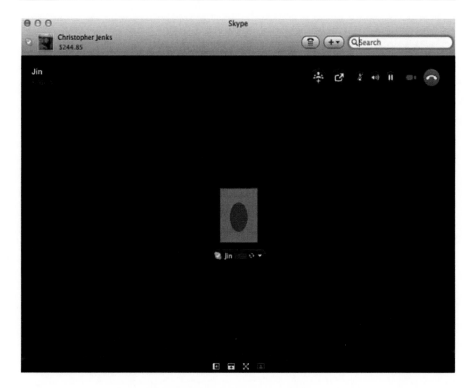

*Figure 4.3    Skype UI: calling*

Most online platforms present the caller with a window that displays the call receiver's avatar or photo. With Skype, the caller will see the call receiver's avatar or photo in the middle of the screen, along with a row of buttons on the top right-hand corner of the window. These buttons allow the caller to change the medium of communication, say from audio-only to video, adjust the volume, add new Skype users to the call, and share what is visible on one screen with other co-users, to name a few. Figure 4.3 is particularly helpful in showing the multimodal nature of CMSI: two Skype users will minimally see each other's avatar or photo when communicating verbally. Figure 4.4 is a screenshot of two interactants communicating via CMSI and text-based CMC.

In Figure 4.4, the text dialogue is located on the bottom of the UI. Skype is graphically designed so that each communication type or modality has a dedicated section (or sub-window) displayed on the UI.

### 4.2.1.2 Skypecasts

While Skype and similar CMSI platforms (e.g. Adobe Connect, MSN Messenger) are used primarily to communicate with family, friends, acquaintances, and colleagues, VoIP technology is also used to establish new friendships and meet unacquainted people in chat rooms. Skype offers one such online service called Skypecast. Skypecasts represent the main data set for this book.

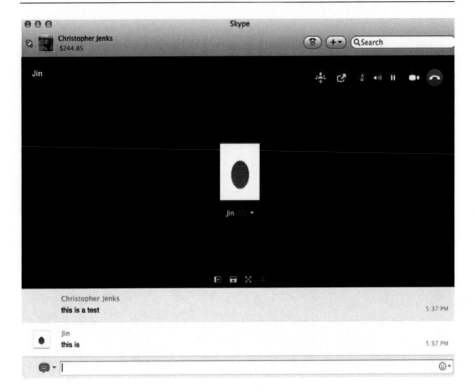

*Figure 4.4    Skype UI: talking and texting*

Skypecasts are multiparty CMSI-based chat rooms hosted by Skype. Although Skypecasts are temporarily unavailable at the time of writing, the multiparty audio conferencing tools that Skype currently offers provide a similar CMSI experience (see also Paltalk). Any Skype user over the age of eighteen can host and/or participate in a Skypecast. A host creates the chat room and is responsible for managing the different levels of participation that exist in Skypecasts (see below). While Skypecasts are sometimes used to conduct business meetings, deliver classroom lessons, and carry out other formal, preplanned speech exchange events, many chat rooms provide forums for unacquainted interactants to meet and discuss topics of common interest (for a detailed discussion of the data collected for this study, see Section 4.5 below). Skypecasts are created with titles and descriptions that are displayed online and within the Skype UI. Skype users can search for, and subsequently participate in, chat rooms based on their interests (e.g. English, religion, political talk, Arabic). Figure 4.5 is a screenshot of three public forums listed on the Skype UI.

Skypecast communication is conducted primarily in the spoken medium, though participants can send private text messages to each other. After joining a Skypecast, participants are bound by three levels of participation: listening, waiting, and talking. Upon entering a chat room, a new user is assigned to the listening section (see "allan" in Figure 4.6). Users in the listening section cannot speak, but can send each other

*Figure 4.5    Skypecast UI: public forums*

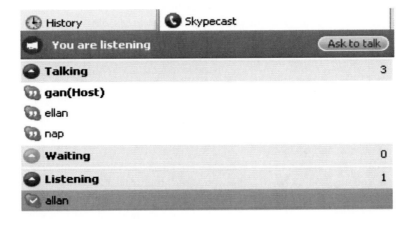

*Figure 4.6    Skypecast UI: chat room*

private text messages and upgrade their status to waiting. Interactants in the listening section can upgrade their status to waiting by pushing the "Ask to talk" button located on the top right-hand corner of the UI. It is not uncommon for Skypecasts users to stay in the listening section for the entire duration of a chat room. That is to say, "lurking" is not uncommon in Skypecasts.

Once in the waiting section, the host of the chat room can move interactants into the talking section—only the host possesses this privilege. In the waiting and talking sections, users can send private text messages—these messages are rarely explicitly oriented to in the main public chat room. Online spoken communication in Skypecasts is similar to telephone interactions in that embodied actions are not visually available to the users. Furthermore, Skypecasts do not offer tools to graphically signal speakership (e.g. a graphical hand to signal the wish to take a turn at talk; cf. Paltalk). In the same vein, when interactants speak, there is nothing located on the UI that signals who the current speaker is (e.g. user names do not illuminate when speaking). Thus, Skypecast users must rely almost entirely on the spoken medium to identify the current speaker. As subsequent chapters demonstrate, this contextual constraint has an impact on how Skypecast users manage their interactions.

## 4.3 KEY TECHNOLOGICAL AND CONTEXTUAL FEATURES OF CMSI

A general assumption in the CMC literature is that online communication is a hybrid language system that comprises elements of written and spoken communication (see Crystal 2011). While this assumption may reflect synchronous text-based CMC, it neglects the technological and contextual differences in, and variation across, online platforms. As revealed in the previous sections on Skype and Skypecasts, online spoken communication is managed according to technological tools. While one CMSI platform may not offer a particular feature of communication (e.g. using hand gestures), other platforms may. In other words, CMSI should always be discussed in relation to the technological tools that are available and the communicative affordances and constraints that result from using a particular online platform. Therefore, before moving on to the analytic chapters, it is necessary to identify the facets of technology and contextual features that are central to the second language chat rooms examined in this study.

The second language chat rooms examined in subsequent chapters have no persistence (see Herring 2007). That is, the words and utterances that are spoken during communication do not visually appear on computer screens. Unlike text-based CMC, where communication remains on the screen until an online platform is shut down, second language chat room participants must rely on their memory to recall previously spoken words and utterances. That is, interactants cannot scroll back to retrieve previous communicative exchanges—it should be noted, however, that with current screen capturing and recording technology, interactants can record online spoken communication for later inspection. The issue of ephemerality is important to how online spoken communication unfolds, and is what distinguishes it from other CMC types (see, for example, Chapter 6).

Another defining technological characteristic of CMSI is granularity. Granularity refers to the level of linguistic detail that is available for communication. This definition should not be confused with Herring's (2007: 14) interpretation of granularity; the latter understanding deals with message transmission types: message-by-message, character-by-character, and line-by-line. CMSI is highly granular in that a substantial amount of information is contained within spoken words and utterances (e.g. changes in voice amplitude and fluctuations in stress and intonation). In other words, a high degree of linguistic detail is transmitted or conveyed in, and through, online spoken communication. For example, variation in pitch allows interactants to shape their identities and affiliate or dis-affiliate themselves with or from a larger community of users. While the granularity of CMSI entails linguistically rich, yet varied ways of, interaction, it also presents CMC researchers with the difficult and time-consuming task of capturing (and transcribing) online spoken communication in a form that is easily disseminated to, and understood by, an academic audience (for the transcription conventions used in this book, see Section 4.4 below). Despite these challenges, capturing the highly granular nature of online spoken communication is crucial to conducting rigorous CMC research, as micro features of talk are central to meaning construction in CMSI environments.

The second language chat rooms examined in this book require interactants to use screen names and/or avatars. While chat rooms cannot fully prevent users from creating fictitious profiles and using pseudonyms in lieu of real names, the granularity of CMSI makes it difficult for interactants to disguise their manner of speaking, and ultimately their "true" identities. It is possible that interactants are less likely to discuss sensitive information on CMSI platforms because online spoken communication does not afford users complete confidentiality, though this is an empirical question that requires further investigation. Although the possibility of being recognized by voice may deter interactants from using CMSI platforms to discuss sensitive information with strangers, high granularity is beneficial for interactants who wish to narrow the sense of social distance that is experienced with text-based CMC (e.g. instant messaging programs). For example, work colleagues, family, and friends often wish to maximize their sense of physical co-presence during online communication, and this is perhaps one reason why CMSI platforms are widely used for communication with acquainted interactants—or conversely, why CMSI chat rooms are less popular than text-based chat rooms for unacquainted interactants. This should come as no surprise, as social distance and physical co-presence are important aspects of human interaction (Tillema *et al.* 2010).

The CMSI platforms discussed above are inherently multimodal in that online communication is minimally conducted with a graphical UI. For example, Skype users minimally see each other's avatar when communicating verbally, and simultaneous texting is possible within the same UI. While having different graphical features located in one UI facilitates multimodal communication, in that users do not have to toggle between different communication windows, the ability to simultaneously communicate in different media presents many interactional challenges. In the final chapter of this book, the multimodal nature of CMSI will be discussed in terms of the methodological challenges of capturing and analyzing how interactants communicate verbally whilst engaging in other modes of communication.

Unlike text-based CMC, capturing and transcribing online spoken communication is not only challenging, but also integral to the analytic process of conducting CMSI research.

Message clarity (or call quality) is also an important technological issue in second language chat rooms. The ability to co-construct meaning during CMSI is dependent not only on the physiology of interactants, but also on the hardware used during communication. That is to say, an interactant may have the ability to clearly articulate thoughts, but these thoughts may not be effectively conveyed if the hardware used during CMSI is problematic. For example, CMSI requires two acoustic devices: one device that emits sound (e.g. speakers) and a second device that transmits speech (e.g. microphone)—often these two devices are built into one unit (e.g. headset). The quality and positioning of these two devices plays an important role in message clarity. Interactants are likely to experience problems with audibleness, background noise, and echoes, as a result of low-quality speakers and/or incorrectly positioned microphones (for a discussion of how this shapes CMSI, see Chapter 7). As a result, it is not uncommon for interactants to report, and indeed diagnose each other's, hardware problems during CMSI. Furthermore, bandwidth speeds are closely connected to message clarity. Slow connections often result in white noise, amplification problems, and choppy sound, to name a few. Although all CMC types are to some degree influenced by hardware issues (e.g. using a keyboard during text-based CMC), technology is more likely to disrupt message clarity in CMSI because of variation in bandwidth capacity and the quality of acoustic devices.

The CMSI platform examined in subsequent chapters can be minimized, allowing users to carry out other computer-based tasks during communication; for example, CMSI can take place while users read and respond to emails, check updates on Twitter, read the news, or get stock quotes. In other words, users may have a number of different application windows running whilst engaging in online spoken communication. This is made possible, in part, because an interactant does not have access to a co-interactant's screen unless this is made available and/or what is running on a screen is made relevant in talk; therefore, interactants are somewhat free to re-focus some of their attention to multitasking. Multitasking is a common feature of CMC that has salient implications with regard to how online communication is managed. The methodological challenges of recording and analyzing multitasking in CMSI will be discussed at the end of this book (see Chapter 10).

The type of multitasking that occurs is also partly influenced by physical space. Increased dependency on mobile and tablet devices, coupled with wider availability of wireless Internet access points (e.g. cafes, libraries, university campuses), has expanded the number of spaces used to engage in online spoken communication. CMSI is no longer limited to computers, and only conducted in the physical confines of an office space or private room. Interactants are increasingly using VoIP to communicate in public spaces, and with and across a number of different computing devices (e.g. laptops, desktops, mobile phones, tablet devices). CMSI is conducted while waiting in line to order food, commuting to and from work, and even during classroom lectures.

The way online spoken communication is managed is also closely connected to graphical tools. In the CMSI platforms discussed above, interactants use graphical tools to adjust volume, add or toggle between channels of communication (e.g. adding text-based CMC to CMSI or switching from CMSI to text-based CMC), incorporate new participants into a conversation, and share documents, to name a few. Interactants rely heavily on these graphical tools to engage in communication and enhance message clarity. Furthermore, some graphical tools determine what is interactionally possible. For example, in Paltalk, an online platform that provides a similar experience to Skypecast, interactants raise graphical hands to signal the desire to take a turn at talk, and a push-to-talk graphical button must be used to speak. As a result of these graphical tools, overlapping talk is not possible in Paltalk. Conversely, Skypecast users do not have a graphical tool that allows them to signal speakership, nor do they need to use a push-to-talk button to speak. As a result, overlapping talk is a common phenomenon in Skypecasts (see Chapter 5).

The discussions contained in this section provided a brief overview of the affordances and constraints of CMSI, as they pertained to the second language chat rooms investigated in this book. The technological and contextual issues identified here will be revisited in subsequent chapters as part of a more detailed analysis and discussion of CMSI. In the following section, the methodological issues of transcribing online spoken communication are introduced. This is followed by a detailed discussion of the data set used in the present study.

## 4.4 TRANSCRIPTION CONVENTIONS

Online spoken communication has been around for many years now, though CMSI studies represent a small portion of the CMC literature. This research gap is due, in part, to the fact that online spoken communication requires far more effort to transcribe than text-based CMC (for other reasons why CMSI studies represent a small portion of the CMC literature, see Chapter 3). Put differently, the challenge in pursuing an investigation of CMSI lies largely in the time, knowledge, and resources needed to prepare detailed transcripts of spoken communication (for a discussion of the practical and theoretical issues of transcribing communication data, see Jenks 2011). This section provides a concise overview of the transcription conventions used in this book.

The transcription conventions used in subsequent chapters have been modified from Atkinson and Heritage (1984). These transcription conventions were originally developed to represent face-to-face and telephone conversations. As such, the transcription system adopted in this study is well suited for CMSI.

The first three transcription conventions relate to turn-taking phenomena, an important aspect of online spoken communication (see Chapter 5):

[[ ]]     Simultaneous utterances—(beginning [[) and (end ]])
[ ]       Overlapping utterances—(beginning [) and (end ])
=         Contiguous utterances (or continuation of the same turn)

Simultaneous utterances occur when two or more interactants begin speaking at the same time. This phenomenon generally occurs after a pause. Overlapping utterances occur when an interactant talks at the same time as another speaker. Overlapping utterances should not be confused with interruption. An interruption is a phenomenon that is made relevant when interactants treat overlapping talk as disruptive (i.e. it is a social phenomenon, rather than an interactional one). Contiguous utterances occur when an utterance spoken by one speaker is immediately followed by another utterance spoken by a different speaker.

Pauses are timed using a software application that measures the precise duration of silence. The two transcription conventions used in the analysis of CMSI are as follows:

(0.4)    Represent the tenths of a second between utterances
(.)      Represents a micro-pause (one tenth of a second or less)

In addition to interactional phenomena, paralinguistic features are important to an understanding of how online spoken communication is managed (see Chapter 7). Five commonly transcribed paralinguistic features are elongation, fall in pitch, slight rise in pitch, abrupt stop, and rise in pitch:

:    Elongation (more colons demonstrate longer stretches of sound)
.    Fall in pitch at the end of an utterance
,    Slight rise in pitch at the end of an utterance
-    An abrupt stop in articulation
?    Rising in pitch at utterance end (not necessarily a question)

Voice amplitude, accentuation, fluctuations in intonation, and quiet talk, are common features of online spoken communication. The conventions used to transcribe these features are as follows:

CAPITAL    Loud/forte speech
__           Underlined letters/words indicate accentuation
↑↓        Marked upstep/downstep in intonation
° °        Surrounds talk that is quieter

Online spoken communication is markedly differently from other types of CMC in that interactants can hear, and attend to, exhalations and inhalations, as well as laughter. These micro features of talk can shape, among other things, turn-taking practices (see Chapter 5). A descriptive analysis of CMSI must be based on transcripts that incorporate these features of speech.

The following conventions are used to represent the different ways in which breathing and laughter occur in online spoken communication:

hhh       Exhalations
.hhh      Inhalations
he or ha   Laugh particle
(hhh)     Laughter within a word (can also represent audible aspirations)
$ $       Surrounds 'smile' voice

In addition to breathing and laughing, pace of speech is used as an interactional resource to manage communication in online settings. The following conventions are used for utterances that are spoken faster and more slowly than surrounding talk:

>>    Surrounds talk that is spoken faster
<<    Surrounds talk that is spoken more slowly

Finally, parentheses are used to add analyst notes and approximations of what may have been spoken in any given stretch of talk, as follows:

(( ))   Analyst notes
( )     Approximations of what is heard

All of the transcription conventions identified above are used to represent, in written form, the highly granular nature of CMSI. These transcription conventions are crucial to conducting rigorous CMC research because they allow researchers to examine and present CMSI as it unfolds in real time, as the interactants themselves construct, hear, and respond to spoken words and utterances. Conversely, transcripts devoid of these conventions restrict researchers to making superficial observations of online spoken communication. Therefore, it is important for CMSI researchers to be somewhat faithful in their representations of online spoken communication, as the nuances of spoken discourse are fundamental to the co-construction of understanding and the organization of social action and practices. Again, detailed transcripts, like the ones provided in subsequent chapters, are necessary for understanding the highly organized nature of CMSI.

## 4.5  THE STUDY AND DATA SET

The data analyzed in this book are conversations between speakers of English as an additional language. Nearly one hundred chat rooms were recorded over a two-year period. The transcripts that were used in the present study represent approximately 20 percent of the data collected (i.e. approximately ten hours of audio data). The chat rooms examined in subsequent chapters were created to practice and use English (for a discussion of how Skype can be used for language teaching and learning, see Godwin-Jones 2005), though interactants rarely treated their conversations as opportunities to engage in formal language learning. For example, interactions were never based on preplanned lessons, interactants rarely assumed the role of language teacher (e.g. explicitly correcting grammatical mistakes), and participatory rights were distributed symmetrically or at least managed organically. English was the main language of the chat rooms, but interactants would occasionally switch to and from different languages.

The interactants that were recorded came from different parts of the world. Countries of origin include, but are not limited to, South Korea, Thailand, Turkey, Egypt, Syria, China, and Japan. Topics of discussion were not predetermined and there were no explicit rules of participation. Interactants would occasionally negotiate rules of participation on the fly, but this can lead to trouble in communication (see Chapter 9).

Conversations were based on anything from favorite movies to political issues. Getting acquainted exchanges were common in the data set because interactants would enter and leave chat rooms with high regularity, which would in turn require self-introductions and the like (e.g. greeting exchanges). The length of conversations varied from a few minutes to two hours.

Most of the chat rooms investigated in the present study comprised three or more participants. A small portion of the chat rooms were created by a research assistant and two doctoral students that assisted in the present study. These recordings represent approximately 25 percent of the data set (i.e. roughly three hours of data). The remaining chat rooms were created by interactants that had already been using the online platform for language practice or informal learning purposes. None of these interactants had any prior knowledge of, and connection with, the present study. Nearly all of the interactants were unacquainted at the beginning of the chat room (i.e. the interactants did not demonstrate prior knowledge of each other).

Data were captured using a software program that, at the beginning of each chat room, notified interactants via text and voice messages that their interactions were being recorded. The software program also notified interactants that the recording would stop if they did not wish to be recorded. Very few interactants did not provide consent. When consent was not provided, the recording was stopped. The names used in the extracts in subsequent chapters are pseudonyms.

# ANALYSIS

5

# TALKING ONLINE: CMSI FEATURES

## 5.1 INTRODUCTION

The aim of this chapter is to describe the basic interactional features of CMSI. In so doing, this chapter contributes to the language and discourse empirical strand. The findings established in this chapter are used in subsequent chapters to make comparisons with synchronous text-based CMC (see Chapter 6), and explore the pedagogical implications of second language chat rooms (see Chapter 8).

Before proceeding with the analysis, two caveats must be made regarding the phenomena examined in this chapter. First, this chapter does not examine every feature of talk and interaction that is associated with conversation analysis (e.g. repair sequences and preference organization). The features of talk and interaction that are examined in this chapter have been selected because (1) few studies have examined such phenomena in CMSI platforms, and (2) they are fundamental to the organization and management of online spoken communication.

Although research may reveal that repair sequences, preference organization, and other sequential aspects of talk are central to how CMSI unfolds, this is not the case for the second language chat rooms investigated in this book (see, however, Chapter 7, for an analysis of how the CMSI environment shapes *what* is repaired). That is not to say that researchers should ignore repair sequences, preference organization, and other sequential aspects of talk when investigating different online platforms. How talk and interaction are managed in other CMSI platforms are empirical questions that must be answered in future research.

The second caveat is concerned with the type of analyses made in this chapter. In the CMC literature, it is common practice to make analytic comparisons across or between communicative settings (e.g. chat rooms versus face-to-face encounters). Although comparative studies are important to the CMC literature, and indeed represent the type of analyses conducted in Chapter 6, this chapter is principally concerned with uncovering the interactional and organizational features of CMSI. The decision to refrain from making extensive comparisons in this chapter allows for more space to offer detailed observations of CMSI; it also helps readers better understand and appreciate the complexities involved in online spoken communication.

This chapter is broken down into three analytic sections: turn-taking, summons-answer exchanges, and identification practices. These three interactional features have been selected because they are exemplary in illustrating how second language chat rooms are managed in the absence of physical co-presence. Because these interactional features have been investigated extensively in the conversation analytic literature, each data analysis section begins with a general overview of the topic of investigation.

## 5.2 TURN-TAKING

Many conversation analytic studies of telephone and face-to-face interactions have shown that turn-taking is methodically organized and crucial to the organization of social structures, activities, and actions. This has been demonstrated most notably in Sacks *et al.* (1974), where the authors revealed that although turn-taking practices differ from one context to another, as a system of rules, turn-taking is incredibly robust. That is not to say, however, that turn-taking rules are static. Rather, turn-taking practices are situated in, and thus created for, the immediate communicative context in which interactants find themselves interacting. This idea underpins most conversation analytic work: researchers have demonstrated that turns, and the talk and interaction that are contained within them, are used methodically by interactants to display their commonsense understanding of each other and their communicative environment (for a seminal investigation conducted in second language classrooms, see Seedhouse 2004). For many conversation analytic studies, turn-taking practices are integral to an understanding of communication.

In the CMC literature, turn-taking is also a key area of research. Turn-taking studies have contributed much to an understanding of how technology mediates communication (e.g. McKinlay *et al.* 1993; Condon and Cech 2001). To date, however, nearly all turn-taking studies have examined text-based CMC, including most notably the study conducted by Herring (1999) on chat rooms (see also Garcia and Jacobs 1999). Turn-taking studies generally possess two analytic objectives: to understand the communicative features of an online platform and to compare these features with face-to-face communication. Studies have focused on, for example, turn allocation practices and sequential coherence, and have juxtaposed what happens in text-based CMC with the turn-taking practices of spoken, face-to-face interaction (see Anderson *et al.* 2010).

While turn-taking studies on text-based CMC have contributed much to an understanding of online communication, few studies have adopted the same level of analytic detail when examining turn-taking practices in CMSI. This section narrows this empirical gap by examining three aspects of turn-taking in CMSI: turn construction and transition, overlapping utterances, and turn allocation.

### 5.2.1 TURN CONSTRUCTION AND TRANSITION

The turn-taking system in CMSI is highly ordered. The turns that make up this system are made up of "turn constructional units" (e.g. a backchannel, phrase, or syntactically complete utterance). Turn constructional units, as opposed to what can be heard as "complete sentences," are used to co-construct meaning and coordinate turn transitions in CMSI. This turn-taking system allows interactants to manage speakership according to an understanding of when a current turn at talk is complete (or nearing completion). The ability to hear a turn as it is being constructed (or as it unfolds in real time) allows interactants to project turn completion and/or take a turn at talk when enough information has been given to do so. Managing turns as they are vocally produced makes CMSI markedly different than synchronous text-based CMC (see Chapter 6). As the examples below demonstrate, turn constructional units and turn transitions represent the basic interactional building blocks of CMSI.

In online spoken communication, turn transitions occur in several sequential locations, including at turn completion. Note, for example, the following question–answer exchange, where two interactants are negotiating a topic of discussion.

```
(1)
11—Skypecast
01:13:36—01:13:43
1     Ryan:      what would you <like to talk about?<
2                (1.1)
3     Hal:       about↑ a simple'er: (0.6) subject
```

In Extract 1, the turn transition occurs after a syntactically complete question. Although the turn-taking system in CMSI allows Hal to take a turn at any point during this exchange (e.g. Hal can interject, begin his own topic of discussion, or ask Ryan a question), he produces an answer after the question is constructed in its entirety. This is significant in that it shows that there is a great deal of collaborative work involved in co-managing an ostensibly simple question–answer exchange. Turn-taking in CMSI requires monitoring and coordinating turn constructions as they unfold in real time. Take, for example, the following extract. In this example, SydneyLove and Dukes have just met and are getting acquainted.

```
(2)
1g—Skypecast
00:45—00:59
1     SydneyLove:     my name's sydney love from south korea
2                     a::nd. (0.5) nice to meet you.
3                     (1.1)
4     Dukes:          you're from austria, is it?
```

Here SydneyLove begins his turn by introducing himself and identifying his country of origin. In line 2, after a pause, SydneyLove completes his turn with a greeting. Thus, this turn comprises two constructional units: an introduction and a greeting. What is particularly interesting in this exchange is that although the half-second pause in line 2 represents a possible turn transition (i.e. a point in the interaction where any participant can begin talking), Dukes does not take his turn until after the greeting.

Closer inspection of the pause in line 2 reveals that it follows a conjunction that is produced with elongation ("a::nd."). This lexical item may signal to Dukes that talk is forthcoming. Indeed, this is how Dukes responds to the entire turn: although Dukes responds to the introduction (i.e. the first turn constructional unit), he begins his turn after the second turn constructional unit (i.e. Dukes lets SydneyLove produce a greeting before providing a response). In other words, Dukes does not orient to the greeting provided by SydneyLove.

Extracts 1 and 2 demonstrate that turn transitions are coordinated with turn constructions. That is to say, the transition from one speaker to another is done in coordination with turn constructional units. In both extracts, turn transitions occurred at turn completion. However, because the turn-taking system in CMSI affords interactants the ability to monitor turns as they are vocally produced, turn transitions can also occur before or near turn completion. This is exemplified in the following extract. In Extract 3, two interactants are negotiating a time to meet again.

```
(3)
1k—Skypecast
00:33—00:46
1    Sal:     you- you mean today or eh:: t-
2             tonight o:r.
3    Han:     i me[an
4    Sal:        [tomorrow?
5    Han:     tonight (.) tonight tonight (0.9)
```

In lines 1 and 2, Sal seeks clarification by listing a series of possibilities (i.e. today, tonight, and tomorrow). Although Sal begins to utter a third option, the first two possibilities provide Hal with enough information to supply a response. This is demonstrated in line 3, where Hal begins to clarify his previous turn ("i mean"). The turn transition occurs before Sal completes his turn (i.e. before Sal provides his third possibility). This is noteworthy, as it shows that although the turn-taking system in CMSI is robust (e.g. participants, by and large, speak one at a time), turn transitions can occur before turn completion. The example also shows the type of interactional work involved in managing turn transitions. By providing a response before Sal completes his turn, Han shows that he is monitoring the series of possibilities as they unfold in real time. Rather than wait until the turn is syntactically complete, Han takes his turn when enough information is provided for him to do so. This phenomenon is further illustrated in the next extract. Extract 4 begins immediately after Extract 3.

```
(4)
1k—Skypecast
00:46—00:51
6    Han:     twelve aye ehm=
7    Sal:     =o:h o[kay!
8    Han:           [will be- (.) will be nine
9             aye ehm wed[nesday
10   Sal:                [okay
```

In line 6, Han offers Sal's local time. As Han closes this turn, Sal provides an acknowledgment token in line 7. The change in speakership occurs in quick succession because Han's turn has revealed enough information for Sal to provide a response and/or Sal is able to project the end of the turn. As with Extract 3, the turn transition occurs near, and not at, turn completion. Extracts 3 and 4 demonstrate that the turn-taking system in CMSI is organized according to turn constructional units (as opposed to syntactically complete sentences). This is further evidenced upon closer inspection of Extract 3, re-presented below as Extract 5.

```
(5)
1k—Skypecast
00:33—00:46
1    Sal:    you- you mean today or eh:: t-
2            tonight o:r.
3    Han:    i me[an
4    Sal:       [tomorrow?
5    Han:    tonight (.) tonight tonight (0.9)
```

As noted before, Han provides a response in line 3 before Sal supplies a third possibility. The precise location of the turn transition is crucial to an understanding of how speakership is managed in CMSI. Just before Han takes his turn, Sal produces a conjunction ("o:r."). Although the grammatical function of "or" is to provide an alternative, the utterance ends with a fall in pitch (as indicated by the period/full stop). Falls in pitch are frequently located at the end of a turn constructional unit, and may signal that a turn is complete (Selting 2000). At this particular moment in the interaction, therefore, Han can orient to either (1) the grammatical function of the conjunction (by letting Sal utter the third option) or (2) the possibility that the fall in pitch represents a turn transition (by taking a turn after the conjunction). By taking his turn after the conjunction, Hal demonstrates that he is implicitly aware of prosodic fluctuations in online spoken communication.

This example establishes that prosody shapes turn-taking practices in CMSI. The turn-taking system in CMSI is dependent on the production and coordination of vocal cues, including micro changes in stress and intonation. Furthermore, this subsection has shown that turn transitions (1) are organized according to turn constructional units, (2) may but need not occur at the end of turns, and (3) are sometimes managed by prosody rather than grammar. The methodological upshot of these observations is that researchers must be aware of the micro details of talk and interaction in order to adequately examine CMSI. This observation is even more apparent when examining overlapping utterances.

## 5.2.2 OVERLAPPING UTTERANCES

Overlapping utterances are a popular topic of investigation in the CMC literature (see Jenks 2009a). Interest in overlapping utterances stems from seminal discussions of whether, and to what degree, interactants follow the so-called one-speaker-at-a-time rule (Searle 1986; Lerner 1989; Searle *et al.* 1992; Schegloff 2000). Comparisons between, and across, modes of communication (e.g. text-based CMC and face-to-face interactions) are often made (see Negretti 1999). It is observed that interactants in synchronous text-based CMC flout the one-speaker-at-a-time rule (Herring 1999; see, however, Marcoccia *et al.* 2008).

In CMSI, overlapping utterances also occur. However, the organization of talk leading up to, and during, two or more simultaneous utterances is different than the organization of overlap observed in text-based chat (see Chapter 6) and face-to-face interaction (see below). Overlapping utterances occur in CMSI partly because turn transitions occur near, and not generally at the end of, turn completions, as demonstrated in the preceding section (cf. face-to-face interactions; see Sacks *et al.* 1974; Schegloff 2000).Overlapping utterances also occur because two or more speakers attempt to speak at approximately the same time. The interaction leading up to the latter type of overlapping utterances sheds light on how technology mediates online spoken communication. In Extract 6, Roci opens the discussion by identifying who is currently present in the chat room.

```
(6)
1h—Skypecast
00:00—00:27
1     Roci:        if you uh- if you try to join us eh
2                  you like to join us here daniel just
3                  moved into the waiting area (1.0) uh::
4                  y- i- i- daniel here is from uh: brunei
5                  (0.7) fro[m brunei
6     Winnie:               [from brunei
7                  (0.6)
```

In lines 2–4, Roci announces that a co-interactant is in the chat room and identifies where is he is from. A pause occurs in line 5, at which point Roci repeats the country of origin. Almost immediately after Roci's repetition, Winnie also states the country of origin. The talk leading up to and following this pause is important to an understanding of the turn-taking system in CMSI. The pause, which follows a syntactically complete utterance ("daniel here is from . . . brunei"), opens up the conversational floor.

In lines 5 and 6, Roci and Winnie orient to this pause as an opportunity to begin talking. The pause, followed by overlapping utterances, illustrates one of the challenges of communicating in CMSI. CMSI participants cannot use body positions, gaze, and/or gestures to project when a co-participant is about to speak. This contextual variable is similar to participating in a multiparty audioconferencing call, where the turn-taking system is constrained by the medium of communication.

Because CMSI participants cannot see each other, pauses can lead to overlapping utterances. To extend this observation further, pauses are potential sources of communication trouble, as they require interactants to project speakership in the absence of physical co-presence. Once talk stops, interactants must effectively guess when it is appropriate to take a next turn (Jenks 2009a). This so-called guessing game some-

times leads to two or more interactants speaking at the same time. Extract 7 begins
with Diamond identifying himself and initiating a getting-to-know-you sequence.

```
(7)
1o—Skypecast
22:35—22:38
1    Diamond:      yeah this is diamond speaking
2                  (1.5)
3    Diamond:      how are [you doing]
4    Allure:               [where are] you from::
5                  (0.5)
```

In this extract, both interactants have oriented to the pause (in line 2) as an opportunity to take a turn, but they have done so at about the same time (i.e. one interactant
speaks, and another speaker follows shortly after). The result is two overlapping questions that seek different information. Because it is a challenge for CMSI participants
to determine who will attempt to take a turn after a pause and when this will happen,
any given lapse in speech may lead to overlapping utterances. This observation is
most evident in the following extract. In Extract 8, several interactants are attempting
to determine which participant is from Poland.

```
(8)
1j—Skypecast
01:56—02:03
1    Val:      i am from poland you know (0.3)
2              do you know::=
3    Zendt:    =pol↑ and↓
4              (1.7)
5    Val:      pol[and
6    Zendt:       [go on
7              (0.4)
8    Val:      do you kn[ow where it is
9    Borno:             [are you from poland
10             (0.7)
```

In this exchange, two instances of overlapping utterances occur with two different
speaker dyads. The first instance occurs between Val and Zendt (lines 5 and 6), and
the second instance occurs between Val and Borno (lines 8 and 9). Both instances
of overlapping utterances follow a pause, and each coinciding utterance begins at
approximately the same time. This demonstrates that the timing of turn initial bids
is crucial to the management of overlapping utterances in CMSI. In this example, all
three interactants "mistime" their attempts to take a turn at talk. The issue of timing
is most evident in line 6, where Zendt explicitly requests Val to continue speaking,
but does so in overlap with the previous turn (N.B. the latching of talk in lines 2 and
3 occurs after a short pause in line 1).

While it is clear that overlapping utterances occur in CMSI, the section has yet to explore how interactants deal with coinciding turns. That is to say, once overlapping utterances ensue, do interactants continue speaking or do they stop shortly after? The answer to this question is important to an understanding of online spoken communication, as it reveals how robust the turn-taking system is in CMSI. In Extract 9, Jin is discussing her current living situation with her co-participants.

```
(9)
1h—Skypecast
00:57—01:05
1     Jin:      hm::. no. actually my husband works
2               here so .hhh that's why I came here
3               (0.6) tsk a:nd, (0.3) .h[hh
4     Roci:                            [oh'rilly.
5               (0.5)
6     Jin:      yes s[o-
7     Roci:          [okay
8               (.)
9     Jin:      basically I'm not doing anything
```

The overlapping audible inhalation in line 3 and the utterance in line 4 are followed by a pause in line 5. Jin's inhalation demonstrates that she is about to take a turn at talk. However, the inbreathing stops immediately after the coinciding turns. In other words, Jin withholds her turn, thus momentarily stopping the possibility for further overlapping talk. The pause acts as a resource for dealing with or avoiding two overlapping turns (cf. Extract 6, line 7). The same sequence of turns occurs later in lines 5–8: talk momentarily stops, two interactants attempt to speak at approximately the same time, and a pause follows. As this and other extracts demonstrate (cf. Extracts 6–8), although overlapping utterances occur in CMSI, they are not long in duration. That is to say, CMSI participants orient to the one-speaker-at-a-time rule (cf. text-based CMC; see Chapter 6).

The observations made in this section contribute to the CMC literature by revealing that a pause in CMSI acts as both a "source" of, and a "resource" for, resolving overlapping utterances (see Schegloff 2000). The dual role creates a somewhat peculiar situation: a pause will often follow the onset of simultaneous talk because it allows at least one interactant to yield the conversational floor, but this same pause may also precede the onset of further overlapping utterances because CMSI participants must project speakership in the absence of physical co-presence. This is demonstrated most vividly in Extract 8, re-presented here as Extract 10.

```
(10)
1j—Skypecast
01:56—02:03
1     Val:      i am from poland you know (0.3)
2               do you know::=
```

```
3     Zendt:      =pol↑ and↓
4                 (1.7)
5     Val:        pol [and
6     Zendt:          [go on
7                 (0.4)
8     Val:        do you kn[ow where it is
9     Borno:                [are you from poland
10                (0.7)
```

Here the interactants use pauses to resolve coinciding turns, but the lapses in speech lead to further overlapping utterances. For example, the latching of talk in lines 2 and 3 is followed by a pause (N.B. latching is not the same as overlapping, but both phenomena result in lapses in speech), which in turn requires both interactants to manage when and who will take the next turn at talk. In this case, both interactants speak at nearly the same time. Similarly, the overlapping utterances in lines 5 and 6 are followed by a pause, which causes further coinciding talk in lines 8 and 9. This example shows that interactants use pauses to re-set the conversational floor back to a one-speaker-at-a-time format, but these floor resetting resources are also a potential source for further overlapping utterances.

The analyses in this section have revealed how overlapping utterances unfold in CMSI. Overlapping utterances occur, in part, because interactants cannot use body positions, gaze, and hand gestures to organize turn initial bids that follow pauses. The absence of physical co-presence shapes turn-taking practices, as evidenced in the sequential organization of interaction leading up to, and following, overlapping utterances. That is, pauses precede and follow instances of simultaneous talk. In contrast, participants in face-to-face encounters are less likely to mistime their turn initial bids after pauses, as interactants typically have a wealth of interactional resources for dealing with speakership. Consequently, pauses are less likely to precede overlapping utterances in face-to-face interactions. In both CMSI and face-to-face encounters, however, pauses are used to yield the conversational floor (see Schegloff 2000: 11).

### 5.2.3 TURN ALLOCATION

Engaging in spoken communication, or any dialogue for that matter (Jenks 2012b), requires interactants to manage who will take a turn at talk and when this will happen. Therefore, turn allocation is an important aspect of any turn-taking system. As with the sequential organization of turn transitions, turns are normatively allocated at, or near, the completion of a turn constructional unit. The mechanics of turn allocation in most mundane (spoken) conversational settings are relatively simple. Broadly speaking, a current speaker can select next speaker or someone else can self-select. The allocation of turns during transition relevant places allows interactants "to minimize gap and overlap" (Sacks *et al.* 1974: 704). Part of the analysis below investigates to what extent gap and overlap are minimized when speakers allocate turns.

Investigations of online communication report that turn allocation in text-based CMC is fundamentally different than the turn-taking system reported in Sacks *et al.*

(1974). In text-based CMC, interactants can, and often do, send messages whenever they want, and as a result, turn transitions and allocation are not closely coordinated with turn construction (see Chapter 6). In theory, CMSI platforms allow interactants to speak whenever they want, though the management of turn allocation during online spoken communication follows, by and large, the turn-taking principles observed in telephone and face-to-face conversations. That is, in CMSI, turns are allocated at, or near, turn completion, and according to one of three "rules": current speaker selects next speaker, next speaker self-selects, or current speaker continues to talk when no selection is made. As extensive reporting has been done on the organization of these practices in telephone and face-to-face conversations (e.g. Larrue and Trognon 1993; Selting 2000), the analysis below focuses on turn allocation phenomena that shed light on the unique affordances and constraints of CMSI.

The first noteworthy example of turn allocation has been taken from Extract 8, re-presented here as Extract 11. The interactants in this example are getting acquainted.

```
(11)
1j—Skypecast
01:56—02:03
1    Val:        i am from poland you know (0.3)
2                do you know::=
3    Zendt:      =pol↑and ↓
4                (1.7)
5    Val:        pol[and
6    Zendt:         [go on
7                (0.4)
8    Val:        do you kn[ow where it is
```

In lines 1–5, the allocation of turns occurs in a relatively straightforward manner. That is, the turn-taking system here follows what can be referred to as the basic rules of turn allocation, as outlined in Sacks *et al.* (1974): Val selects next speaker by asking a question (lines 1 and 2), Zendt answers the question and thus becomes the current speaker (line 3), and finally Val regains current speaker status by selecting himself after a transition relevant pause (line 5).

What is remarkable, however, is the turn allocation practice that occurs in line 6. Here Zendt explicitly assigns Val as next speaker. This turn orients to the relatively long pause in line 4, as demonstrated in the interactional imperative "go on." In so doing, Zendt moves beyond the basic rules of turn allocation: the utterance "go on" not only selects next speaker, but it also relinquishes control of the conversational floor and explicitly invites next speaker to continue speaking. Zendt's assignment of next speaker treats the relatively long pause in line 4 as an issue that is procedurally consequential to the interaction at hand. That is, the next speaker must be given "the green light" to continue speaking. In other words, Zendt must engage in additional interactional work in order to manage the pause in line 4, so as to minimize gap and overlap (interactional imperatives like the one discussed above are used in other examples to manage interruptions; see Section 6.2.2).

The interactional imperative in line 6 is a phenomenon that occurs throughout the corpus of data for different reasons, though in most instances, "go on" and variations of it (e.g. "go ahead"), are sequentially embedded within, and used for the management of, turn-taking practices. This is further demonstrated in the next example (the horizontal arrows in the extract below indicate the line where the interactional imperative is used). In Extract 12, several interactants have just entered a chat room and are determining who should speak first.

```
(12)
A39—Skypecast
00:33—00:53
1      Ego:               ((static noise))
2                         he:l↓lo↑
3                         (2.3)
4      Shawn:             hello:.
5                         (0.5)
6      Ego:               can↓ you↑ hear↓ me↑
7                         (0.8)
8      Joseph:            yeah
9                         (0.4)
10     Shawn:             yes we can hear you
11                        (0.4)
12     Ego:               ok oh↓ yeah↑ so should i just uh::m
13              →         go ahead o:r are you guys talking on
14                        something.
15                        (0.6)
16     Shawn:   →         yes. (.) uh you can go ahead is this
17                        uh:m (0.4) eh- eee-goo is very
18                        confusing i don't know what to
19                        call↓ you↑
```

In this exchange, Ego joins the conversation in line 2. After all parties perform a series of sound checks (see Chapter 7), Ego begins his first extended turn at talk by establishing whether he can continue speaking ("should i just go ahead"). Although Ego selects himself as next speaker in lines 12–14, his question topicalizes (or makes relevant explicitly) the issue of who can take a turn at talk and where in the interaction a turn can be taken. Shawn subsequently provides confirmation by explicitly assigning Ego as next speaker ("you can go ahead").

The use of interactional imperatives in CMSI represents one of many ways in which technology shapes communication. Although the practice of explicitly assigning next speaker occurs in face-to-face settings (e.g. to manage overlapping talk during an argument), the location of "go on" in the larger sequence of turns suggests that CMSI participants use interactional imperatives to minimize gap and overlap (Extract 11), as well as to establish who is sequentially in a position to continue speaking when first joining a conversation (Extract 12). The latter function of interactional imperatives is particularly important to the management of turn-taking in CMSI, as it allows inter-actants to deal with the fact that co-interactants are entering and leaving chat rooms, as well as conversations, with high regularity.

The last two extracts presented in this section provide further examples of how technology shapes CMSI. Both examples show how communicating in the absence of physical co-presence creates challenges when attempting to establish who the next speaker will be. In Extract 13, several interactants have just entered a chat room.

```
(13)
A12—Skypecast
00:29—00:46
1       Amir:       ye::ah↓ (0.6) so::::: we have
2                   porn-peeve with↑ us↓
3                   (2.1)
4       Sam:        >yeah.>
5                   (0.5)
6       Amir:       hello?
7                   (1.9)
8       Amir:       he:llo?=
9       Ming:       =hi. (.) ehm ((clears throat))
10                  (0.8)
11      Amir:       okay↓
12                  (0.7)
13      Amir:       sah-rhee-ma (.) tell us about yourself
```

The extract begins with Amir announcing the presence of a co-interactant ("we have porn-peeve with us"). In conversational openings in second language chat rooms, announcements lead to an acknowledgment of some sort (e.g. greeting token; see Extract 17 below). In other words, announcements are often treated as utterances that require a response, and as such, perform the function of selecting next speaker (cf. question–answer exchanges). However, "porn-peeve" does not provide a response, as evidenced in the approximately two-second pause in line 3. That is, the selected next speaker does not take a turn at talk, despite being inter-actionally "obliged" to do so (Sacks *et al.* 1974: 704, Rule 1a). The lack of uptake is treated as procedurally consequential to the talk at hand, as Amir follows his turn with two greeting tokens (lines 6 and 8). These greeting tokens provide further invi-tations to speak (e.g. to provide a greeting token in return). Later in line 11, Amir appears to accept the fact that "porn-peeve" is not in the room or does not wish to be selected as next speaker or is perhaps too busy to do so, as he selects a new next speaker.

In the above example, the absence of physical co-presence creates a situation where an attempt to allocate a turn is unsuccessful because the selected next speaker is not "verbally present." This situation is characteristic of communicating in many online chat settings. Being online in a chat room does not necessarily demonstrate a willing-ness and/or ability to communicate. The difference between having a screen name displayed on the user interface and actively attending to the talk at hand is something that needs to be managed in CMSI (see Section 7.3).

In the same vein, screen names function as interactional resources for the management of turn-taking in CMSI. In the following extract, for example, a next speaker is selected, but some interactional work is required in order to figure out who that interactant is. In Extract 14, several interactants are in a chat room discussing languages. Suzi has been in the chat room for some time, but has contributed minimally to the conversation.

```
(14)
A21—Skypecast
1:20:25—1:20:35
1       Raj:        so, can you introduce yourself
2                   (1.6)
3       Suzi:       eh? (0.4) me?
4                   (0.9)
5       Raj:        ye⌊ah↑
6                   (0.8)
7       Suzi:       .hhhhhhh
8                   (1.6)
9       Suzi:       uhm (0.5) hi. (0.3) >hehe>
10                  .hhhh (0.7)
```

The extract begins with Raj asking Suzi to introduce herself. In so doing, Raj, the current speaker, selects next speaker. In face-to-face conversations, this turn allocation technique is often coupled with mutual gaze, change in body orientation, or head turn (see Lerner 2003). These acts of embodiment serve to assist interactants in understanding who, for example, a question is directed to. In CMSI, interactants can engage in similar interactional practices when using screen names to allocate turns (see Section 5.4 below).

In this exchange, however, Raj simply asks a co-interactant to speak, which leads to Suzi seeking clarification. The trouble that occurs here begins in line 1, and stems from the fact that the question does not identify the recipient. As with Extract 11, this example demonstrates that CMSI participants must engage in additional interactional work in order to allocate turns in the absence of physical co-presence (i.e. naming speakers when allocating turns). This observation suggests that the basic rules of turn allocation reported in face-to-face and telephone interactions do not adequately address the type of work required to allocate turns in a setting where interactants frequently enter and leave chat rooms and conversations.

The turn-taking phenomena investigated in this chapter establish that technology shapes CMSI in small, but important, ways. From turn transitions to turn allocation, interactants engage in turn-taking practices that reflect the affordances and constraints of speaking online. These observations will be revisited at the end of this chapter. For now, it is worth mentioning that this section contributes to an understanding of online communication by describing the turn-taking system in

CMSI, a phenomenon that has not received a great deal of analytic attention in the CMC literature. Although future research must continue investigating the extent to which the turn-taking system reported here is similar to other CMSI platforms, this section has established an empirical foundation from which future research can make such comparisons.

## 5.3 SUMMONS–ANSWER EXCHANGES

Talk does not simply happen. In most communicative settings, interactional work is needed in order to begin a conversation. For instance, in telephone communication, all conversations begin with a summons-answer exchange. First one interactant must pick up a phone and enter a phone number. The ringing of the telephone in turn summons the call receiver. These two actions—that is, the ringing and answering of the phone—precede all talk conducted on a telephone.

In addition to playing an important sequential role in telephone conversations, the summons-answer exchange serves the interactional function of placing interactants into mutual orientation (Schegloff 1986: 129). That is, the summons-answer exchange tells both interactants that they are available to talk. For example, deciding not to answer a ringing telephone signals to the caller that the call receiver is unavailable to talk. Conversely, answering a ringing telephone (with a greeting token) signals to the caller that the business of talk can begin.

In face-to-face encounters, mutual orientation is accomplished by establishing eye contact, pointing a finger and turning a head, or adjusting spatial positions, to name a few (see Goodwin 1981). Therefore, the co-production and management of summons-answer exchanges vary according to the type of interactional resources available to interactants. In settings where spoken communication occurs in the absence of physical co-presence (e.g. talk radio; see Hutchby 1999), summons-answer exchanges are typically embedded within conversational openings. In conversational openings, greeting tokens often coincide with, and/or immediately follow, summons-answer exchanges. To illustrate this point, an opening sequence from a telephone conversation is presented below (see Hutchby and Barnett 2005: 153).

```
(15)
1                    ((summons: i.e. telephone ring))
2      Nancy:        H'llo?
3      Hyla:         Hi:,
4      Nancy:        ↑Hi::.
```

In Extract 15, the telephone ring performs the function of the summons, and the answer turn consists of the call receiver picking up the phone and providing a greeting token (line 2). In this telephone opening, the greeting exchange (lines 3 and 4) immediately follows the answer turn.

In CMSI, summons-answer exchanges occur during conversational openings. That is to say, summons-answer exchanges in CMSI and telephone conversations occur in the same sequential location. However, CMSI is somewhat remarkable in that summons-answer exchanges do not always lead to talk, as they do in other communicative settings. This is because interactants enter and leave conversations with high regularity, and not all newly admitted participants are spoken to or verbally accounted for. It is not uncommon for an interactant to remain silent many minutes after engaging in a summons-answer exchange. Before presenting an illustrative example, it is important to first examine how a summons-answer exchange is managed in CMSI.

```
(16)
1c—Skypecast
00:00—02:00
1                    ((1:48—Jin is humming with music
2                    in the background))
3                    ((1:56—Jin turns down the music))
4    Jin:            HELLO.
5                    (1.8)
6    Hinaka:         hell:o::↑
7                    (0.5)
```

In lines 1–4, Jin is in the chat room by herself and there has been no prior talk. As Jin turns down her music, she accepts Hinaka's request to join the chat room. This request is done electronically. That is, Hinaka's request to join the chat room is accomplished by clicking on a button located on her user interface. As with the ringing of a telephone, this button functions as a summons, as it gives Jin the option of answering or ignoring the request to talk. Sometime near line 4, Jin answers the summons—by clicking on another button located on her user interface—with a greeting token.

In sum, the summons-answer exchange occurs in the opening of the chat room, allows both interactants to establish mutual orientation and thus establish talk proper, and is reliant upon performing two electronic actions (i.e. clicking on two buttons: "summons" and "answer"). The summons-answer exchange is interactionally obligatory, as admission into, and subsequent talk in, chat rooms is not possible without performing these two electronic actions (cf. the ringing and answering of a telephone).

What distinguishes CMSI from other audio-only settings (e.g. telephone conversations) is the fact that summons-answer exchanges do not always lead to talk. Although electronic summons-answer exchanges are interactionally obligatory and incipient, interactants that are presently in a chat room do not have to begin conversing with a newly admitted interactant, nor does the summoner (i.e. the newly admitted interactant) have to speak upon entering the chat room. For example, if talk is ongoing during a summons-answer exchange, then the participants that are actively talking in the chat room may not greet a newly admitted interactant. Similarly, a newly admitted interactant may not talk without being greeted and/or asked to participate in an ongoing conversation (see Chapter 7).

Because a conversation with an interactant may not immediately follow admission into a chat room, greeting exchanges and other talk that generally accompanies summons-answer exchanges may be displaced from a conversational opening. For instance, in Extract 17, Roci admits Jin into the chat room, but does not immediately greet her. The extract begins with Roci announcing who is in the chat room.

```
(17)
1h—Skypecast
00:00—00:27
1     Roci:       if you uh- if you try to join us eh
2                 you like to join us here daniel just
3                 moved into the waiting area (0.5) uh::
4                 y- i- i- daniel here is from uh: brunei
5                 (0.7) fro[m brunei
6     Winnie:              [from brunei
7                 (0.6)
8     Roci:       °yeah° (0.7) oh we have sailor jin mee
9                 ((mumbling for 3.0 seconds)) okay uh
10                (1.0)
11                jin rhee mee hello?
12    Jin:        hello?
```

In Extract 17, Roci has electronically answered several summonses, including those made by Jin and Winnie. In lines 1–5, Roci announces to the chat room that Daniel is in the waiting section. As with talk radio hosts, Roci uses the screen names listed on the user interface as resources to announce, identify, and greet potential contributors (see Hutchby 1999). In line 8, although Jin is already in the chat room, Roci announces her presence. This turn is then followed by an other-identification and greeting token in line 11.

What is particularly interesting in this example is the sequential displacement of turns that exists between the electronic summons-answer exchange and the work done to establish mutual orientation with Jin. That is, Roci does not verbally establish mutual orientation with Jin until sometime after they engage in a summons-answer exchange. This displacement demonstrates that establishing mutual orientation in CMSI can be accomplished in two ways: electronically and verbally.

Interactants establish mutual orientation through an electronic summons-answer exchange. However, as Extract 17 demonstrates, establishing a state of electronic mutual orientation does not necessarily mean that talk will follow. In order for talk to begin, interactants must engage in some verbal interactional work in order to establish whether the other interactant is free to talk.

In Extract 17, this work includes an announcement (line 8), other-identification, and greeting token (line 11). Verbally mutually orienting to each other is necessary in CMSI, as interactants cannot see, and often do not know, each other. Interactants may be lurking, busy attending to something in their immediate physical space, or pursuing different tasks on their computers.

The observations made in this section have shown that the interactional organization of talk following summons-answer exchanges is shaped by several contextual factors that are unique to CMSI (e.g. electronic summonses, absence of physical co-presence, multiparty talk). This section has also demonstrated that the sequential location and interactional function of summons and answer turns are similar to those observed in telephone openings (see Extract 16). In CMSI, however, talk may not immediately follow a summons-answer exchange (see Extract 17). Talk between summoner and answerer may never occur or the prototypical greeting exchange that follows a summons-answer exchange may occur long after both interactants establish a state of electronic mutual orientation.

The sequential displacement of the electronic summons-answer exchange and greeting exchange is a consequence of communicating in a multiparty setting where unacquainted interactants are entering and leaving chat rooms with high regularity. Because talk is inherently ongoing, CMSI participants may not verbally establish a state of mutual orientation after completing an electronic summons-answer exchange—some verbal interactional work is needed in order to begin a conversation. That is to say, CMSI participants have two ways of establishing a state of mutual orientation: electronically and verbally.

## 5.4 IDENTIFICATION PRACTICES

Talking in CMSI requires establishing a state of mutual orientation, as was demonstrated in the previous section. However, the ability to participate, and later engage, in a conversation is partly dependent on how interactants identify each other. Identification practices are especially important in CMSI, as interactants must communicate in the absence of physical co-presence.

The ability to see who is participating in a conversation is a taken-for-granted aspect of communication. This is because in many communicative settings, especially in face-to-face encounters, identification practices are accomplished with ostensible ease. For instance, four able-bodied interactants in a busy cafe could simply begin talking without the need to ask who is presently at the table and ready and able to communicate.

In telephone conversations, however, slightly more interactional work is needed. For example, opening a telephone conversation requires interactants to minimally identify and recognize caller and call receiver. This is often done through a greeting exchange (Schegloff 1979), though occasionally greeting tokens do not provide enough contextual information to identify and recognize caller and call receiver. Therefore, it is not uncommon for telephone conversationalists to explicitly ask who is on the other end of the line. In mobile phone openings, interactants similarly use voice recognition and greeting exchanges to identify each other (Hutchby and Barnett 2005), though caller identification technology can be used to bypass the interactional work that is involved in telephone openings (Arminen 2005).

Identification practices differ from one setting to another because of technological affordances and constraints. Generally speaking, interactants engage in comparatively more identification work when fewer interactional resources are available to them (e.g. requesting identification when receiving an unexpected telephone call). CMSI is similar to telephone conversations in that both communication types require comparatively more identification work than in face-to-face encounters. However,

CMSI possesses several unique interactional challenges that do not exist in telephone conversations. Namely, in CMSI, and especially of the chat room variety investigated here, interactants (1) enter and leave conversations with high regularity, (2) cannot see each other, and (3) are not fully acquainted. The aim of this section is to discuss how these contextual features shape identification practices.

In telephone conversations, identification practices occur during conversational openings (see Schegloff 1979). This is also the case for CMSI. However, identification practices in CMSI can additionally occur long after a conversational opening (cf. mutual orientation after a summons-answer exchange). In CMSI, identification practices occur each time mutual orientation is lost (e.g. an interactant does not participate in a conversation for a long period of time) and/or when a newly admitted interactant joins an ongoing discussion (N.B. an interactant can join a conversation multiple times throughout a chat room).

Before analyzing such examples, it is important to note that this section is concerned with what practices are used to identify interactants and how talk is organized during identification work. This analytic focus departs from how identification practices are traditionally investigated in the conversation analytic literature, where a single sequential location, say a conversational opening, is examined (see Schegloff 1979).

The first example examined in this section deals with the work required to identify an interactant that joins an ongoing discussion. In Extract 18, Jin, Samir, and Veronica are discussing movie genres. After nearly ten minutes of interaction, Velson joins the conversation in line 8.

```
(18)
1a—Skypecast
09:47—10:13
1      Jin:        horror mo↓vie↑
2                  (0.8)
3      Samir:      ho:r↑ror↓ movie↑
4                  (0.9)
5      Jin:        yeah sca↑ry↓ >y'know> horror movi:e
6                  (3.0)
7      Samir:      o↑kay.
8      Velson:     talk about mo↓vie↑
9                  (1.0)
10     Jin:        >yeah yeah> we are talking about
11                 movie
12                 (0.6)
13     Jin:        hi↑ [hello::
14     Velson:         [(who i- speaks)
15                 (0.4)
16     Velson:     hi.
17                 (0.8)
18     Jin:        w- (0.4) who↑ is↓ it↑=
19     Velson:     =you are?
```

```
20                     (1.3)
21    Jin:             <who↑ is↓ i:t↑<
22                     (0.7)
23    Velson:          .hh i'm velson
24                     (1.2)
25    Velson:          and you are?=
26    Veronica:        =velson?
27                     (0.6)
28    Jin:             a:::h my name is (.) jin.
29                     (1.1)
```

After Velson makes his first verbal contribution, Jin responds to his turn in lines 10 and 11. In so doing, Velson and Jin verbally establish a state of mutual orientation (i.e. by completing a question–answer exchange). In theory, both interactants could carry on with the topic of movies. Sequentially, however, their question–answer exchange bypasses the interactional work that typically occurs in conversational openings (i.e. greeting and identifying each other). In line 13, Jin accounts for this, as she provides two greeting tokens ("hi" and "hello"), which Velson later responds to in line 16 ("hi"). After several requests for self-identification (lines 18, 19, 21, and 25), both interactants establish who is on the other end of the line (lines 23 and 28).

This extract demonstrates that talk in CMSI is partly dependent on knowing who is in the chat room. Although an interactant can join a conversation by simply talking on topic, generally some form of identification work is needed. Take, for example, the following extract. In Extract 19, Shiho has just entered the conversation and is greeted by her co-interactants.

```
(19)
'nice and gentle talk'—Skypecast
(time unavailable)
1     Shiho:           hello=
2     Kris:            =hello:::↑
3     Shiho:           nice to meet you (0.3) hello
4     Yam:             oh sounds like woman
5     Kris:            o:h ye::ah
6                      (1.0)
7     Shiho:           can you hear me↑
8                      (1.0)
9     Kris:            oh=
10    Hally:           =ah yah we can
11                     (0.9)
12    Jenson:          i think that (.) you can you can
13                     (0.1) intro- duce yourself↑
14                     (1.0)
15    Shiho:           yeah i'm (0.7) i'm from japan↑ and
16                     i'm sixteen↑
```

```
17                      (1.0)
18      Kris:           O::KAY↑
19      Shiho:          a::nd my name is shiho
20                      (1.0)
21      Kris:           [shiho]
22      Jenson:         [seho]oka::y (0.1)
23      Shiho:          shi shi shiho (0.5)
24      Jenson:         shiho shihak
```

Shiho joins the conversation in line 1 with a greeting token, but she does not self-identify herself (e.g. "hello, my name is Shiho"). Although this omission is not procedurally consequential for Kris and Yam in their next turns (e.g. they do not ask who has just provided a greeting token), Jenson in line 12 requests Shiho to introduce herself. In so doing, Jenson makes the conversation in the chat room contingent upon knowing who has just provided a greeting token.

In Extracts 18 and 19, the sequential location of the identification practice is noteworthy. In both examples, a request for self-identification occurred *after* an interactant attempted to participate in an ongoing discussion. Put differently, both interactants were admitted into their respective chat rooms, but no attempts were made to identify Velson and Shiho until after they had verbally established their online presence (for a discussion of how online presence is managed in CMSI, see Section 7.3).

Thus, an important distinction must be made with regard to identification practices in CMSI. Identification is not always needed unless someone has made their presence verbally known to the chat room. In such instances, identification work will often take the form of a request for self-identification. However, in other situations, identification work occurs before an interactant attempts to join an ongoing discussion. Here the identification work will generally take the form of other-identification. In Extracts 20 and 21, for example, an existing interactant identifies the presence of a co-participant that has not spoken in the chat room.

```
(20)
A12–Skypecast
00:29–00:46
1       Amir:           ye::ah↓ (0.6) so::::: we have
2                       porn-peeve with↑ us↓
3                       (2.1)
4       Sam:            >yeah.>
5                       (0.5)

(21)
1h–Skypecast
00:00–00:27
1       Roci:           if you uh- if you try to join us eh
2                       you like to join us here daniel just
```

```
3                       moved into the waiting area (0.5) uh::
4                       y- i- i- daniel here is from uh: brunei
5                       (0.7) fro[m brunei
6      Winnie:                  [from brunei
7                       (0.6)
```

Several noteworthy observations can be made regarding the different types of identification work that takes place in CMSI. In Extracts 20 and 21, the identification turn preempts the possibility for the named interactant to identify herself at a time of her liking. Put differently, the identification turn sequentially obliges the named interactant to make a verbal contribution to the ongoing conversation (though, in some cases, the named interactant will not acknowledge the identification turn). In contrast with Extracts 18 and 19, Amir and Roci other-identify their co-interactants. Here the identification turn verbally accounts for an interactant that is visually present via a screen name, but not speaking. Furthermore, the identification work is addressed to all of the interactants in the chat room (i.e. the identification turn functions as an announcement).

The identification work that takes place in CMSI is significant in light of what happens in telephone conversations. As noted above, in telephone conversations, interactants normatively establish mutual orientation before engaging in identification work. That is, the ringing and answering of a telephone puts both interactants into a state of mutual orientation, which in turn makes it possible for them to identify each other. With telephones, identification work is partly reliant upon recognizing the voice of the person on the other end of the line.

In CMSI, voice recognition is also an important aspect of identification: CMSI participants must be able to match voice with screen names. Although interactants can actively attend to their screens when managing identification work, screen names are only one of two resources that are used in CMSI. "Real" names, as opposed to names listed on computer screens, are also used (N.B. the term real should be interpreted with caution, as it is virtually impossible to determine whether a name given in a chat room is genuine or a pseudonym). In the next two extracts, for example, screen and real names are used for identification purposes.

```
(22)
1e–Skypecast
08:16–08:38
1      Gadi:      yes (.) uh: excuse me (0.5) thi:s uh:
2                 (0.3)
3                 outstanding gu:y↓
4                 (1.4)
5      Mustafa:   yeah.
6      Gadi:      who:. (0.4) you (.) yes (0.6) uh:↓ your-
7                 your aye dee is?
8                 (1.3)
9      Mustafa:   ((inaudible)) (.) add a dee ee (0.2) and
```

```
10                      my name is (mustafa)
11                      (1.0)
12      Gadi:           ye:s mu↓-sta↑-fa.
13                      (0.2)
14      Mustafa:        yea (0.2) yea
15      Gadi:           mu↓-sta↑-fa. (.) my brother's name is
16                      mu↓-sta↑-fa too
17                      (0.6)
18      Mustafa:        is it? heheha good
```

(23)
A39—Skypecast
00:33—00:53

```
1       Ego:            ((static noise))
2                       he:l↓lo↑
3                       (2.3)
4       Shawn:          hello:.
5                       (0.5)
6       Ego:            can↓ you↑ hear↓ me↑
7                       (0.8)
8       Joseph:         yeah.
9                       (0.4)
10      Shawn:          yes we can hear you
11                      (0.4)
12      Ego:            ok oh↓ yeah↑ so should i just uh::m
13                      go ahead o:r are you guys talking on
14                      something.
15                      (0.6)
16      Shawn:          yes. (.) uh you can go ahead is this
17                      uh:m (0.4) eh- eee-goo is very
18                      confusing i don't know what to
19                      call↓ you↑
20      Ego:            oh okay sorry i'm gonna write my name o-
21                      over there i'm so sorry for using
22                      that .hh (0.9) actually one of my friend
23                      gave that but i- my names (mel↓ amer↑)
```

In Extracts 22 and 23, screen and real names are used as interactional resources for identification. In Extract 22, Mustafa treats a request for self-identification as an opportunity to reveal his screen and real names. In other words, Mustafa uses his screen and real names as resources to respond to a request for self-identification. In Extract 23, Shawn uses a screen name to account for his confusion identifying a co-participant. Ego, the named interactant, orients to this confusion by revealing his real name.

These examples show that screen names are fundamental to identification practices in CMSI. Screen names allow interactants to establish, and distinguish between, co-participants that are present and those that are ready to communicate. Screen names are especially useful in CMSI, as interactants cannot see, and do not know, each other. The analysis also established that screen names do not always provide sufficient information for identification purposes, and indeed some interactants rely on real names when engaging in identification work. Despite the use of real names in CMSI, interactants must first identify each other with screen names (i.e. the identification of screen names precedes the use of real names).

The practice of using real names demonstrates that interactants have multiple resources for identification purposes. This finding is especially interesting in light of existing observations of text-based chat rooms, where interactants almost exclusively rely on screen names (see Yi 2009). The practice of using real names is noteworthy given the fact that screen names are prominently displayed on computer screens. It is possible that real names are used because they allow interactants to narrow the social distance that is inherent in online communication, and move beyond the anonymity that is offered by screen names, though this is an empirical question that requires further investigation.

This section has also demonstrated that if an interactant begins speaking without initiating some form of identification, then the work involved in establishing mutual orientation and identification will not occur in one continuous sequence as it does in telephone openings. In such situations, the identification work will often take the form of a request for self-identification (cf. Extracts 18 and 19). In other situations, identification work occurs before an interactant begins speaking. Here the identification work will generally take the form of other-identification (cf. Extracts 20 and 21). Other-identification turns are interactionally and sequentially interesting, as they oblige named interactants to make verbal contributions, whether they intend to or not. In both situations, identification work is often initiated by an interactant that has been participating in a conversation. Furthermore, the analysis of both self- and other-identification showed that talk is contingent upon knowing who is in the chat room. Talk cannot, and does not, simply happen.

## 5.5 DISCUSSION AND CONCLUSION

This chapter has reported on three aspects of communication that are central to how CMSI is managed: turn-taking, summons-answer exchanges, and identification practices. Although turn-taking practices have been examined somewhat extensively in the CMC literature, most observations are based on text-based CMC (for a comparison of turn-taking practices in CMSI and text-based CMC, see Chapter 6). Furthermore, summons-answer exchanges and identification practices have not been examined in any detailed way in the CMSI literature. Thus, this chapter contributes to current understanding of online communication by uncovering and describing several aspects of talk that have been deemed important in the CMC literature, but have been rarely investigated from a social-interaction perspective.

This chapter also contributes to the CMC literature by demonstrating that CMSI is highly complex and organized, and as such, should be examined using detailed transcripts of talk and interaction. While a number of CMSI studies have been conducted over the years, observations of online spoken communication are only occasionally based on detailed transcripts (see Section 3.2.4).

Findings showed that turn construction, transition, allocation, and overlapping utterances are shaped by technological affordances and constraints. The analysis of turn construction and transition demonstrated that the management of CMSI is dependent on the production and coordination of vocal cues, including micro changes in stress and intonation. Interactants use pauses to deal with overlapping utterances, but prolonged spells of silence also lead to simultaneous talk. This is because CMSI participants cannot use body gestures, gaze, or other embodied actions to manage speakership. In the same vein, CMSI participants use interactional imperatives to manage speakership (e.g. "go on"). This observation shows that although the turn-taking system in CMSI is robust, it is sometimes necessary to explicitly manage speakership during online spoken communication.

The section on summons-answer exchanges demonstrated that the sequential location and interactional function of summons and answer turns is similar to that observed in telephone openings. Summons-answer exchanges allow interactants to establish a state of mutual orientation, and are sometimes followed by greeting exchanges. Unlike telephone openings, however, talk may not follow summons-answer exchanges. CMSI is unique in that greeting exchanges can occur long after conversational openings.

The management of summons-answer exchanges and the establishment of mutual orientation show that talk does not simply happen in CMSI. Talk is preceded by electronic summons-answer exchanges and the talk-based practices that are required to take part in an ongoing conversation. This interactional work gets accomplished on top of the practices involved in identifying co-interactants and determining whether they are actually willing to participate in a conversation.

The final section in this chapter uncovered how interactants identify each other in the absence of physical co-presence. The analysis of data established that screen names are fundamental to identification practices. Screen names are visible for all participants to see, and are thus used as resources to determine who is in the chat room. Identification work is needed throughout a conversation (cf. conversational openings in telephone interactions) because interactants enter and leave chat rooms and conversations with high regularity. The findings also showed that CMSI participants use real names for identification purposes. This is noteworthy, as it demonstrates that CMSI participants have multiple resources available to them during identification.

All of the findings reported in this chapter shed light on how technological affordances and constraints shape online spoken communication (e.g. the situation where interactants enter and leave conversations with high regularity and its impact on identification practices). Although some of the technological affordances and constraints identified here have been discussed in studies of telephone conversations (e.g. speaking in the absence of physical co-presence), the findings reported in this chapter revealed how interactants manage online spoken communication with multiple, unacquainted interactants. This type of communication has rarely been investigated in both the CMC and conversation analytic literature.

Despite the empirical contributions made in this chapter, many interactional features were not investigated (e.g. repair organization and opening sequences). Researchers must continue to examine online spoken communication in order to determine whether such features are fundamental to the management and organization of CMSI. Additionally, researchers must build on the findings reported here by examining different online platforms, uncovering new features of talk that are shaped by technology, and exploring whether interactional features that are fundamental to the management of other communicative settings (e.g. telephone conversations or audio-only communication) are similar to those observed here.

# 6

# TURN-TAKING IN CHAT ROOMS:
# TEXTING VERSUS TALKING

## 6.1 INTRODUCTION

The analysis has thus far established that the turn-taking system in second language chat rooms is robust and capable of handling multiparty interactions that take place in the absence of physical co-presence. The CMSI features identified and examined in the previous chapter demonstrate that technology shapes communication in small, but important ways. The findings provided a glimpse into how CMSI is organized interactionally and sequentially, though it is not clear to what extent online spoken communication is similar to other CMC types. This chapter addresses this issue. Specifically, this chapter compares the turn-taking systems in CMSI and text-based chat.

Few people would argue that texting and talking are the same communicative endeavor. Outside of academia, texting and talking are understood to present different communicative demands and possess different interactional purposes. For instance, this is evident in the way mobile communication providers market their subscription packages (for a report on the important role mobile phones play in communication, see Meeker *et al.* 2010). Mobile communication providers have different price points for texting and talking. Price differences partly reflect the costs associated with running such endeavors, but also reflect the fact that demand for texting and talking varies. That is to say, mobile communication providers do not randomly select price points for texting and talking. These prices, which vary according to subscription packages, reflect consumer preferences and needs. Texting and talking also serve different social and interactional purposes, and this is evident in the many online platforms that provide single modality communication (e.g. online platforms that are for texting only).

Although it is commonly understood outside of academia that texting and talking present different interactional challenges, CMC researchers have for many years conflated these two forms of communication. For instance, text-based CMC is often used to investigate theories associated with speaking (Yanguas 2010). Similarly, theories and methodologies associated with spoken communication are often used to examine text-based CMC (see Negretti 1999). In some cases, CMC is used synonymously with text-based CMC (see Georgakopoulou 2006: 550). While many researchers understand that texting and talking are linguistically different, few studies have attempted to uncover the interactional nuances (and differences) that exist between text- and

CMSI-based chat rooms (for a largely quantitative analysis of repair in text-based CMC and CMSI, see Jepson 2005).

This chapter narrows this empirical gap by comparing the turn-taking systems in text- and CMSI-based chat rooms. Specifically, multiparty text-based chat rooms are compared with multiparty synchronous CMSI-based chat rooms. In the interest of simplicity, text-based CMC and CMSI will be used henceforth, respectively. In order to make this comparison, the turn-taking findings established in Chapter 5 will be juxtaposed with what the literature says about turn-taking practices in text-based CMC.

Although the space devoted to this chapter does not deal exclusively with CMSI, the analysis below provides a different perspective to online spoken communication by incorporating an understanding of text-based CMC. A comparison of this type is needed because it builds on what is currently known about how technology shapes communication. For example, this chapter demonstrates that significant differences exist in how turns are constructed and managed in text-based CMC and CMSI. Such a comparison advances the field by providing an empirical foundation from which future studies can be conducted. For instance, the interactional similarities and differences that exist between text-based CMC and CMSI can help researchers and language teachers select online communication platforms that best suit their pedagogical goals (see Chapter 8).

Before proceeding with the analysis, several methodological issues, as well as analytic shortcomings, must be identified. First, online platforms that support text-based CMC vary, sometimes greatly, with regard to what users can do communicatively. For example, several text-based platforms provide the ability to see when a co-user is typing a message (e.g. a graphical symbol of some sort, like a pencil, will begin moving when someone is typing a message), whereas others do not. Many text-based platforms do not, however, allow users to see what other co-users are typing until a message is deemed ready to be sent. These differences have been reported to shape the management and construction of turns. Such differences must be highlighted when making comparisons across different online platforms and settings.

Second, the dearth of studies that investigate, and make comparisons between, the turn-taking practices in text-based CMC and CMSI means that this chapter has a modest amount of empirical data to build on. A search through the literature revealed that few transcript-based, empirically driven comparisons of text-based CMC and CMSI have been made. Furthermore, while the comparisons made below draw on several studies that examine text-based CMC, not much has been done in the way of turn-taking practices in CMSI. In other words, the CMSI data used to make the comparisons in this chapter are limited to the observations made in Chapter 5.

Third, the comparisons made in this chapter are limited to turn-taking practices (see Section 5.2). Although summons-answer exchanges and identification practices were examined in the previous chapter, they are not included in the analysis below, as there is not enough text-based CMC research on these phenomena to make useful comparisons.

Finally, the findings reported in Chapter 5 have been informed by conversation analytic principles. Although text-based CMC has been examined from a conversation analytic perspective, most studies that examine chat rooms are informed by discourse analytic principles (for a book-length discussion on the differences between conversation analysis and discourse analysis, see Wooffitt 2005). As a result, the CMC literature possesses different terminology for understanding turn-taking practices in text-based CMC. The comparisons made below draw on terminology adopted from both conversation and discourse analytic approaches.

Despite the analytic issues and shortcomings identified in this discussion, this chapter makes a small, but important contribution to the CMC literature by uncovering the different ways in which turns are constructed and managed in text-based CMC and CMSI. The aim of this chapter is to increase awareness of the important interactional differences that exist in online settings and platforms.

## 6.2 TURN-TAKING

CMC researchers come from a number of different disciplinary backgrounds and possess varied empirical interests (see Chapter 3). Despite this diversity, most CMC research is directly or indirectly interested in understanding whether, and to what extent, a particular online platform is similar to another communicative setting. For instance, the CMC literature comprises many studies that make comparisons between asynchronous and synchronous CMC, text-based CMC and face-to-face interactions, and text-based and telephone chat. For many studies, the main investigatory aim is to make comparisons (e.g. Abrams 2003; Freiermuth 2011). If not explicitly comparative in design, then a study will often use the analytic observations of one online platform as a springboard to discuss similarities and differences across or between communicative settings (e.g. Garcia and Jacobs 1999).

Comparisons are helpful in understanding how facets of technology shape communicative practices, and are thus central to expanding the CMC literature and advancing an understanding of online communication. The analytic sections below are organized into three parts: turn construction and transition, overlapping utterances, and turn allocation.

The comparisons made in this chapter are based on extensive analyses of data extracts taken from Chapter 5 and the literature on turn-taking practices in text-based CMC. However, in the interest of space, clarity, and simplicity, this chapter does not include all of the data extracts used to make these comparisons. Rather, each analytic section includes a small set of exemplary data extracts. Sections then end with a table that summarizes the analyses made of the data extracts taken from Chapter 5 and the text-based CMC literature.

## 6.2.1 TURN CONSTRUCTION AND TRANSITION

The turn-taking systems of most online platforms are highly organized, and partly based on the simple principle that when interactants take turns, they do so according to an understanding of what has been said and what is currently being said. Although the turn-taking systems of text-based CMC and CMSI follow this principle, there are major differences in how turns are constructed and managed in these two settings. These differences stem largely from two aspects of communication: turn recall and turn monitor. These two terms have been coined specifically for the comparisons made below.

Turn recall is related to how interactants retrieve information that has been uttered or typed in previous exchanges. Although Herring's (2007: 15) "persistence of transcript" is used in a similar way, turn recall is preferred because it places special attention on how "persistence" shapes turn-taking practices.

Turn monitor is related to whether interactants have access to turn construction (i.e. the ability to see messages or hear utterances as they are being typed or spoken). Herring's (2007: 17) "message format" has a similar meaning, but turn monitor provides a more context sensitive understanding of how turns are shaped by the ability to see or hear turn construction.

Turn recall and turn monitor are not associated with any particular methodology (e.g. they are not conversation analytic terms), but they are useful in understanding how turns are constructed and speakership is managed in text-based CMC and CMSI.

All CMC platforms possess turn recall. In text-based CMC, interactants can scroll back to see what has been typed (N.B. the number of messages that are kept in a buffer varies from program to program). Turn recall in text-based CMC is possible because messages are permanently displayed on computer screens. Herring (2007: 15) refers to this feature of communication as "persistence of transcript"—this chapter uses "message persistence." The latter term is more suitable for the comparisons made in this chapter because CMSI participants are not presented with "transcripts" when speaking online.

In CMSI, interactants use memory to recall spoken words and utterances. CMSI participants must actively attend to what is being said because spoken words and utterances are not stored as transcripts and permanently displayed on computer screens. Although turn recall is likely to influence how CMSI is managed, this aspect of communication is difficult to investigate from a social-interaction perspective because it is not a readily observable phenomenon. That is, CMSI participants rarely topicalize this issue. For instance, CMSI participants seldom talk about how they can or cannot remember what has been said in past exchanges. The upshot is that turn recall can only be discussed from a social-interaction perspective when it is made procedurally consequential for the interactants under investigation (for a study of how turn recall shapes the management and organization of word searches in face-to-face encounters, see Brouwer 2003). Similarly, few studies have investigated whether, and how, turn recall shapes turn-taking practices in text-based CMC. Therefore, this section is concerned primarily with turn monitor. Unlike turn recall, significant variation exists with regard to whether, and to what degree, turns are monitored in text-based CMC and CMSI.

The turn-taking system in CMSI is dependent on the ability of interactants to monitor turn construction. For some aspects of interaction and communicative contexts, turn monitor is a technological affordance. For example, turn monitor allows CMSI participants to manage speakership according to what has been said. Furthermore, and in contrast with text-based CMC, turn monitor also allows CMSI participants to take turns according to what is currently being said. That is to say,

CMSI participants are afforded the ability to speak before a current turn is complete. Take, for instance, the following CMSI example. In the question–answer exchange in Extract 1 (for a detailed analysis of this extract, see Section 5.2), Hal provides a second-pair answer before the first-pair question is complete.

```
(1)
1k–Skypecast
00:33–00:46
1    Sal:      you- you mean today or eh:: t-
2              tonight o:r.
3    Hal:      i me[an
4    Sal:         [tomorrow?
5    Han:      tonight (.) tonight tonight (0.9)
```

Hal does not need to wait until the question is syntactically complete before providing an answer. Because Hal can hear the turn unfold in real time, he provides an answer when enough information allows him to do so. When turn monitor is available to participants, it is not uncommon for turn transitions to occur near turn completion.

In text-based CMC, it is rare for an online platform to possess turn monitor. Consequently, most text-based platforms do not afford interactants the ability to monitor when a co-interactant momentarily pauses, re-starts, and/or self-corrects. That is, text-based CMC participants cannot see turn constructional units unfold in real time. Text-based CMC that does not possess turn monitor is often referred to as one-way transmission (see Cherny 1999). The absence of turn monitor means that turn transitions always occur after turn completion (i.e. after a message is constructed and sent in its entirety). As a result, turn construction and transition in text-based CMC are handled differently than in CMSI (for a conversation analytic investigation of a text-based platform that shares some turn-taking characteristics of CMSI, see Garcia and Jacobs 1999).

Extract 2 illustrates how the absence of turn monitor shapes turn construction and transition. In this example, the interactants are communicating with an instant messaging program. The extract begins with two interactants closing a conversation. For comparison and presentation purposes, all of the text-based CMC extracts used in this chapter have been given new line numbers and are presented in a font that is different from the one used for the analysis of CMSI data.

```
(2)
Baron (2010: para. 3)
1    Gale:     hey I gotta run
2    Sally:    Okay.
3    Sally:    I'll ttyl?
4    Gale:     gotta do errands.
5    Gale:     yep!!
6    Sally:    Okay.
```

In Extract 2, every instance of turn transition occurs after turn completion. The sequential implication of communicating in the absence of turn monitor is second-pair part turns (e.g. a response to a declarative statement) cannot occur before the completion of first-pair part turns. For example, Sally cannot respond to Gale until the message in line 1 is deemed complete (i.e. considered ready to be sent), as turns are only visible when an interactant clicks the carriage return key. Because turns are only displayed as "complete" units, the smaller lexical and/or syntactic components that make up messages do not shape turn-taking practices in text-based CMC (see Schönfeldt and Golato 2003: 248). That is to say, although a message may consist of a series of lexical and/or syntactic components, turn transitions cannot occur near or between turn constructional units.

The absence of turn monitor shapes turn-taking practices in other ways. In addition to second-pair part turns occurring only after first-pair part turns, second-pair part turns are often sequentially disjointed from constituent first-pair part turns in multiparty text-based CMC (see Herring 1999). For example, Sally asks whether she will be able to communicate with Gale at a later date (line 3), but the next turn does not answer the question (line 4)—instead, Gale provides a reason for needing to leave the chat room. Although Gale provides a response in line 5, the question–answer exchange is disjointed (i.e. both turns are not adjacent).

Closer inspection of this exchange reveals that the message in line 4 is being constructed as and/or after Sally clicks the carriage return key in line 3. Although the message in line 4 is interactionally tied to the declaration made in line 1—that is, the message in line 4 provides justification as to why Gale must leave the conversation—Sally is able to post her question before Gail's turn. This example demonstrates that the absence of turn monitor can shape the sequential organization of interactional exchanges by disjointing first- and second-pair parts (see Smith and Gorsuch 2004). A poorly coordinated exchange of turns can potentially lead to trouble in communication, though message persistence in text-based CMC allows interactants to maintain a sufficient level of interactional coherence and comprehension (Herring 1999). Table 6.1 summarizes the observations made thus far. Again, this table also represents the data extracts that are not presented in this chapter.

Table 6.1 shows that there is only one sequential location for turn transitions in text-based CMC (i.e. after turn completion). Conversely, turn transitions occur in multiple sequential locations in CMSI. With regard to turn adjacency, turns are generally adjacently placed in CMSI, but it is not uncommon for them to be disjointed in (multiparty) text-based CMC. In text-based CMC, interactants cannot see

Table 6.1   Text versus talk: turn-taking

| Aspects of turn-taking | Text | Talk |
| --- | --- | --- |
| Turn transitions | After turn completion | Before and after turn completion |
| Turn adjacency | Often disjointed | Often adjacent |
| Turn constructional units | Does not shape turn-taking practices | Shapes turn-taking practices |

each other typing messages, and therefore turn constructional units do not shape turn-taking practices. In CMSI, interactants can hear turns unfold in real time, and therefore turn constructional units are often used to manage speakership.

Many of the differences in turn-taking practices reported here exist because of turn monitor. The findings reported in Table 6.1, consequently, should not be extended to text-based CMC platforms that provide turn monitor. If interactants have visual access to turn construction, then they are likely to engage in different turn-taking practices than those reported above (see Herring 2002).

For instance, in Extract 3, two interactants are participating in a text-based CMC platform that supports turn monitor. This online platform is called VAX. In VAX, a text box that each interactant uses to type and post messages is available for everyone to see. As a result, VAX participants are able to take turns before and after turn completion. Although VAX and other similar programs have not been investigated in detail, and indeed most current instant messaging and text-based CMC platforms do not support turn monitor, Extract 3 provides an excellent illustration of how technology shapes communication.

(3)
Anderson *et al.* (2010: Transcript)

| 1 | B: | are you saying diverse experiences in |
| 2 | | different work situations |
| 3 | A: | no [, diverse experience as far as the |
| 4 | B: | [among professors in the same field |

The interaction that takes place in this example is a question–answer exchange. Speaker B asks a question and Speaker A provides an answer. Unlike text-based CMC platforms that do not support turn monitor, the answer in line 3 is provided before the question is complete. Speaker A does not wait until the previous turn is complete, but rather provides an answer when enough information is available to do so (cf. CMSI). In this example, the turn transition occurs before turn completion, first-pair and second-pair parts are adjacent, the next speaker is able to anticipate or project turn completion, and the change in speakership occurs after the completion of a "smaller" turn constructional unit (i.e. before the clause that starts with "among").

Although Extract 3 shows that VAX can lead to turn-taking practices that are similar to those observed in CMSI, at the time of writing, turn monitor is not a common feature in text-based CMC. For many text-based CMC platforms, turn construction and transition are managed differently than CMSI. This is further demonstrated in the next two sections on overlapping utterances and turn allocation.

## 6.2.2 OVERLAPPING UTTERANCES

A fair amount of attention has been given to whether, and how, overlapping utterances occur in CMC. As with many aspects of online communication, most observations of overlapping utterances are based on text-based CMC, and use face-to-face interactions as a point of comparison. Studies of overlapping utterances in text-based

CMC have led to several important findings. The most notable observation is that text-based CMC participants do not follow the same turn-taking principles used by interactants in face-to-face encounters (see Herring 1999; Anderson *et al.* 2010). Namely, researchers have observed that text-based CMC participants do not follow the "no overlap" rule found in face-to-face communication (Herring 1999: Turn-taking, para. 1).

The "no overlap" rule is based on the observation that interactants in face-to-face communication predominately speak one at a time, with the exception of turn transitions, where changes in speakership occur in slight overlap. When simultaneous talk does occur in face-to-face encounters, interactants use a number of different resources to rectify overlapping utterances, including hesitation and restarts (Schegloff 2000). The "no overlap" rule has been useful in understanding how overlapping utterances are managed in online settings, making comparisons between different CMC types, and comprehending how technology shapes communication (e.g. Marcoccia *et al.* 2008; Jenks 2009a). This section contributes to this body of knowledge by examining overlapping utterances in text-based CMC and CMSI.

Two contextual variables are important to an understanding of overlapping utterances in text-based CMC and CMSI: seeable and hearable (N.B. seeable and hearable are used somewhat loosely here, and do not refer to the conversation analytic use of the terms; see Liddicoat 2011). In CMSI, overlapping utterances are hearable in that interactants have access to turn construction. That is, interactants can respond to, react to, or otherwise manage simultaneous talk as it unfolds in real time.

Conversely, in text-based CMC platforms with one-way transmission (i.e. no turn monitor), overlapping utterances do not occur because turns are presented linearly, according to when the carriage return key is pressed. However, interactants can, and often do, type at the same time (see Marcoccia *et al.* 2008). This phenomenon is referred to as overlapping typing (N.B. some researchers use the term overlapping exchanges; see Herring 1999). Overlapping typing is not seeable. That is, interactants in text-based CMC do not have visual access to turn construction.

The issue of what is seeable and hearable is important to an understanding of how overlapping utterances are managed in online settings. In text-based CMC and CMSI, communication is conducted in the absence of physical co-presence, which consequently constrains the turn-taking system in both online settings. For instance, as demonstrated in Chapter 5, it is difficult to know when to take a turn at talk when communication has momentarily stopped. Despite the constraints of communicating without gestures, gaze, and body positions, interactants in both settings have ways of dealing with overlapping utterances once they occur. In CMSI, one such method is to stop talking momentarily.

```
(4)
1j–Skypecast
01:56–02:03
1     Val:        i am from poland you know (0.3)
2                 do you know::=
3     Zendt:      =pol↑and↓
```

```
4                       (1.7)
5       Val:            pol [and
6       Zendt:              [go on
7                       (0.4)
8       Val:            do you kn [ow where it is
9       Borno:                      [are you from poland
10                      (0.7)
```

In Extract 4, two instances of overlapping utterances occur (lines 5 and 6; lines 8 and 9). In both instances, a pause follows the overlap (lines 7 and 10). These pauses perform the action of yielding the conversational floor. That is, talk is withheld during these pauses, which in turn allows interactants to rebid for speakership. By withholding talk near the onset of overlapping utterances, these interactants demonstrate an orientation to a one-speaker-at-time format (see also line 4). That is to say, CMSI participants can, if deemed necessary, rectify simultaneous talk in real time, once it occurs. Again, this is possible because overlapping utterances in CMSI are hearable.

Although overlapping utterances are not possible in text-based CMC, overlapping typing is an ordinary part of communication. In text-based CMC, interactants cannot manage the onset of overlapping typing. Again, this is because text messages are displayed linearly and not as messages are being constructed. While overlapping typing is not seeable, the interactional consequence of this phenomenon is. That is, overlapping typing can lead to overlapping floors (and/or disjointed turns, as was demonstrated in the previous section). For instance, the interactants in Extract 5 engage in overlapping typing, which leads to simultaneous conversations (see also Simpson 2005).

(5)
(Paolillo 2011: example 2)

| 1 | ashna | hi jatt |
|---|---|---|
| 2 | Dave-G | kally i was only joking around |
| 3 | Jatt | ashna: hello? |
| 4 | kally | dave-g it was funny |
| 5 | ashna | how are u jatt |
| 6 | LUCKMAN | ssa all |
| 7 | Dave-G | kally you da woman! |
| 8 | Jatt | ashna: do we know eachother?. I'm ok how are you |

In Extract 5, ashna and Jatt are engaging in a greeting exchange at the same time Dave-G and kally are conversing with each other. The lack of turn adjacency in these exchanges demonstrates that overlapping typing occurs (cf. lines 1 and 3; lines 2 and 4). Although the interactants cannot manage the onset of overlapping typing, they have ways of dealing with overlapping floors.

Specifically, the interactants manage to overlap the two conversations by naming the recipient of their message. In line 3, for example, Jatt provides a second-pair part greeting token by naming the recipient. The practice of naming recipients allows text-based CMC participants to maintain comprehension and coherence while communicating in a setting that lacks turn cohesion and adjacency.

This example demonstrates that the turn-taking system in text-based CMC is robust during moments of overlap. The ability to scroll back and read messages, coupled with the turn construction strategy of naming recipients, allows text-based CMC participants to type at the same time without significant communication trouble. That is, although the transmission of overlapping typing is not seeable, the interactants do not appear to experience any communicative difficulty when turns become disjointed and conversations fracture.

In CMSI, conversely, the turn-taking system is less robust during moments of overlap. For instance, in the following extract, the onset of two simultaneous conversations is treated as an interruption. The extract begins with Dukes and SydneyLove getting acquainted.

```
(6)
1g—Skypecast
02:23—02:41
1     Dukes:          are you- are you- are you- (in korea)
2                     are you working
3     SydneyLove:     yeah (0.7) i'm work[ing (* *)
4     Jin:                              [james what are you
5                     talking about? i'm still here and
6                     i'll be here too
7                     (1.7)
8     James:          excuse me can you hear my voice?
9                     (0.5)
10    Dukes:          h[ello? hell]o? hello? (0.7) p- please=
11    James:           [excuse me ]
12    Dukes:          =please wait til, we- we till we
13                    complete our chat okay?
14                    (0.7)
15    Jin:            i'm sorry yeah go'head
```

In lines 1 and 2, Dukes asks SydneyLove where he is from and whether he is working. As SydneyLove begins to provide an answer, Jin enters the conversation by asking James a question and stating that she is currently in the chat room (lines 4–6). This instance of overlap marks the onset of two simultaneous conversations: SydneyLove provides a second-pair part answer to Dukes's question, and Jin directs her talk to James.

It is important to note that all four interactants do not compete for the floor (e.g. talking faster or louder), nor do they continue with their respective conversations. In this instance of overlap, SydneyLove withholds his talk, and thus yields the conversational floor to Jin. In line 8, James orients to Jin's conversation by providing a response. In so doing, the conversation between Dukes and SydneyLove is put on hold. In line 10, Dukes attempts to resume his conversation with SydneyLove.

However, Dukes does not simply begin talking; rather, he waits until the conversation between Jin and James momentarily stops (line 9). In lines 12 and 13, Dukes treats the conversation between Jin and James as an interruption.

The conversation between Jin and James demonstrates that the floor space in CMSI is rigid. Although the spoken medium can theoretically handle long spates of simultaneous talk, when overlapping utterances or floors occur, interactants often treat it, explicitly (cf. Dukes in lines 12 and 13) or implicitly (e.g. withholding talk), as problematic.

Conversely, as demonstrated in Extract 5, the floor space in text-based CMC can handle multiple conversations. Studies of text-based CMC have shown that the text medium affords interactants a high degree of flexibility in floor space because turns can be referred to long after message transmission (see Herring 1999; Simpson 2005).

The extracts examined thus far establish that text-based CMC and CMSI possess different types of message persistence, and that this contextual issue partly determines how interactants manage overlap in online communication (cf. "persistence of transcript"; see Herring 2007). In CMSI, there is no message persistence, and so interactants do not have technological resources to manage overlapping utterances and floors. In text-based CMC, message persistence is high because of technological affordances (e.g. the ability to scroll back).

Message persistence is so important in online communication that overlapping typing is sustainable and not treated as problematic even when text-based CMC participants can monitor turn construction. To illustrate this point, Extract 7 presents an exchange taken from the VAX platform (cf. Extract 3). The interactants in the following exchange have access to turn construction, but the ability to see messages unfold in real time does not demonstrably shape how overlapping utterances are managed.

(7)
Anderson *et al.* (2010: Transcript)
```
1    B:        Does an[yone feel they know where we are
2              headed with this?]
3    A:                  [Well, if we decide that one category
4              is more important the]n the others
5    B:        did that help?
```

In lines 3 and 4, Speaker A starts to type a message shortly after Speaker B begins constructing a question (lines 1 and 2). Despite this, both interactants continue typing until their turns are fully constructed. The overlapping turns do not contain any floor-yielding interactional features (e.g. hesitation or restarts). That is to say, both interactants do not orient to the one-speaker-at-a-time rule. In this exchange, message persistence allows both interactants to construct their turns at the same time without signaling in any way that the overlap is problematic.

Although further research is needed in order to fully understand how technological factors, like message persistence, shape online communication, it is clear that the medium in which online communication takes places has a significant impact on how turn-taking is managed (for a list of medium factors, see Herring 2007).

To further illustrate this point, a final CMSI extract is presented. In this example, several interactants are communicating in an experimental CMSI program that adjusts voice amplitude according to conversational topics. As a result, the interactants in the following extract are able to engage in long spates of overlapping utterances and manage multiple conversational floors—this phenomenon is known as schisming (see Egbert 1997). In Extract 8, the arrows next to each line number indicate "Topic 1," whereas the line numbers without arrows correspond to "Topic 2."

```
(8)
(Aoki et al. 2003: Excerpt I)
1     Y:    →      would you rather: (.) have to wear big
2           →      clown shoes
3     K:           four ounces isn't that- isn't
4                  [that much, I wo]uld say liquid
5                  detergent
6     B:    →      [big what shoes?]
7     Y:    →      big clown shoes (.) you know the
8           →      big [clumsy shoes] that a clown wears,
9     A:                [what was that?]
10    K:           i don't know, i'll
11                 let you choose that one,
12                 [since i chose the first] one,
13    B:    →      [okay, i would rather:]
```

The two conversations in this example unfold simultaneously, and in the same way as text-based CMC (cf. Extract 5). Turns associated with one topic are sometimes disjointed (cf. the question in lines 1 and 2 and the response in line 6), there is no explicit orientation to minimize gap and overlap (e.g. interactants do not pause or hesitate at or near the onset of overlap), and the floor space—because the medium has been technologically "enhanced"—is flexible to the extent that multiple interactants can contribute to different topics at the same time. Despite the experimental nature of this online platform, Extract 8 shows that technology is a great mediating factor in communication. Technology can enhance online communication and create new interactional possibilities. For example, technological enhancements, like the ones examined here, have the potential to blur the boundaries between CMC types.

Although Extracts 7 and 8 demonstrate that technology can bridge some of the interactional differences that exist between text-based CMC and CMSI, both examples are based on platforms that are not available for mainstream use. Therefore, Table 6.2, which summarizes the findings made in this section, does not take into consideration Extracts 7 and 8.

Table 6.2 demonstrates that there are significant differences in the construction and management of overlapping utterances in text-based CMC and CMSI. In text-based CMC, although overlapping utterances are not possible, interactants can, and often do, engage in overlapping typing. This phenomenon is not seeable, though the consequences of it are (e.g. disjointed turns and simultaneous conversations). In

Table 6.2   Text versus talk: Overlapping utterances

| Aspects of overlap | Text | Talk |
| --- | --- | --- |
| Type of overlap | Typing | Utterances |
| Transmission of overlap | Not seeable | Hearable |
| Onset of overlap | Exists, but is not an issue | Treated as problematic |
| One-speaker-at-a-time | No orientation | Orientation |
| Floor space | Flexible | Rigid |
| Conversational floors | One or more | Typically only one |
| Interactional consequence of overlap | Leads to disjointed turns | Leads to simultaneous talk |

CMSI, overlapping utterances occur, are hearable, and are often treated as problematic. CMSI participants treat overlapping utterances as problematic by, for example, withholding talk or performing interactional imperatives (e.g. "go on"). The onset of overlap is not an issue in text-based CMC because interactants cannot see what the other interactant is typing. Although overlapping typing leads to disjointed turns and simultaneous conversations, the floor space in text-based CMC allows interactants to disregard the one-speaker-at-a-time rule. Conversely, the floor space in CMSI is rigid, and one conversation is often the norm.

Many of these differences exist because of turn monitor and message persistence. Turn monitor affords interactants the ability to manage overlap in real time (e.g. CMSI participants can withhold talk near the onset of overlapping utterances), and message persistence influences how overlap is managed once it occurs (e.g. text-based CMC participants can engage in overlapping conversations by scrolling back to re-read messages).

Although message persistence affords interactants the ability to engage in overlapping typing, research has shown that text-based CMC participants attempt to minimize the consequences of it. To end this section, a final extract is presented to illustrate this point. In Extract 9, the researchers of this study were able to capture overlapping typing by video recording participants in a computer room.

(9)
Smith and Gorsuch (2004: 568)

| seeable interaction | | unseen simultaneous typing |
| --- | --- | --- |
| 1 H: | so I have no idea about | K: ~~cuz if I present~~ ((K deletes message |
| 2 | other food.. | after reading H's message)) |
| 3 K: | ok have u ever known | |
| 4 | Tom yum kung | |
| 5 H: | Is it sour soup? | K: it's kind of spicy shrimp |
| 6 K: | it's kind of spicy shrimp | |

In lines 1 and 2, Speaker H sends his message before Speaker K. This results in Speaker K, the slower typist, modifying, and thus aligning, his turn according to the previous message. This exchange demonstrates that text messages are constructed progressively, as participants monitor what other co-interactants have transmitted. Although overlapping typing is not an observable phenomenon (i.e. Speaker H cannot see what Speaker K is typing), the example shows that there is much more interactional work going on than what is visually displayed on computer screens. Indeed, what happens behind computer screens and how this "offline" behavior shapes online communication is an interesting line of research worth investigating.

### 6.2.3 TURN ALLOCATION

The two previous sections have demonstrated that turn monitor and message persistence affect turn construction, transition, and overlapping utterances. Turn monitor and message persistence also shape turn allocation practices in text-based CMC and CMSI. In text-based CMC, the absence of turn monitor constrains the ability to project when next speakers bid for next turns—it is equally difficult to project when a message will be transmitted (Garcia and Jacobs 1999; Panyametheekul and Herring 2003). In CMSI, interactants have access to turn monitor (see Chapter 5): the interactional and sequential implication is that CMSI participants allocate turns at, or near, turn completion. Conversely, the absence of turn monitor in text-based CMC means turns are always allocated after turn construction.

These small, but crucial interactional differences influence whether, and how, participants of online communication follow the turn allocation rules identified in the conversation analytic literature (see Sacks *et al.* 1974): current speaker selects next speaker, next speaker self-selects, or current speaker continues to talk when no selection is made.

The first rule, current speaker selects next speaker, occurs in both text-based CMC and CMSI. However, because the floor space in text-based CMC is flexible (see Table 6.2)—that is, interactants can engage in two or more simultaneous conversations without significant incomprehensibility—it is not uncommon to have two or more current speakers. For instance, Current Speaker A may select Next Speaker B at approximately the same time Next Speaker D responds to Current Speaker C. In sequential terms, current speakers in text-based CMC may not select next speaker, but rather a "future" speaker (see Garcia and Jacobs 1999: 356). Take, for example, Extract 10. The example begins with ashna selecting Jatt as next speaker. However, the next turn is sequentially occupied by Dave-G's utterance to kally.

(10)
(Paolillo 2011: example 2)

| 1 | ashna | hi jatt |
| 2 | Dave-G | kally i was only joking around |
| 3 | Jatt | ashna: hello? |
| 4 | kally | dave-g it was funny |
| 5 | ashna | how are u jatt |
| 6 | LUCKMAN | ssa all |
| 7 | Dave-G | kally you da woman! |
| 8 | Jatt | ashna: do we know eachother?. I'm ok how are you |

Other instances of current speaker selecting future speaker occur throughout Extract 10, including lines 2 and 4, and 5 and 8. In nearly all instances of turn allocation, one turn displaces current and "future" turns. For example, line 3 displaces the adjacency pair in lines 2 and 4. The observation that current speakers select future speakers is yet another example of text-based CMC participants somewhat freely engaging in simultaneous conversations. However, closer inspection of the turn allocation practices reveals that current speakers name their recipients, a strategy that allows interactants to deal with the displacement of turns that results from overlapping floors (see Negretti 1999). For instance, in line 3, Jatt directs his greeting token to ashna by naming her.

In CMSI, the current speaker selects next speaker rule occurs with high frequency. However, the floor space in CMSI cannot handle simultaneous conversations in the same way as reported in text-based CMC. Sequentially, this means next speakers predominately take their turns in next sequential position (see, however, Extracts 13 and 14). Extract 11 illustrates this point. This example begins with current speaker selecting next speaker; next speaker then takes her turn in next position.

```
(11)
1a—Skypecast
09:47–10:00
1    Samir:      horror movie?
2                (0.9)
3    Jin:        yeah sca⌈ry⌊ y'know horror movi:e
4                (3.0)
5    Samir:      o⌈kay
6    Velson:     talk about mo⌊vie⌈
7                (1.0)
8    Jin:        >yeah yeah> we are talking about
9                movie
```

The change in speakership from line 1 to line 3 is noteworthy, in particular with regard to how turns are allocated in text-based CMC. In this exchange, a nearly one-second pause in line 2 follows the current speaker's turn. Although the current speaker has selected Jin as the next speaker, the pause allows other interactants to adopt the next speaker self-selects rule. In this particular exchange, however, this does not happen. Rather, Jin assumes the current speaker position by taking her turn in line 3.

One reason why Jin is able to take the next turn in next turn position is because the floor space in CMSI does not normatively include two or more simultaneous conversations (see Table 6.2). Although Velson could initiate a topic change in line 2, the exchange between Samir and Jin would be either temporarily put on hold or terminated (see Extract 6). If two or more next speakers attempt to take a turn at the same time, at least one speaker will typically orient to the one-speaker-at-a-time rule (see Chapter 5). This example also demonstrates that only one speaker normatively has the "right" to allocate a turn (i.e. there is only one current speaker).

In contrast, as noted previously, it is not uncommon to have two or more current speakers in text-based CMC. The interactional implication is that more than one interactant can adopt the self-select rule in text-based CMC. In Extract 12, for example, Fred constructs a long message that is posted in two parts (lines 1 and 2, and 5 and 6), but two interactants self-select after the first message construction (lines 1 and 2).

(12)
(Garcia and Jacobs 1999: 358)

| 1 | Fred: | the biggy is that CMU is the 3rd ranked school of |
|---|---|---|
| 2 | | music in the country and SU isn't even ranked |
| 3 | Mr. White: | so? |
| 4 | Silver: | so you transferred here from SU |
| 5 | Fred: | so they have to ensure a certain level of skills from |
| 6 | | their graduates |

Although Fred's second message construction in lines 5 and 6 appears to be posted in response to his co-interactants' turns (i.e. Mr. White and Silver both begin their turns with "so," which is followed by Fred's "so"), a video recording of this exchange shows Fred typing before Mr. White and Silver. In other words, Mr. White and Silver respond to the first message construction in lines 1 and 2 without knowing that Fred has not completed his message (cf. turn monitor). In this instance, Mr. White and Silver apply the next speaker self-selects rule while Fred is typing a message.

Mr. White's turn is displayed first, as it is the shortest message. Despite this, Fred continues constructing his message. That is, Fred does not orient to Mr. White's turn. Fred does not, for example, postpone his turn as a result of, or re-type his messages according to, Mr. White's question. In other words, Mr. White fails to select Fred as next speaker.

In CMSI, interactants allocate, and deal with, turn singly, as demonstrated in the final two extracts. To illustrate how the second rule of turn allocation (next speaker self-selects) is dealt with in CMSI, one extract is presented in two parts (Extracts 13 and 14). In Extract 13, Diamond and Allure allocate turns at approximately the same time.

```
(13)
1o—Skypecast
22:35—22:38
1    Diamond:    yeah this is diamond speaking
2                (1.5)
3    Diamond:    how are [you doing]
4    Allure:             [where are] you from::
5                    (0.5)
```

In line 2, a prolonged pause follows Diamond's turn. This pause allows Allure or any other interactant to apply the second turn allocation rule. The pause also allows

Diamond to continue speaking if no attempt is made to talk (i.e. the third turn allocation rule). In line 3, Diamond applies rule three, though in slight overlap with Allure's attempt at the second turn allocation rule. Although the turns are allocated in overlap, only one turn allocation rule is normatively dealt with at a time in CMSI, as demonstrated in Extract 14.

```
(14)
1o–Skypecast
22:38–22:45
5                       (0.5)
6       Zana:           welcome [diamonds]=
7       Diamond:                [fine]=
8       Allure:         =just good just good (.) what about
9                       you
10                      (0.5)
11      Diamond:        well i'm fine i am: from Sweden
```

Diamond and Allure answer their respective questions (Extract 13, lines 3 and 4): in line 7, Diamond responds to Allure's question; in line 8, Allure responds to Diamond's question. Although multiple interactants have allocated turns (Zana also nominates herself to speak after a short pause in line 5), each turn is dealt with singly. That is, only one interactant will normatively control the floor even after multiple attempts by different interactants have been made to allocate turns. This observation is further demonstrated by the non-response that follows Zana's turn. Although Diamond has the option of responding to Zana (e.g. by thanking her), he decides to converse with Allure.

The third rule, current speaker continues to talk when no selection is made, is applied by interactants in both text-based CMC and CMSI. A crucial difference exists, however, in how this rule is managed. In text-based CMC, interactants can simultaneously self-select while the current speaker applies the third rule of turn allocation (cf. Extract 12). In CMSI, interactants do not normatively self-select while the current speaker applies the third rule. If overlap occurs, then again, interactants deal with each turn singly (cf. Extract 14).

Table 6.3 summarizes the analyses of turn allocation.

The analysis conducted in this section has established that all three rules of turn allocation occur in text-based CMC and CMSI. However, as Table 6.3 illustrates,

Table 6.3  Text versus talk: turn allocation

| Aspects of turn allocation | Text | Talk |
| --- | --- | --- |
| Number of current speakers | One or more | Typically only one |
| Next turns | Can occur in next and future positions | Can occur in next and future positions |
| Concurrent turn allocation | Can happen, and are dealt with, singly or simultaneously | Can happen, but are dealt with singly |

several notable differences exist. In text-based CMC, message persistence allows interactants to manage multiple, simultaneous conversations. Thus, it is not uncommon to have several current speakers in text-based CMC. Although overlap may occur in CMSI, only one interactant will generally hold the floor. In both online platforms, next turns can occur in next and future positions. In other words, when allocating turns in text-based CMC and CMSI, turns can become disjointed. This is characteristic of communicating in multiparty settings of any type. Interactants in both text-based CMC and CMSI can engage in concurrent turn allocation (i.e. more than one turn is allocated). In text-based CMC, interactants deal with concurrent turns singly or simultaneously. In CMSI, concurrent turns are managed one at a time.

## 6.3 DISCUSSION AND CONCLUSION

This chapter has compared the turn-taking systems of text-based CMC and CMSI. The analyses revealed that turns are constructed and managed differently in these two online platforms. For example, turn transitions occur in one sequential location in text-based CMC and in multiple locations in CMSI. Turns are often adjacently placed in CMSI, but are typically disjointed in text-based CMC. In CMSI, turn constructional units unfold, and are monitored, in real time. In text-based CMC, turn constructional units are displayed after message transmission. With regard to overlapping utterances, text-based CMC participants do not normatively orient to the one-speaker-at-a-time rule, as the floor space can handle multiple conversational floors. When overlap occurs in CMSI, at least one interactant will normatively yield the conversational floor. Many of the interactional differences identified were connected to two contextual issues: turn monitor and message persistence. The comparisons made in this chapter demonstrated that turn monitor and message persistence are crucial to how interactants manage the turn-taking systems of text-based CMC and CMSI.

Although some interactional and sequential similarities exist (e.g. second-pair parts can be displaced when allocating turns in text-based CMC and CMSI), the chapter revealed that texting and talking must be treated as distinct communicative endeavors. Specifically, care must be taken when using spoken discourse analytic approaches to investigate text-based CMC (Simpson 2005). In the same vein, text-based CMC may not be a suitable site of investigation for testing hypotheses based on oral communication (Yanguas 2010).

Finally, despite calls for CMC research to move beyond descriptions of the language and discourse of online communication (see Androutsopoulos 2006a; Georgakopoulou 2006), this chapter has proven that much more descriptive level work is needed in order to better understand different CMC types. Descriptive level work is needed because online communication can be conducted in a number of different ways. Communication varies across online platforms (e.g. text-based CMC and CMSI), as demonstrated in the comparisons made in this chapter. Communication also varies within CMC types (e.g. one-way transmission text-based CMC and two-way transmission text-based CMC). For example, turn-taking practices in text-based CMC vary according to whether turn monitor exists (cf. Extracts 2 and 3). Furthermore, future CMC research must examine more closely how different programmatic features, like the ability to know when a co-interactant is typing, shape online communication.

Descriptions and comparisons of CMC are also needed because the bulk of research is based on text communication, and comparatively few studies have been conducted on CMSI. Furthermore, descriptions and comparisons advance the study of CMC, move researchers away from the notion that online communication is a hybrid writing system, and are helpful in making practical suggestions for people that need to use technology for professional purposes (see Chapter 8). Although this chapter has provided a better understanding of turn-taking practices in text-based CMC and CMSI, many other interactional features must be examined and compared. Notable interactional features that have not been investigated in this chapter, but may prove useful for comparative purposes, include opening and closing sequences, topic decay, and backchannels.

# 7

# CONTEXTUAL VARIABLES IN CMSI

## 7.1 INTRODUCTION

The analyses have thus far focused on the interactional practices that are used to co-manage talk in, and the sequential organization of, CMSI. While Chapters 5 and 6 establish that turns and turn-taking are central to an understanding of how online spoken communication is managed, and offer insights into the degree to which chat rooms are similar to other online settings, these chapters present a limited picture of CMSI. For example, although the meaning that is co-constructed between interactants is organized by, and revealed through, turns (Schegloff 2007; see also Garcia and Jacobs 1999, for how technology shapes turn-taking practices in text-based CMC), there are several contextual variables that shape the type of work that is involved in achieving intersubjectivity in online settings (e.g. Simpson 2005; Dresner and Herring 2010). Some of these contextual variables were discussed superficially within a more focused analysis of turns and turn-taking, but these issues deserve more attention than given previously.

This chapter uncovers several contextual variables that shape the management of CMSI (for an exemplary conversation analytic study that examines context in radio communication, see Luff and Heath 2002). The aim, in so doing, is to provide a more complete picture—than what has been offered thus far—of what CMSI is and how online spoken communication is managed. While previous chapters examined sequence organization and interactional practices, the analysis below is concerned with how CMSI shapes the ability to talk with multiple interactants in the absence of physical co-presence (e.g. responding to, and dealing with, background noises). This chapter builds on the observations made in Chapters 5 and 6, and provides an empirical foundation for the discussions that take place in Chapters 8 and 9.

Similar attempts to identify contextual variables have been made in the literature. Most notably, Herring (2007) devised a system for classifying different facets of communication that shape CMC—her classification system, which comprises ten factors related to the medium of communication (i.e. synchronicity, message transmission, persistence of transcript, size of message buffer, channels of communication, anonymous messaging, private messaging, filtering, quoting, and message format) and eight situational factors (i.e. participant structure, participant characteristics, purpose, topic/theme, tone, activity, norms, and code), was devised principally for making distinctions between different CMC types (e.g. asynchronous discussion boards versus asynchronous text-based chat rooms). Though Herring's (2007) facets of technology move researchers away from the idea that CMC is a genre of communication (cf. "net speak"; see Crystal 2004), her system is not particularly helpful in uncovering the ways in which interactants deal with the contextual issues that are unique to CMSI.

For example, while the category Herring (2007) refers to as "synchronicity" allows researchers to classify the different types of CMSI that exist, it does not offer any analytic tools to uncover how interactants synchronously orient to turns. In the same vein, "participant structure" is helpful in distinguishing one communicative context from another (e.g. dyadic versus triadic talk), though this situational factor is not useful in understanding the interactional practices that take place when, for example, interactants cannot see each other, but must somehow negotiate a place in an ongoing multiparty conversation. That is to say, the eighteen (medium and situational) factors are useful for classification purposes, but the system does not provide the methodological tools for describing how online spoken communication is managed sequentially and interactionally.

Although Herring's (2007) classification system is incorporated below at various points in the discussion of context, this chapter provides new insights into CMC by revealing how interactants organize their talk according to, and around, several contextual issues that are unique to CMSI. The excerpts examined in this chapter do not reflect any pre-defined CMC category or classification system, and the contextual variables were selected if an issue or circumstance was both reoccurring (i.e. happened with high regularity throughout the data set) and characteristic of online spoken communication (i.e. specific to verbally and synchronously communicating in the absence of physical co-presence).

Five contextual variables are analyzed in this chapter: background noises, online presence, pauses, ongoing talk, and audibility. These contextual variables have been selected because they are made relevant by the interactants and for their interactions (see Luff and Heath 2002). In other words, this chapter provides an emic perspective to how contextual variables are oriented to by the participants themselves (for a discussion of what an emic perspective is, see Section 2.2). These contextual variables are not meant to replace, or build on, Herring's (2007) classification system. Rather, the objective is to identify some of the unique challenges of speaking online in a multiparty chat room.

## 7.2 BACKGROUND NOISES

Background noises are defined as sounds that are not vocally produced by CMSI participants and/or are extraneous to the immediate conversational exchange. The range of background noises is wide, spanning from sounds that mask verbal communication (e.g. white noises) to ambient noises that can be heard, but do not drown out spoken words and utterances (e.g. emphatic typing sounds and physically co-present people talking in the background). Background noises are not uncommon in CMSI because online spoken communication is dependent on high-quality sound transmission (see Ackerman *et al.* 1997). An audio channel that supports high-quality sound transmission is necessary for interactants to hear each other and make sense of what is being said. Unfortunately, however, high-quality sound transmission also amplifies background noises. Although background noises are not usually intended to add meaning to CMSI, very often interactants treat these sounds as interactionally relevant to the management of talk.

For instance, a long period of white noise is accounted for by both interactants in Extract 1. The extract begins at the opening of a chat room. Both interactants have not been acquainted.

```
(1)
11–Skypecasts
00:05–00:43
1     Sanchez:          uh:: who are speaking
2                       ((for 5.7 seconds, faint typing sound
3                       in the background))
4                           (.)
5                       ((for 4.1 seconds, white noise))
6     Sanchez:          whoaw ((noise continues))
7                       ((for 1.1 seconds, white noise))
8     Michele:          what↓ is↑ that↓ ((noise continues))
9                           (4.8)
10    Sanchez:          what's your name hhh
11                          (1.0)
12    Michele:          me?
13                          (1.1)
14    Sanchez:          yeah
15                          (0.7)
16    Michele:          i'm michele
17                          (2.5)
18    Sanchez:          me::chelle↓
19                          (1.7)
20    Sanchez:          what's your nickname over here
21                          (0.6)
22    Michele:          eh:m ((the letter M)) la↓bo↑da↓
```

In line 1, Sanchez initiates a getting acquainted sequence by asking Michele to identify herself (see Jenks 2009b). The question represents the first part of a two-part exchange. That is, the delivery of the question means that Michele is interactionally and sequentially obliged to provide an answer. However, what follows in lines 2 and 3 is a long pause with sporadic faint typing sounds in the background. Although the typing sounds are loud enough to be heard in the chat room, both interactants do not topicalize the noise nor do they do anything in response. This is noteworthy in that it shows that not all background noises are accounted for verbally. Background noises can occur at various points in a conversation (e.g. in this case the typing sounds occupy the second-pair part position), and interactants have the option of making background noises procedurally consequential to the ongoing management of talk.

After a micro spate of silence in line 4, a relatively long period of white noise occurs in line 5. Unlike the faint typing sounds, the interactants topicalize the white noise, beginning with Sanchez's emphatic utterance in line 6 ("whoaw"). The white noise continues to line 8, at which point Michele inquires about the sound. For unknown reasons, the white noise stops, and after a long pause in line 9, both interactants continue with the task of getting acquainted (lines 10–22).

In this exchange, the interactants talk over, or through, the white noise. The white noise is interactionally relevant in that the interactants verbally account for its manifestation. Although both interactants continue talking as the extraneous sound unfolds, the white noise postpones the getting acquainted sequence between Sanchez and Michele. This is significant, as it demonstrates that background noises can momentarily stop ongoing conversations.

In CMSI, the medium of communication can only handle a limited number of competing sounds. CMSI participants cannot simply talk at the same time without experiencing considerable incomprehensibility, and multiple background noises will likely have interactional and/or sequential consequences (cf. multiple conversational floors; see Chapter 6). In Extract 1, the typing sounds occupied the sequential position where an answer should have been given and the white noise postponed an interactional exchange. Although Sanchez and Michele resume their getting acquainted exchange after the typing sounds and white noise end, background noises can terminate ongoing conversations.

In Extract 2, for instance, an ongoing conversation terminates when the chat room experiences some background noise. In this conversational exchange, the extraneous sound is Jin talking to someone in the background. The interactants in the extract below have been engaging in an extended discussion about their favorite movies. The extract begins with Veronica asking her co-interactants about a movie.

```
(2)
1a–Skypecast
11:07–11:35
1    Veronica:      have you ever seen (the field
2                   green)↑
3                   (1.2)
4    Jin:           ((for 2.2 seconds, Jin closes a conversation
5                   with someone in the background))
6                   (7.0)
7    Jin:           hello?
8                   (1.5)
9    Andregee:      hello.
10                  (0.8)
11   Jin:           yeah sorry i was on the phone
12                  (10.1)
```

```
13    Jin:              nobo(h)dy's talk(hh)ing at
14                      a(h)ll (0.3) .hh
```

Veronica's question in the beginning of this extract represents the first part of a two-part exchange, and as such, sequentially and interactionally obliges one of her co-interactants to provide a second-part answer. A pause of approximately one second ensues in line 3, which is followed by an audible conversation between Jin and someone in her physical space. Veronica and her co-interactants do not topicalize the background conversation as it unfolds, nor do they say anything about it after the extraneous sound ends. For instance, they do not at any point in the exchange ask Jin to stop talking. Furthermore, during and after the nearly two seconds of background noise, Veronica does not receive an answer to her question. The background noise is then followed by a seven-second pause.

In this example thus far, the conversation begins with a discussion of movies, but Jin's conversation in the background assumes the second part of a two-part question–answer exchange. Interactionally, the background noise holds the conversational floor because no one says anything during Jin's conversation.

After a long pause in line 6, Jin ends her background conversation and makes a verbal contribution to the chat room. Andregee responds with a greeting token, and thus both interactants establish a state of mutual orientation. That is, both interactants can begin talk proper. Although Jin and Andregee have the option of taking about movies, the conversation that eventually begins moves away from this topic. The topic of discussion ends in three interactional parts: the background noise (1) is inserted into a sequential position where talk should occur, (2) holds the conversational floor for a fixed period of time, and (3) allows an interactant to initiate or propose a new topic of discussion.

To further illustrate this interactional phenomenon, a final extract is examined. In Extract 3, the extraneous sounds are white noise and audible background typing. As with Extract 2, these sounds hold the conversational floor, as no interactants attempt to talk as the background noises unfold. The interactants in the extract are discussing karaoke singing.

```
(3)
1a—Skypecast
04:29—05:01
1     Veronica:         ye::s (0.2) just (1.0) just sing to
2                       myse:lf
3                       (1.1)
4     Jin:              a:::h
5                       (0.9)
6     Jin:              why did you go there by yourself↓
7                       (2.9)
8                       ((white noise for 1.5 seconds))
9                       ((typing noise for 3.7 seconds))
10                      (1.4)
```

```
11                          ((white noise for 2.2 seconds))
12                              (0.8)
13      Jin:                    hello::?
14                              (2.0)
15      Samir:                  i'm back.
16                              (1.0)
17      Jin:                    oka::y (.) good.
18                              (1.8)
19      Samir:                  what was the- subject we are talking
20                              about now.
```

The extract begins with Veronica confirming that she sings in karaoke rooms by herself. Later in line 6, Jin asks a follow-up question. This question forms the first part of a two-part exchange. Although Veronica is obliged to provide an answer, the question is followed by white noise (line 8), audible typing sounds (line 9), and further white noise (line 11). During this spate of background noise, Jin and Veronica do not continue talking, nor do they comment on the series of extraneous sounds. The pauses that occur in lines 7, 9, and 12 are also not taken up as opportunities to speak (i.e. the pauses are not oriented to as transition relevant places).

The long spell of silence and background noise leads to a greeting token in line 13. This utterance checks whether someone is on the other end of the line, and allows Jin to establish mutual orientation with her co-interactant if a response is given (cf. Extract 2). In other words, Jin accounts for the background noise by soliciting a response from one of her co-interactants. This greeting token also gives Veronica the opportunity to provide a second-pair part answer, though one is not immediately given. Instead, Samir, a participant who has not spoken for some time, states that he has returned to the chat room (line 15).

As with Extracts 1 and 2, the background noise here begins in second-pair part position, holds the conversation floor, and ends by placing an interactant in a position to either continue talking on topic or propose a new conversation. Although Samir is in a position to propose a new topic of discussion, he asks what his other participants have been talking about (lines 19 and 20).

This section has demonstrated that the spoken medium cannot handle multiple, competing sounds (cf. simultaneous conversations in multiparty text-based CMC; see Chapter 6). The idea that sounds are competing is important to an understanding of CMSI, as background noises occupy sequential positions that would otherwise be used for talk. Although CMSI participants can talk over background noises, such sounds often have interactional and/or sequential implications. That is to say, background noises are procedurally consequential to the management of CMSI. Extraneous sounds stop ongoing conversations, permanently or momentarily. These sounds also sequentially disjoint talk and interaction. In other situations, background noises lead to a loss in mutual orientation. Although it is not uncommon to re-establish mutual orientation after experiencing background noise in face-to-face encounters (e.g. in a busy cafe or construction site it would not be unusual for someone to say, "So, where were we?" after a sound disruption), there is often no need for people in such settings to check whether their co-interactants have left the conversation (e.g. "Are you still there?"). This type of interactional work is necessary in CMSI. Managing presence, or online presence to be more precise, is the focal point of analysis in the next section.

### 7.3  ONLINE PRESENCE

Online communication requires dealing with a number of different contextual issues. Very often these contextual issues act as both a communicative affordance and constraint. For instance, as the previous section illustrated, an audio channel that supports high-quality sound transmission affords interactants with the ability to clearly hear each other, but also constrains communication by amplifying extraneous noises. In text-based CMC, message persistence makes it possible for interactants to engage in simultaneous conversational floors, but also constrains discourse cohesion and coherence. Likewise, a setting that involves communicating in the absence of physical co-presence facilitates anonymity, but also challenges communication by requiring interactants to manage speakership without the use of gaze, body positions, and gestures. Chapter 5 examined how this contextual issue shapes the turn-taking system of CMSI. This section also examines the issue of communicating in the absence of physical co-presence, but the analysis below is concerned with how this contextual issue shapes the interactional work involved in distinguishing between the different types of online presence that exist in CMSI.

In CMSI, there are broadly two types of online presence: "electronically present" and "verbally present." The former type of presence is established after an electronic summons-answer exchange (i.e. when a host admits an interactant into the talking section; see Chapter 4; Section 5.3). CMSI participants have visual access to who is electronically present: usernames are listed of all interactants in the chat room. Electronic presence is established only once, unless an interactant exits and re-enters a chat room.

Being electronically present does not mean that an interactant is verbally present. The latter type of presence is established when an interactant makes a verbal contribution. However, talk does not simply happen. Some interactional work is needed in order to determine whether an interactant that is logged in wishes to speak. It is not uncommon for CMSI participants to explicitly establish their verbal presence many times in a chat room (e.g. "hi, I'm here" or "I didn't go anywhere"). This is because interactants frequently enter and leave chat rooms, prolonged pauses and background noises can signal that an interactant has left the discussion and/or is unable to participate, and CMSI participants do not have visual access to what their co-interactants are doing behind their computer screens.

In uncovering how interactants make sense of these two types of online presence, the analysis below demonstrates that complex, collaborative interactional work is needed in order to distinguish between being logged in and wanting to talk.

A common way of determining whether an interactant is electronically or verbally present is to make an announcement. Announcements frequently occur after an interactant is admitted into a chat room, and generally come from the participant who has created the chat room, also known as the host. The host is responsible for admitting new interactants (see Chapter 4), and is therefore the first participant to know when someone has joined the talking section. Although usernames establish that CMSI participants are logged in, announcements make the state of being electronically present procedurally consequential to the talk at hand.

An announcement minimally identifies an interactant's screen name, but can also include a greeting token. In Extract 4, for instance, Roci identifies and greets a new interactant.

```
(4)
1h—Skypecast
00:00—00:27
1    Roci:       °yeah° (0.7) oh we have sailor jin mee
2                ((mumbling for 3.0 seconds)) okay uh
3                (1.0)
4                jin rhee mee hello?
5    Jin:        hello?
```

The first part of the turn includes the collective pronoun "we," which demonstrates that Roci is speaking on behalf of his co-interactants. Announcements are also spoken to the entire chat room, including the interactant that has just joined the talking section. Roci's announcement directs his co-interactants' attention to Jin's electronic presence. The announcement turn does not, however, establish whether Jin is verbally present. Jin could be away from her computer, busy attending to something else on her computer screen, or reluctant to talk. The announcement only verbally acknowledges the fact that Jin is electronically present.

The second part of the announcement turn includes a greeting. Note that Roci does not simply say "hello": he addresses Jin by name, and therefore allocates next speaker position to her. Addressing interactants by name is common practice in CMSI, where participants have no way of gesturally embodying speakership. This practice is integral to distinguishing between the two types of online presence that exist in CMSI, as two or more interactant can successively join a chat room.

More importantly, the utterance in line 4 allows Roci to determine whether Jin is simply logged in or if she is in fact ready and able to take part in the ongoing discussion. In other words, a response (or a non-response) to the announcement turn establishes which of the two online presences is relevant to Jin.

The formulation of Roci's announcement turn reflects the type of interactional work that is involved in distinguishing between electronic and verbal presence. Although all of the interactants have access to screen names (i.e. they know who is logged in), some work is needed in order to determine whether Jin is in fact on the other end of the line. For instance, in the above example, the interactants do not go straight into a conversation with Jin. Before this happens, Roci announces, addresses, and greets. In addition to announcing, addressing, and greeting, this work performs the function of determining whether an interactant is verbally present, as the next extract demonstrates further.

Extract 5 has been taken from a different chat room, but Jin is again the newly admitted interactant. The participants in the chat room have been talking for over six minutes, at which point Menn makes Jin's electronic presence procedurally consequential to the talk at hand.

```
(5)
1e–Skypecast
06:13–06:39
1                       (1.9)
2    Menn:              uh:: (0.2) good morning (.) and uh: good
3                       uh- welcome to jin rhee mee
4                       (0.8)
5    Jin:               he:y (.) hello:
                        ((all of the existing interactants provide
                        self-introductions))
6    Jin:               o::kay↑ (0.8) so (.) a'oh::mean (0.3) i
7                       didn't want to disturb you guys before?
8                       so i was just listening what you guys
9                       (are) talking about
```

After a prolonged spell of silence, Menn greets Jin by name and welcomes her to the chat room. In so doing, Jin's electronic presence is treated as procedurally consequential to the ongoing conversation. The announcement functions as a way of positioning everyone's orientation to a new interactant, but it also allows Menn to initiate a conversational exchange with Jin. If a response is given to the announcement, then Menn, as well as his co-interactants, know that Jin is on the other end of the line.

Jin establishes her verbal presence in lines 6–9. However, responding to an announcement or greeting does not mean that an interactant wishes to maintain this type of online presence. As Jin's turn reveals, CMSI participants may wish to simply lurk in the talking section ("i didn't want to disturb you guys before . . . i was just listening"). That is, being admitted into in a chat room does not necessarily mean that an interactant is present to speak.

Extract 5 shows that determining whether talk is possible with an interactant requires some interactional work. This is further demonstrated in the next extract. Here the topic of discussion is related to William Ohna (also referred to as Will or Bill), an interactant that has been admitted into the talking section, but is not currently participating in the current discussion. The extract begins with Roci announcing William's electronic presence.

```
(6)
1h–Skypecast
01:53–02:16
1    Roci:              and uh will here oh:ma: ohna is uh:::
2                       (0.3) actually is in japan now teaching
3                       english she- he's from hawaii
```

```
4                             (0.4)
5      Jin:                   mmhm=
6      Winnie:                =he- e- [is- actually
7      Roci:                          [actually from hawaii
8                             (0.2)
9      Winnie:                is he a half asian
10                            (1.2)
11     Jin:                   me?=
12     Roci:                  =uh- no uh=
13     Jin:                   =ah sorry
14     Winnie:                will (.) no sorry i- i- say william
15                            (0.6) o:: o-oh[na
16     Roci:                               [>oh will>
17                            (0.8)
18     Roci:                  bill? are you there? can you answer the
19                            question bill?
                ((interactants continue to talk about Bill))
```

In line 1, Roci orients to the electronic presence of William by stating that he is in the chat room ("will here"). William's electronic presence is later distinguished from his geographical location (line 2), which also highlights the fact that space and place are highly liminal concepts in CMSI. Unlike the two previous extracts, the announcement turn is not constructed with a greeting token. Rather, the announcement that William is in the chat room acts as a conversational springboard. For several lines of interaction, Roci and his co-interactants talk about William as if he were not logged into the chat room—note, for example, the use of the third-person singular pronoun "he" in the description of William in line 6, as well as the question regarding his ethnicity in line 9. This is particularly noteworthy, as William is electronically present, as marked by his username displayed on the user interface, and indeed as Roci has made this fact relevant during his announcement turn.

The fact that Roci and his co-interactants talk about William in the third person—despite making William's electronic presence interactionally relevant to the ongoing discussion—demonstrates that talk with a new interactant does not simply happen. Mutual orientation must be established with a new interactant, and this, as previous extracts have demonstrated, can be accomplished with a greeting token. Establishing mutual orientation is necessary for interactants to begin talk proper, and this work also determines whether CMSI participants are willing and able to actively take part in a conversation. In this example, the interrogative "are you there?" is used to determine whether William is in fact on the other end of the line (line 18).

The interrogative "are you there?" is used regularly in CMSI to determine verbal presence. To illustrate this point further, a final extract is examined. Unlike previous examples examined in this section, the interrogative comes from a newly admitted interactant. In Extract 7, two interactants are in the chat room. Jin is the newly admitted interactant and Sayed is the host. Because Sayed has just admitted Jin into the chat room, both interactants have established their electronic presence. That is, both interactants know that they are logged in. They do not, however, know whether their co-interactant is verbally present.

```
(7)
1d—Skypecast
00:00—00:11
1     Jin:       hello
2                (1.8)
3     Jin:       HELLO
4                (0.2)
5     Sayed:     yeah i hello uh-
6                (0.6)
7     Jin:       hi are you there?
8                (3.2)
9     Sayed:     yes (.) hi
10               (1.3)
```

The extract begins with Jin providing a greeting token in line 1. This greeting token requires a response in kind, and thus allows Jin to determine whether Sayed is available to talk. However, no response is given, and after nearly two seconds of silence, Jin delivers a second greeting token with increase voice amplitude. In line 5, Sayed provides a response. Although Sayed's turn should signal to Jin that he is verbally present, Jin treats the greeting token delivered by Sayed as insufficient in establishing the second type of online presence. This is evidenced in line 7. Here Jin upgrades her previous attempts to determine Sayed's verbal presence, as demonstrated in the interrogative "are you there?" This turn requires an answer that explicitly confirms whether Sayed in on the other end of the line. In other words, the greeting exchange does not allow Jin and Sayed to fully establish that they are ready and able to take part in talk proper. Sequentially, the interrogative "are you there?" follows some interactional trouble in lines 1–3 (i.e. nonresponse to Jin's first greeting token), which may be the reason why Jin upgrades her attempt to determine whether Sayed is verbally present.

This section has established that beginning a conversation with an interactant first requires engaging in some interaction work, as there are two types of online presence in CMSI. For example, a participant must first notice that a new interactant is in the chat room before determining whether talk is possible. However, verbally acknowledging that an interactant is logged in does not mean that talk is possible, nor does it always lead to an attempt to determine whether an interactant is willing and able to talk (cf. Extract 6). CMSI participants determine the second type of online presence by greeting an interactant and/or seeking confirmation that someone is on the other end of the line.

Because CMSI is managed in the absence of physical co-presence, participants must engage in intricate, collaborative interactional work in order to determine which interactants are willing to actively take part in a conversation. Often this work is carried out in subtle ways (e.g. greeting each other, completing summons-answer exchanges). In other situations, CMSI participants explicitly orient to the fact that being logged in does not mean that an interactant is "in" the chat room (cf. the are-you-there interrogative).

While speaking in the absence of physical co-presence requires interactants to engage in interactional work that is otherwise unnecessary in many face-to-face and video-based CMC settings, online presence can act as an affordance (see Ackerman *et al.* 1997: 55). For instance, interactants can appear to be present, as manifest in their usernames that are displayed for everyone to see, but can be in fact busy attending to tasks unrelated to the chat room. In the same vein, interactants can engage in tasks unrelated to the chat room while simultaneously embodying the second type of online presence by engaging in active listening (e.g. providing backchannels to a co-interactant while playing a computer game). Despite these affordances, there are other contextual issues involved in speaking online that constrain the type of work that is required to maintain a sense of verbal presence in CMSI, as the next section demonstrates.

## 7.4 PAUSES

The length, sequential placement, and management of pauses vary from one setting to another, and the social norms and conventions that are established, and co-constructed *in situ*, help determine how pauses are dealt with and whether they are treated as problematic. Prolonged pauses are socially acceptable in face-to-face contexts that require interactants to engage in interactions whilst carrying out different tasks (e.g. cooking and talking in a kitchen). In other situations, spells of silence are evaluated according to institutional norms and treated as a deficiency in communication (e.g. language proficiency interviews). In push-to-talk radio communication, where participants are not physically co-present, long pauses of over two minutes are the norm, and sometimes unanswered utterances are not treated as problematic (Woodruff and Aoki 2004: 425).

In addition to social norms and conventions, technology shapes how pauses are managed in synchronous CMC settings. For example, in the two-way synchronous text-based CMC platform investigated by Anderson *et al.* (2010), pauses were infrequent though relatively long in duration (i.e. approximately 12 seconds on average). Pauses were especially long in this setting because the text medium afforded interactants the ability to re-read old messages (cf. message persistence; see Chapter 6).

In CMSI, pauses have an important mediating role in online spoken communication. Although pauses are used as interactional resources to deal with the onset of overlapping talk, spates of silence constrain the turn-taking system of CMSI by making it difficult to manage speakership (see Chapter 5). In other words, pauses can cause overlapping utterances to occur. This section builds on these observations by examining the sequential organization of pauses. More specifically, this section is concerned with how pauses are responded to in sequential locations where talk is expected. It is argued that an examination of pauses reveals a great deal about CMC in general, CMSI in particular.

Two sequential locations are examined in this section. The first location is a pause that follows an ostensibly incomplete turn (e.g. an utterance that is cut off). The second location is a pause that occurs where a second-pair part utterance should have been given (e.g. an answer to a question). These sequential locations are examined because they reveal how pauses are made procedurally consequential to CMSI. The analysis begins with the first location.

In Extract 8, several interactants are conversing. The extract begins with Gadi discussing relationships.

```
(8)
1e—Skypecast
19:08-19:38
1    Gadi:      it's quite conventional to:: for example
2               (0.2) uh:: be familiar with ay- uh:: (.)
3               friend (.) i mean have a girlfriend or::
4               boyfriend and after that (0.2) for
5               example (0.5) proposing for:
6               (2.1)
7    Mustafa:   hello?
8               (0.3)
9    Jin:       hello? (.) huh::
10              (0.2)
11   Mustafa:   uh- we: (0.3) i think we lost him huhhuh
12              (.) we lost contact
13   Ang:       nono we're we are with-
14              (0.2)
15   Jin:       so what's his- what's his name? (.) who:
16              was [just talking?
```

In lines 1–5, Gadi holds the conversational floor for several lines of talk with no apparent technical or communicative difficulty (e.g. no background noise or audible perturbations). Although the final word uttered in Gadi's turn signals syntactically that talk is forthcoming ("for:"), for unknown reasons no additional talk is given after line 5. What follows is a prolonged pause in line 6.

The interactional work that follows this pause is noteworthy. In line 7, Mustafa responds to the pause with a greeting token. The greeting token allows Mustafa to establish whether Gadi is verbally present (N.B. if Gadi had left the chat room, then his username would have disappeared from the user interface, and there would be little doubt over his online presence). By responding to the pause with a greeting token, Mustafa treats the silence as interactionally consequential to the ongoing discussion. Put differently, Mustafa does not wait to see if Gadi will continue talking. Rather, Mustafa attempts to re-establish mutual orientation with Gadi after two seconds of silence. This exchange shows that talk cannot simply stop in CMSI without the pause leading to some interactional work. This is further illustrated in the next example.

In Extract 9, Dukes and SydneyLove are getting acquainted. In this exchange, the pause occurs in second-pair part position. The extract begins during the first few seconds of the opening of a chat room.

```
(9)
1g—Skypecast
00:00—00:11
1    Dukes:        [eh- eh- i'm- i'm dukes,] dukes from sri
2                  lanka
3                  (2.0)
4                  hello i'm dukes from sri lanka
5                  (.)
6    SydneyLove:   yea:h, nice to meet you <sri lanka<
```

In lines 1 and 2, Dukes introduces himself to SydneyLove. This utterance represents the first part of a two-part exchange, as self-introductions are normatively responded to with talk of some sort (e.g. greeting token). Put differently, the self-introduction creates an expectation that a second-pair part will be given. However, SydneyLove does not immediately provide a response. By repeating his self-introduction in line 4, Dukes treats the silence as noticeably absent (i.e. procedurally consequential and interactionally problematic).

This exchange sheds light on how the management of pauses is intertwined into the commonsense practices of CMSI participants. Although pauses vary in duration and are responded to in different ways in the data set (e.g. pauses of three or more seconds may not be treated as procedurally consequential), in this exchange, Dukes waits for two seconds before repeating his self-introduction. That is, for Dukes, two seconds appears to be enough time to wait before treating the silence as problematic.

While different expectations exist with regard to what is a sufficient amount of time to wait when talk is expected (e.g. waiting for an answer to a question), and these expectations no doubt change from one context to another, for the interactants examined in these extracts, there appears to be a threshold for silence. In Extract 9, the two-second pause passed the threshold for Dukes to wait for SydneyLove to provide a response. In Extract 8, approximately the same amount of time was given to a current speaker to continue with his turn after a pause. In the next extract, a similar amount of time is given in two instances where talk is expected (i.e. lines 3 and 7).

```
(10)
A12—Skypecast
00:29—00:46
1    Amir:   ye::ah↓ (0.6) so::::: we have
2            porn-peeve with↑ us↓
3            (2.1)
4    Sam:    >yeah.>
5            (0.5)
6    Amir:   hello?
7            (1.9)
```

```
8    Amir:    he:llo?=
9    Ming:    =hi. (.) ehm ((clears throat))
10            (0.8)
11   Amir:    okay↓
12            (0.7)
13   Amir:    sah-rhee-ma (.) tell us about yourself
```

In lines 1 and 2, Amir makes an announcement that a new participant is in the chat room. Amir does not provide a greeting token, which would sequentially oblige the new participant to provide a response (see Section 7.3). However, announcements are spoken to an entire chat room, and thus provide the opportunity for any verbally present interactant to topicalize the arrival of a new participant. Despite this, no response is given to the announcement. After two seconds, Sam provides an acknowledgment token, which is followed by Amir's "hello." This greeting token demonstrates that Amir expected a response from the new participant rather than from someone else in the chat room (N.B. Amir does not respond to Sam's turn). After two seconds of silence in line 7, Amir provides another greeting token in line 8.

Both of Amir's greeting tokens represent the first part of a two-part exchange. As such, a second-pair part utterance is expected. These greeting tokens also show that both pauses of two seconds are procedurally consequential to the arrival of a new participant. To extend this observation further, prolonged pauses are noticeably absent when located in second-pair part position. Although the same could be said for many settings that involve spoken communication (see Schegloff 2007), the difference in CMSI lies in the interactional work that takes place after prolonged pauses. For example, both of Amir's greeting tokens not only treat the prolonged pauses as procedurally consequential, but they also explicitly seek to confirm that an interactant is in fact present in the chat room.

With this observation in mind, the examination of pauses builds on the findings established in the previous section on online presence. In situations where a prolonged pause follows either an incomplete turn or a first-pair part utterance, interactants will normatively check whether the current speaker or recipient is present in the chat room. The interactional work that follows pauses in both of these sequential positions shows how context shapes online spoken communication. Although mutual orientation is established before talk occurs in CMSI (i.e. during an electronic summons-answer exchange), communicating in the absence of physical co-presence requires monitoring, and sometimes re-establishing, online presence after a conversation has begun. Conversely, in face-to-face and video-enabled online communication, interactants do not need to regularly monitor online presence. Monitoring and re-establishing online presence is necessary in CMSI because interactants do not know whether a spell of silence means that a current speaker is experiencing technical difficulties, has momentarily left the chat room, or is busy attending to a different computer task.

Although this section has demonstrated that pauses are a central organizing feature of CMSI, much more work is needed in this area of investigation. For instance, the possibility that a threshold for silence exists must be examined with a larger collection of data. That is, it is too early to say whether CMSI participants have a temporal preference for responding to prolonged pauses. For example, is two seconds the threshold for silence in CMSI settings? Not only would a larger collection of data, as well as a focused analysis of pause length, shed light on whether a threshold for silence exists, but such a study could also help determine to what extent CMSI is similar to other technology-enabled communication (e.g. two-way radios). Furthermore, future research would contribute to the CMC literature by closely examining the turns that follow long spells of silence, as response types may vary according to pause length (e.g. repeating a turn after a pause of one second versus explicitly determining online presence after a pause of two seconds). Despite these limitations and research gaps, the analytic observations made in this section show that the interactional work that takes place after prolonged pauses is noteworthy in light of what happens in other communicative settings.

## 7.5 ONGOING TALK

Participating in a conversation requires managing a number of different interactional resources and possessing an understanding of context. For example, participating in a classroom discussion requires understanding how and when to make a contribution. Students can raise their hands to bid for the conversational floor, but this in no way guarantees that talk will follow. This is because contributions to a lesson are dependent on several contextual variables, including the number of students raising their hands, where students are positioned in the classroom, and whether the teacher is looking for one or several contributions, to name a few. In text-based chat rooms, the written medium presents interactants with a context where contributions to a conversation can break into multiple topics of discussion. The interactional resources that are used to manage conversational schisms include typing faster, postponing message transmission, and addressing specific interactants. In multiparty face-to-face interactions (e.g. cocktail party), participating in a conversation where multiple discussions are unfolding at the same time involves adjusting voice amplitude, body positions, and proximity to others.

In each of these multiparty talk settings, there are several unique contextual variables that influence the type of interactional work that is involved in participating in a conversation. These contextual variables may be related to social and interactional norms and conventions (e.g. classroom rights and rules) and/or communicative affordances and constraints, including technology-based factors (e.g. message persistence). An examination of how these contextual variables shape talk and interaction is crucial to understanding a communicative setting.

In CMSI, there are two aspects of communication that are somewhat exceptional, but by no means exclusive, to online spoken interactions. That is, talk is inherently ongoing and interactants enter and leave conversations with high regularity. In this section, ongoing conversation refers to talk that has been started by a group of interactants but is later joined by new participants.

With these contextual variables in mind, one of the unique challenges of communicating in CMSI is knowing when and how to join an ongoing conversation. As discussed in previous sections, one way to join an ongoing conversation is to wait for an existing member of the chat room to elicit a response from a newly admitted inter-actant (e.g. announcing the arrival of, and greeting, a new interactant). Alternatively, a newly admitted interactant can join an ongoing conversation by eliciting a response from an existing member of the chat room.

As Section 7.3 has already established how existing members of chat rooms elicit talk from newly admitted interactants, this section uncovers the interactional work that takes place during the latter situation.

In Extract 11, the newly admitted interactant is Samir. Veronica and Jin are dis-cussing geographical locations and their countries of origin. The extract begins 30 seconds into the chat room.

```
(11)
1a—Skypecast
00:32—00:48
1      Veronica:    ye:s (.) an::d, (0.3) it's
2                   really near china right?
3                   (1.6)
4      Jin:         yeah it's near china too
5                   (2.0)
6      Samir:       hello:?=
7      Veronica:    =yes I'm chinese hhh.
8                   (0.4)
9      Jin:         ahh are you chinese↑ okay nice
10                  to meet you
11                  (0.8)
12     Veronica:    yes (0.2) nice to meet you too:
13                  (1.3)
14     Jin:         so are you in china↑ right now↓
```

The extract begins with Veronica and Jin getting acquainted (lines 1–4). In line 6, Samir delivers a greeting token. Although Samir does not address a specific person, his greeting token seeks a response from a co-interactant (e.g. a second-pair part greeting). However, no greeting token or response is provided, and Veronica and Jin continue getting acquainted (lines 7–14). This is particularly noteworthy, as the greeting token occurs during a transition relevant place and after a prolonged pause. Sequentially, the greeting token is delivered in the appropriate location: Samir selects himself as next speaker after no attempts are made to allocate the next turn. However, closer inspection of this exchange reveals that Veronica's turn latches onto the greet-ing token. Thus, both turns compete for the conversational floor, as Veronica and Samir apply the third rule of turn allocation at nearly the same time (see Section 5.2.3).

In the next turn, Jin chooses to topicalize Veronica's country of origin. Although it is impossible to determine the precise reason why Samir has failed to establish himself as an active participant in the ongoing conversation, it is possible that he does not receive a response because he does not greet a specific co-interactant, nor is his turn on topic (i.e. his turn does not build on the ongoing discussion).

Indeed, examination of additional extracts reveals that topic management is an important interactional issue when contributing to an ongoing conversation. Take, for example, the following extract. In Extract 12, the newly admitted interactant has not been identified by name (see line 6). The existing members of the chat room are discussing countries of origin. Unlike the previous extract, the newly admitted interactant here receives a response after his turn. Despite this, talk does not extend beyond a two-part exchange.

```
(12)
1a–Skypecast
16:27–16:51
1       Andregee:    yes. where↓ are↑ you↓ now↑
2                    (1.0)
3       Jin:         i::'m in↑ yeah i'm in england
4                    now i'm from korea and i'm .hhh
5                    currently liv[ing in (.) england
6       ???:                      [hi:: veronica
7                    (1.3)
8       Andregee:    for how long are you there now↓=hh
9                    (.)
10      Veronica:    hell::o:↑
11                   (0.7)
12      Jin:         wer::: i:'ve been living here for hhh
13                   er: four months right now↑ (0.2) .hhh
14                   (0.3) and the::n, (0.3) tsk .hhh i guess
15                   i'm gonah::↑ hh .hh stay here for a
16                   long time↓ (0.6) i think (1.0)
```

The extract begins with Andregee and Jin getting acquainted. In line 5, as Jin nears the end of her turn, the newly admitted interactant provides a greeting token. Although the greeting token does not occur during a transition relevant place, the newly admitted interactant is able to elicit a sequentially delayed response from Veronica (line 10). While Veronica and the newly admitted interactant complete a greeting exchange, and have as a result established a state of mutual orientation, they do not continue speaking. Instead Jin proceeds to further explain her current living situation.

This extract uncovers several important issues with regard to becoming an active member of an ongoing conversation. Although greeting tokens can lead to talk, they do not guarantee that an extended conversation will follow. In order for an interactant to establish him- or herself as an active member of an ongoing conversation, he or she must not only know whom to address, but also what the current topic of discussion is and when in the interaction it is appropriate to make a contribution.

For instance, the newly admitted interactant greets Veronica, a participant that is in the chat room, but not participating in the ongoing conversation. Veronica's response, despite forming the second part of a two-part greeting exchange, is off topic. This is because Andregee and Jin have established, and are controlling at the time of this greeting exchange, the conversational floor. As this example illustrates, joining an ongoing conversation requires knowing what to say, when to say it, and whom to say it to, as the final extract in this section demonstrates.

In Extract 13, several interactants are talking about movies, including Jin, Samir, and Veronica. The newly admitted interactant in this exchange is Velson. The existing members of the chat room are discussing movie genres.

```
(13)
1a—Skypecast
09:47—10:13
1      Jin:        horror mo↓vie↑
2                  (0.8)
3      Samir:      ho:r↑ror↓ movie↑
4                  (0.9)
5      Jin:        yeah sca↑ry↓ >y'know> horror movi:e
6                  (3.0)
7      Samir:      o↑kay.
8      Velson:     talk about mo↓vie↑
9                  (1.0)
10     Jin:        >yeah yeah> we are talking about
11                 movie
12                 (0.6)
13     Jin:        hi↑ [hello::
14     Velson:         [(who i- speaks)
15                 (0.4)
16     Velson:     hi.
17                 (0.8)
18     Jin:        w- (0.4) who↑ is↓ it↑=
19     Velson:     =you are?
20                 (1.3)
21     Jin:        <who↑ is↓ i:t↑<
22                 (0.7)
23     Velson:     .hh i'm velson
24                 (1.2)
25     Velson:     and you are?=
26     Veronica:   =velson?
27                 (0.6)
28     Jin:        a:::h my name is (.) jin.
29                 (1.1)
```

The extract begins with Jin and Samir discussing horror movies. In line 8, Velson makes his first contribution to the chat room ("talk about movie"). Here Velson does not address a specific person, but he is able to elicit a response from Jin in line 10, and subsequently engage in extended talk in lines 13–29.

Velson may be successful in establishing himself as an active member of the ongoing conversation partly because his interrogative occurs at a transition relevant place (i.e. after a turn-ending fall in intonation). Because his turn does not occur in overlap, Velson does not have to compete with his co-interactants for the same floor space. Furthermore, the sequential placement of the interrogative minimizes the possibility that the turn will be heard as background noise (i.e. not heard as a meaningful contribution). Perhaps more importantly, in contrast to previous first contributions in the last two extracts, the interrogative is related to the ongoing conversation. That is, the question requires an answer that is related to the current topic of discussion.

This section has identified the interactional work that takes place when interactants attempt to join an ongoing conversation, as well as demonstrating that CMSI participants face several challenges when engaging in talk for the first time. Sequence organization is crucial to whether a response is given to a first contribution by a newly admitted interactant. In other words, CMSI participants must know when, sequentially speaking, it is appropriate to provide a first contribution. In addition, Extract 12 demonstrated that knowing whom to elicit a response from is important to whether a newly admitted interactant is able to engage in talk beyond a two-part exchange. For instance, a greeting token may elicit a response from a co-interactant, but this does not guarantee that a newly admitted interactant will be incorporated into the talk at hand. Similarly, Extract 13 showed that topic management may be important to whether newly admitted interactants are able to establish themselves as active members of the chat room. That is, the likelihood of joining an ongoing conversation may be partly dependent on whether a first verbal contribution is related to what is being discussed at the time. Although additional research is needed in order to confirm these observations, the analysis has revealed that joining an ongoing conversation requires sequentially sensitive interactional work. This work reflects the unique contextual variables of CMSI.

## 7.6 AUDIBILITY

CMSI is dependent on a number of different technologies. Online spoken communication is not possible without a stable network connection, CMSI participants must have hardware devices that enable sound transmission, and appropriate software is needed in order to connect with other co-interactants. While these technologies enable CMSI, the actual management of online spoken communication—for example, whether and how interactants co-construct meaning—is dependent on the ability to hear and to be heard. That is to say, audibility is a key element in achieving comprehensibility in CMSI.

In CMSI, the technologies that enable the ability to hear and be heard typically operate behind the communicative scene. That is, audibility in CMSI is a taken for granted aspect of communication. However, when technologies fail or constrain the ability to hear and/or be heard, audibility shapes the management of talk and interaction. In other situations, CMSI participants topicalize the issue of audibility when there are no ostensible troubles in communication. The analysis below identifies how audibility is made procedurally consequential to the management of CMSI.

The issue of audibility is made relevant in two ways. The first way occurs when a current speaker performs a sound check. The second way takes place when something said in a preceding turn is treated as the source of hearing trouble. The analysis begins with the first way.

In Extract 14, several interactants are in a chat room getting acquainted. The extract begins with Shiho entering the chat room and providing a greeting token.

```
(14)
'nice and gentle talk'—Skypecast
(time unavailable)
1    Shiho:    hello=
2    Kris:     =hello:::↑
3    Shiho:    nice to meet you (0.3) hello
4    Yam:      oh sounds like woman
5    Kris:     o:h ye::ah
6              (1.0)
7    Shiho:    can you hear me↑
8              (1.0)
9    Kris:     oh=
10   Hally:    =ah yah we can
```

Shiho and Kris mutually orient to each other as a result of their greeting exchange in the beginning of this extract (lines 1–3). Although Shiho can now, as a result of entering into a state of mutual orientation with Kris, begin conversation proper, her next turn is used to perform a sound check ("can you hear me"). Here the issue of audibility is made procedurally consequential, as the interrogative requires an answer that confirms whether there is a hearing issue. The sequential placement of the interrogative demonstrates that talk is contingent upon audibility. Shiho does not simply begin talking, but rather engages in interactional work that requires her co-interactants to address the issue of audibility.

Although sound checks are not interactionally obligatory (i.e. interactants can begin conversations without them), when used, they occupy an important sequential position in CMSI. In Extract 15, for instance, the sound check immediately follows a greeting exchange, forming a part of a larger conversational opening sequence.

```
(15)
A39—Skypecast
00:33—00:53
1    Ego:      he:l↓lo↑
2              (2.3)
3    Shawn:    hello:.
4              (0.5)
```

```
5       Ego:        can↓ you↑ hear↓ me↑
6                   (0.8)
7       Joseph:     yeah.
8                   (0.4)
9       Shawn:      yes we can hear you
10                  (0.4)
11      Ego:        ok oh↓ yeah↑ so should i just uh::m
12                  go ahead o:r are you guys talking on
13                  something.
```

In line 5, the sound check elicits a response from Joseph (line 7) and Shawn (line 9). Because sound checks are often delivered as interrogatives, they form the first part of a two-part exchange (i.e. sound check exchange). In providing an answer, Joseph and Shawn establish that they can hear Ego. The sound check exchange occurs before all three interactants begin their conversation. This extract demonstrates that sound checks can be sequentially embedded in the interactional work that takes place to establish a state of mutual orientation. That is, for some interactants, simply greeting each other is not enough to begin a conversation.

The issue of audibility is also made relevant when newly admitted interactants are requested to participate in an ongoing conversation. In these situations, sound checks precede conversations and are performed by the newly admitted interactant. In Extract 16, for example, Stevie requests Gale to introduce herself. Before providing an introduction, Gale performs a sound check.

```
(16)
'talk talk talk'—Skypecast
(time unavailable)
1       Stevie:     we have another participant
2                   (.) day↑ dreamer↓ (.) uh
3                   please introduce yourself
4                   (2.9)
5       Gale:       yeah hello (0.1) can you
6                   hear↑ me↓
7                   (0.8)
8       Stevie:     yes::
9                   (1.2)
10      Francis:    hi
```

The sound check exchange functions as a pre-sequence (lines 5–8), as Gale delays her self-introduction until she determines whether her co-interactants can hear her. In other words, the pre-sequence allows Gale to preface her conversation with an exchange that establishes whether there is a hearing issue (see Schegloff 2007). The sound check also allows Gale to establish a state of mutual orientation with her co-interactants. Similarly, in Extract 17, Menn asks Jin to share her experience of living in England. However, before doing so, Jin performs a sound check in line 13.

```
(17)
1e—Skypecast
09:25—10:04
1    Mustafa:    i'm an english teacher and i'm teaching
2                uh: (.) uh: at a high school in france
3                ** (de academy)
4                (2.1)
5    Menn:       uh: jin young lee uh:: what
6                [do you uh:::
7    Jin:        [yes?
8    Menn:       it- i (.) uh i think you speak in
9                english more than us (0.8) because uh:
10               you are living in the (0.4) england
11               (0.2) right? a mee-ley
12               (1.4)
13   Jin:        so can you guys hear me?
14   Menn:       yes (.) we hear you
```

In this extract, the sound check exchange precedes talk about living in England, makes relevant the issue of audibility, and allows Jin and Menn to establish a state of mutual orientation (lines 13 and 14).

In all of the extracts examined in this section thus far, the issue of audibility is made interactionally relevant despite the fact that there are no explicit indications of sound problems. In other situations, however, the issue of audibility is made interactionally relevant because of a problem in hearing.

In Extract 18, for example, Jin performs a sound check after Sayed states that there is a hearing problem. Jin is the newly admitted interactant. Sayed is the only interactant in the chat room.

```
(18)
1d—Skypecast
00:09—00:38
1    Jin:      okay so what are you doing alone?
2              (2.6)
3    Sayed:    c-c-can you- i'm sorry but can you
4              raise your voice?
5              (1.6)
6    Jin:      uh:: can you hear me?
7              (1.9)
8    Sayed:    ya i can hear you now ya
9              (0.4)
10   Jin:      oh good (0.4) okay (0.8) so (.) what
11             are you doing alone here (0.1) alone
12             here
13             (2.9)
```

```
14    Sayed:      ↑oh: (0.2) i just stop at uh skype
15                waiting for the audience to come in
16                (0.5)
```

The extract begins with Jin asking why Sayed is alone in the chat room. This interrogative creates some hearing difficulties for Sayed, as he requests Jin to raise her voice. In line 6, Jin adjusts her voice amplitude and performs a sound check. Unlike previous extracts, the sound check is used as a repair device (note also the change in voice amplitude), as it follows an utterance (or repair initiation turn) that identifies a hearing problem.

This observation can be used to extend the analyses made in Extracts 14–17. In these previous extracts, sound checks are used as a preemptive repair device. That is, the issue of audibility is addressed, or made interactionally relevant, before hearing manifests into a problem in communication. Conversely, in Extract 18, the sound check is used to retroactively deal with a past hearing trouble. In both situations, sound checks are used as interactional resources to make audibility procedurally consequential to CMSI. Furthermore, Extract 18 demonstrates that audibility is a repairable phenomenon. CMSI participants can engage in interactional work to calibrate the degree to which they can hear and be heard.

This section has shown that audibility is made relevant in different sequential locations. Sound checks occur after greeting tokens, requests to speak, and repair initiation turns, and are used to preempt troubles in hearing or retroactively deal with past hearing troubles. Often sound checks occur during conversational openings, but can also take place long after a conversation has begun. CMSI requires dealing with audibility throughout a conversation because background noises, voice amplitude, and technical failures, to name a few, can affect an interactant's ability to hear and to be heard. Although the issue of audibility is not unique to online spoken communication, it is crucial to the management of CMSI.

## 7.7 DISCUSSION AND CONCLUSION

The popularity of CMSI has increased in recent years with the help of Skype and other similar programs that offer cost-effective ways of speaking online. Many researchers see this growth as an opportunity to expand the CMC literature, especially in areas of study pertaining to language education where there is a tradition of testing theories of oral development and proficiency in text-based settings (Yanguas 2010). While CMSI platforms have been investigated in the CMC literature (see Kenning 2010), there is still much to be examined with regard to how contextual issues shape online spoken communication.

This chapter has demonstrated that CMSI is shaped by a number of different contextual variables. The analysis showed that background noises vary in type and length, and often occur during a two-part exchange. Background noises are interactionally consequential to the management of CMSI: they can stop ongoing conversations, compel interactants to check whether someone is on the other end of the line, and force participants to re-establish mutual orientation. In other words, dealing with background noises is part and parcel of talking online.

The analysis of online presence uncovered the complex, collaborative interactional work that takes place when interactants determine who is in the chat room. This section showed that there are both subtle and explicit ways to manage online presence in CMSI (e.g. greeting tokens and are-you-there interrogatives, respectively). While this contextual issue represents a technological constraint, in that interactants must engage in interactional work that is otherwise unnecessary in many communicative settings, online presence can also act as an affordance. For example, CMSI participants can engage in a number of different computer-mediated tasks while passively displaying online presence.

Pauses were also shown to be a central organizing feature of CMSI. Specifically, the interactional work that follows pauses illustrated the type of challenges that interactants face when communicating in the absence of physical co-presence. Although mutual orientation is established before a conversation begins (cf. electronic summons-answer exchange), communicating without visual access to what other participants are doing requires monitoring—for example, re-establishing—online presence after a conversation has begun. The analysis showed that prolonged pauses result in such interactional work.

The section on ongoing talk uncovered the challenges of participating in a conversation for the first time. The analysis demonstrated that the timing (or the sequential placement) of a first contribution affected the likelihood of participating in a chat room. Knowing whom to elicit a response from also appeared to be an important factor in joining an ongoing conversation. Furthermore, knowing what is being discussed, and designing a first contribution accordingly, may affect whether a newly admitted interactant is able to join an ongoing conversation. Thus, joining an ongoing conversation requires knowing what to say, when to say it, and whom to say it to.

Lastly, the ability to hear and to be heard is interactionally consequential to the management of online spoken communication. The analysis in this section demonstrated that sound checks are often used to address the issue of audibility. Sound checks vary in their sequential position, and are used in different ways. Although the issue of audibility is not unique to CMSI, it is crucial to establishing mutual orientation and initiating talk proper. Sound checks are used as a preemptive repair device. In other situations, sound checks are used to retroactively deal with a past hearing trouble.

Although this section has identified five contextual variables that shape CMSI, there are several issues and circumstances that must be examined in future research. Contextual issues and circumstances that would build on the observations made in this chapter, and provide a better understanding of CMSI, include backchannels (i.e. how interactants embody active listening), topic management (i.e. how topics of discussion are opened and closed), and social presence (i.e. how the perceived distance between interactants is made interactionally relevant). In other words, this chapter has provided a glimpse into the ways in which online spoken communication is managed, but much more work is needed in order to fully understand CMSI.

Despite these limitations, the five contextual variables examined in this chapter provide an empirical foundation for future research to build on.

# APPLICATION

# 8

# TEACHING AND LEARNING

## 8.1 INTRODUCTION

For over two decades, CMC research has covered a wide range of pedagogical issues (for a review of studies, see Liu *et al.* 2002), including language learning theories (Doughty and Long 2003; Gonzalez-Lloret 2003; Bower and Kawaguchi 2011; Vinagre and Munoz 2011), teaching materials (Abrams 2001; Chou 2001), intercultural awareness (Chung *et al.* 2005; Kabata and Edasawa 2011), pragmatic competence (Bloch 2004; Yang 2011), target language practice (Gonzalez-Lloret 2003; Lund 2006; Peterson 2006; Barrs 2012), and language teaching strategies and approaches (Meskill and Anthony 2005).

Within this body of work, there is a strand of research that aims to understand language teaching and learning issues by investigating online communication (i.e. CALL-CMC research; see Section 3.2). CALL-CMC studies have investigated formal and informal learning settings (e.g. Chun 1994; Payne and Ross 2005; Blake 2009; Sauro and Smith 2010; Wang and Vasquez 2012), adopted a number of different theoretical and methodological approaches (Lamy and Hampel 2007), and examined a range of CMC types and online communication platforms.

This chapter contributes to the CALL-CMC literature by exploring the pedagogical implications of second language chat rooms. The discussion of teaching and learning issues is based on observations made in previous analytic chapters. The premise of this chapter is that what second language users do in informal learning settings should inform what is taught in classrooms. This is especially true given the amount of target language exposure the Internet provides students. Furthermore, students are now more than ever engaged in, and committed to, self-access learning, and computers and other technology-enabled devices are an integral part of communication in today's world.

Second language chat rooms are ideal pedagogical sites because they provide students with opportunities to practice speaking in a setting where participation is not bound by traditionally classroom norms and practices (Levy and Kennedy 2004). Second language chat rooms are rich with authentic input and allow students to engage in communication that is socially meaningful (see Hampel and Hauck 2004; Heins *et al.* 2007; Alastuey 2010; Guichon 2010; Sindoni 2011). This chapter argues that the interactional competencies that are required to communicate in second language chat rooms have some pedagogical value.

Indeed, researchers have thus far observed that CMSI platforms promote vocabulary acquisition (Yanguas 2012), provide opportunities to negotiate for meaning (Yanguas 2010), enhance oral proficiency (Yang and Chang 2008), and improve students' pragmatic knowledge of spoken communication (Sykes 2005). While these studies provide important insights into how CMSI can be used for language teaching and learning purposes, few investigations to date have examined CMSI from a social-interaction perspective (see Section 3.2.4).

The utility in examining CMSI from a social-interaction perspective lies in its ability to uncover the competencies that are required, and the resources that are used, to co-construct meaningful communication. As such, this chapter identifies the interactional competencies that are required of interactants to engage in CMSI. This chapter also explores how an understanding of CMSI can be used to design pedagogical tasks. Both of these analytic foci contribute to the study of SLA.

## 8.2  SECOND LANGUAGE ACQUISITION

CALL-CMC research is heavily influenced by SLA theories and hypotheses, and more specifically, psycholinguistic interpretations of language learning (i.e. psycholinguistic SLA). The popularity of psycholinguistic SLA in CALL-CMC research has been partly driven by the idea that comprehensible language input is the main determiner for second language development (Krashen 1985). Other influential hypotheses include the belief that negotiated interactions are necessary for learners to acquire a language (Long 1996) and the idea that acquisition is not possible without language production (Swain 1993).

SLA researchers that subscribe to, and examine, these hypotheses are commonly referred to as interactionists (see Long 1996). As mentioned in Chapter 3, the interactionist paradigm is based on the belief that conversational exchanges that deal with meaning negotiation, like recasts and clarification requests, provide opportunities for learners to internalize linguistic items (see Mackey and Philp 1998). Accordingly, the interactionist approach is concerned primarily with the "nature of interaction" (Doughty and Long 2003: 51). That is, interactionists do not directly examine what is happening inside of the brain, but rather what occurs during, and cognitively as a result of, interaction.

While the interactionist approach to SLA represents one of many perspectives, the "nature of interaction" is at the heart of all CALL-CMC research. That is, the essence of CALL-CMC research is to examine the nature of online interactions with the aim of showing whether and how technology-driven applications support language learning. Several methodological approaches have been used to investigate CMC, and a plethora of theories have influenced this endeavor (see Section 3.2.1).

The present discussion is concerned with *how* the nature of interaction has been examined in the literature, and *what* online platforms have been investigated in doing so. In this regard, CALL-CMC research can be divided into four domains of study.

The most common way of investigating the nature of interaction is to code and quantify linguistic features and communicative exchanges in text-based CMC. A prototypical example is Bower and Kawaguchi (2011). In their study, corrective feedback moves that occur during a communicative task were counted (e.g. repetition, confirmation, comprehension checks, clarification requests). Statistical measures were then used to discuss the pedagogical efficacy of text-based CMC. This approach represents the bulk of CALL-CMC research (see Table 3.1).

The second domain of study entails examining language learning qualitatively, though comparatively few studies of this type have been conducted. Here the nature of interaction is examined as a complex phenomenon. Attention is given to how interactants achieve intersubjectivity and construct an understanding of their communicative setting. Research of this type treats every interactional exchange as unique, and inextricably tied to interactants' immediate communicative needs and purposes. For example, Ware and Kramsch (2005) examine how opportunities for cross-cultural and language learning are realized through an extended text-based dialogue between students from different geographical regions. The researchers do not code and quantify linguistic features, but rather uncover how learning is embedded in an unfolding dialogue. Most qualitative CALL-CMC research examines text-based CMC platforms.

The third domain of study examines whether speaking proficiency can be promoted by engaging in text-based CMC. In this type of study, the implicit assumption is that second language competency can be transferred from one mode of online communication to another (see Payne and Ross 2005). For example, the effects of text-based CMC on the development of oral proficiency have been investigated in numerous studies (see Payne and Whitney 2002; Abrams 2003; Payne and Ross 2005; Blake 2009). Quantitative methods are typically used in this approach, though several researchers have also anecdotally claimed that oral proficiency can be developed in text media because texting shares many interactional similarities with speaking (e.g. Chun 1994; see, however, Chapter 6).

The fourth domain of study entails the examination of CMSI. Most CMSI studies investigate the nature of interaction deductively and statistically (seeTable 3.1). That is, language learning is examined by quantifying linguistic features and interactional exchanges. In Heins *et al.* (2007), for example, comprehensible input and output are coded and quantified in order to explore whether a video-enabled CMSI platform is conducive to language learning. Wang (2006) runs a number of statistical measures on interactional modifications in order to discuss the pedagogical value of a video-enabled CMSI tool. Similarly, Yanguas (2010) counts the number of interactional breakdowns that occur in audio and video conferencing platforms (as well as face-to-face interaction), and discusses his findings in relation to a psycholinguistic understanding of language learning.

Several themes emerge from the discussion of these four domains of study. First, text-based CMC is the platform of choice for many CALL-CMC researchers working within SLA. Second, spoken interaction is an important investigatory issue, as demonstrated in two of the four domains discussed above. Third, quantitative analysis is the preferred methodological paradigm when examining language learning. Fourth, although there has been a paradigm shift in the study of language learning in applied linguistics (i.e. from cognitive to social and interactional approaches; see Block 2003), CALL-CMC is seen overwhelmingly through an interactionist (cognitive) lens.

These themes all demonstrate the need to examine CMSI with greater qualitative rigor. While interactional and sociocultural approaches have been applied to the investigation of language learning in text-based CMC, the same cannot be said for CMSI. Furthermore, although spoken interaction represents an important pedagogical issue for CALL-CMC researchers, comparatively little is known about how spoken interaction is managed in online settings. This is because when online spoken communication is examined, it is often presented numerically and with minimal attention to the sequential context in which meaning is achieved. Greater qualitative rigor can be applied to CMSI by examining online spoken communication as a co-constructed endeavor that is reflexively tied to context. This requires moving away from the idea that linguistic features and interactional exchanges reside inside the minds of language learners. From a social-interaction perspective, the focus should be on how language is used as an interactional resource to address communicative goals.

While the second language chat rooms examined in this book are not formal classrooms that possess teacher–student dynamics, the analyses conducted in previous chapters uncovered several competencies that are important to an understanding of language learning (see Chapters 5–7). Like grammatical competence, the competencies that are involved in communicating in second language chat rooms can be incorporated into teaching materials. Put differently, CMSI can represent both the medium of communication and the content of language instruction. This line of thought is based on the idea that learning a language requires, among other things, developing interactional competencies.

### 8.2.1 INTERACTIONAL COMPETENCE

When discussing what is required of students to acquire an additional language, researchers working with social-interaction approaches have found interactional competence (IC) to be a useful construct. IC is the command of "the discourse parameters of language *in use*" (Kramsch 1986: 369; my emphasis). It is "the knowledge and ability to participate in social interactions through the use of linguistic and other semiotic resources" (Ishida 2009: 351; see also Young 2008). In other words, IC is the ability to communicate in setting-specific ways; it is about using communicative resources to co-construct understanding and accomplish context-specific goals (see also Hall *et al.* 2011). IC in CMSI is thus the capacity to navigate an online platform for the purpose of engaging in online spoken communication, and knowing how to socially and interactionally manage the affordances and constraints of communicating in an electronic medium.

Researchers have shown that IC is one of several important aspects of learning a second language (e.g. Young and Miller 2004). Like grammatical competence, IC consists of different competencies (see Hall *et al.* 2011). These competencies represent both the resources used to engage in social interaction and objects of learning (see Kasper 2006: 87). As objects of learning, interactional competencies can form the basis for pedagogical activities (e.g. teaching students how to engage in a summons-answer exchange during the opening of a telephone call). But before pedagogical activities can be developed, researchers must determine which discursive practices are significant to the target language environment, and identify the interactional resources that are used to carry out social actions and practices in said context.

Several interactional competencies exist in CMSI (for an extended list of competencies related to face-to-face interactions, see Kasper 2006: 86; Barraja-Rohan 2011: 481–2). As IC is chiefly about what is accomplished collaboratively *in situ*, many of the competencies discussed in this chapter are related to the turn-taking practices identified in Chapters 5 and 7.

One of the most salient ICs in CMSI is the ability to know when and how to take, and yield, a turn at talk. Although this ability is in no way unique to CMSI, the turn-taking system in second language chat rooms is notable in that it requires interactants to engage in multiparty talk while speaking in the absence of physical co-presence. The turn-taking system is further constrained by the fact that co-participants engage and disengage in conversations with high regularity.

The turn-taking system in second language chat rooms is robust despite these contextual variables, but projecting when a turn will end requires students to manage speakership at the turn constructional unit level (see Section 5.2.1). This is because turn transitions in CMSI do not occur precisely at the end of turns, but rather near or before turn completion. Thus, the turn-taking system in second language chat rooms can be severely disrupted if students do not possess the receptive skills to understand when a turn is nearing completion. The additional cognitive strain of monitoring speech in the absence of physical co-presence is likely to challenge many language learners, especially in multiparty settings. For instance, speaking in the absence of physical co-presence requires a higher level of prosodic sensitivity than what is typically required of students in face-to-face encounters.

Given these observations, CMSI platforms present different linguistic and interactional demands on language learners than, and thus provides opportunities to develop competencies that cannot be acquired through, text-based CMC (see Chapter 6). When designing pedagogical activities, language teachers and researchers must be cognizant of how online platforms demand different interactional competencies (for an example of how this can be done with CMSI- and text-based tasks, see Section 8.2.1.1 below).

To extend this observation further, the turn-taking practices of text-based CMC cannot be transferred over to CMSI. CMSI is ephemeral, and so learners must minimize gap and overlap when engaging in online spoken communication. For instance, students cannot, without experiencing considerable incomprehensibility, delay second-pair part answers to questions when multiple interactants are conversing (see Herring 1999). With regard to interactional competencies, students must be able to respond to first-pair part utterances in a time that is appropriate to the speed at which the conversation is taking place. Multiparty talk in second language chat rooms can be somewhat difficult to manage, and participation in these online spaces is dependent on students' ability to engage in a rapid turn-taking system. Although the turn-taking system in CMSI is not as expeditious as the one observed in text-based CMC, online spoken communication is more interactionally demanding than dyadic face-to-face interaction given the contextual variables identified in Chapter 7.

Language teachers, course designers, and CMC researchers can benefit from knowing that ICs vary from one online platform to another. Although CMC researchers have argued that text-based CMC promotes competencies in spoken interaction (see Payne and Ross 2005; Blake 2009), the findings presented in Chapter 6 demonstrate that turn-taking practices differ, sometimes significantly, in CMSI and text-based CMC. Therefore, language teachers should not assume that text-based CMC will demand from students, and thus promote, the same type of turn-taking competencies as those required in CMSI.

Consider, for example, the following extract taken from Chapter 5. This exchange provides a vivid example of what ICs are required to take turns in CMSI. In Extract 1, Sal and Han are negotiating times to meet.

```
(1)
1k—Skypecast
00:33—00:46
1    Sal:    you- you mean today or eh:: t-
2            tonight o:r.
3    Han:    i me[an
4    Sal:       [tomorrow?
5    Han:    tonight (.) tonight tonight (0.9)
```

This example shows that the ICs associated with taking turns in CMSI are much different than those required in text-based CMC. Han takes a turn in line 3 before Sal completes his question. Though some overlap occurs in lines 3 and 4, the sequential location of Han's turn initial utterance demonstrates that he is monitoring Sal's question. Specifically, Han takes his turn immediately after a grammatical conjunction that ends with slight fall in intonation. Han treats this as turn transition because he has gleaned enough information in the previous utterance to begin speaking.

This exchange shows that students must possess a heightened awareness and sensitivity to stress, intonation, and voice amplitude. Managing speakership in CMSI is not simply a matter of waiting until a turn is complete before taking the next turn. Rather, in second language chat rooms, students must co-produce talk in a way that reflects an understanding that prosodic and interactional features, like a slight fall in intonation, create different interactional possibilities and impossibilities (e.g. turn transition place).

CMSI also requires knowing how to deal with different communicative affordances and constraints. For instance, pauses can act as both an affordance and a constraint in CMSI. IC in CMSI entails the ability to jointly coordinate the deployment of, and verbal responses that follow, pauses. The following extract taken from Chapter 3 illustrates this point. Several interactants are getting acquainted at the opening of a chat room.

```
(2)
1j—Skypecast
01:56—02:03
1    Val:    i am from poland you know (0.3)
2            do you know::=
```

```
3       Zendt:      =pol↑and↓
4                   (1.7)
5       Val:        pol[and
6       Zendt:         [go on
7                   (0.4)
8       Val:        do you kn[ow where it is
9       Borno:               [are you from poland
10                  (0.7)
```

Because a spate of silence can signal a number of different things, including difficulties in articulating a thought, technical problems, or a floor-yielding move, students must understand that pauses have different social functions. However, IC in CMSI is not about the accumulation of pragmatic knowledge. IC in CMSI is projecting, in the absence of physical co-presence, whether a momentary break in speech signals that talk is forthcoming by the current speaker or that a turn should be taken by someone else. That is, the ability to successfully deal with pauses in CMSI requires the competence of not just one student, but all participants engaged in communication during a spate of silence.

This is a central concept of IC. Interactional competencies are not contained within the minds of individual learners, but are rather co-constructed by students, and inextricably tied to context. This is evident in the interactional resources used to allocate turns in CMSI.

In Extract 3, for example, an unidentified participant is unable to initiate a conversation after he self-selects himself to speak in line 3. Several interactants are in the chat room, and Veronica and Jin are talking about speaking Mandarin. The unidentified interactant has not spoken before the start of this extract.

```
(3)
1a–Skypecast
15:47–16:20
1       Veronica:   (she called me cuz it really nice)
2                   (1.9)
3       ?:          yo what's up
4                   (.)
5       Jin:        yea'-
6                   (0.7)
7       Jin:        .hhh >i used to> know↑- i used to know
8                   (.) more chinese befor:e from my↑
9                   chinese friend but i forgot actually
```

In this exchange, the unidentified interactant speaks at the appropriate sequential time, that is, during a transition relevant place (i.e. during a prolonged pause in line 2), but he does not identify the recipient of his utterance. This makes it difficult for Veronica and Jin to determine whether the unidentified interactant is talking to one of them, another participant, or indeed the entire chat room. In the turns that follow, the unidentified interactant is unable to establish himself as an active contributor to the chat room. While the unidentified interactant would be more likely to elicit a response if he had identified a recipient, the interactional onus is also on Veronica and Jin to establish and maintain talk with the new member (e.g. asking who the unidentified interactant is and/or stopping their conversation to begin a new one). That is to say, talk does not simply happen in CMSI. It requires all interactants involved to utilize different interactional resources with varying degrees of effort.

The interactional work that is required of students is further constrained by the fact that co-interactants regularly enter and leave chat rooms in the absence of physical co-presence. Accordingly, an integral IC in CMSI is identification practices. For instance, students must know that simply talking upon entering a chat room may not be the most effective way of beginning a conversation. However, as established in Extract 3 above, IC in CMSI is jointly accomplished, and thus communication is not only contingent upon the identification practices carried out by one interactant, but also the interactional work performed by other co-members.

This section has demonstrated that context-specific interactional competencies are required of students when speaking online. IC in CMSI requires the ability to co-manage turns at the turn constructional unit level, take turns while speaking in the absence of physical co-presence, engage and disengage in conversations with multiple interactants, recognize and respond to pauses, and know what turn allocation and identification practices to utilize and when to use them.

As mentioned previously, these competencies represent both the interactional resources used to engage in CMSI and objects of learning (Kasper 2006). This section has identified the interactional resources used in CMSI, and discussed how they can be considered objects of learning. Thus, the next section deals with how these objects of learning can inform the decisions that are made when designing teaching materials, namely task-based learning activities.

### 8.2.1.1 CMSI-BASED TASKS

A discussion regarding how an understanding of IC in CMSI informs the design of task-based learning activities must begin with a definition of task. A task can be defined as a plan or blueprint (Ellis 2003). A plan is made up of decisions that are based on intended learning outcomes (Skehan 2003; Nunan 2004). That is, tasks are designed with an idea of what students are meant to do communicatively during, and achieve pedagogically and linguistically as a result of, task completion (Ellis 2000). Although students occasionally deviate from intended learning outcomes (Seedhouse 2005), research has demonstrated that a plan or blueprint can somewhat reliably determine how tasks are completed (e.g. Long 1983; Ellis 2000; Jenks 2009c; Gass et al. 2005; Robinson 2005).

The utility in designing and selecting tasks according to an understanding of IC in CMSI is based on the belief that teachers need to make "rational choices among the numerous technological options available for foreign language teaching" (Doughty and Long 2003: 50). Rational choices are underpinned by an understanding of several pedagogical issues and factors. Language teachers must know the communicative and linguistic needs of their students, how technology mediates communication, the degree to which students are familiar with the technology of choice, and the pedagogical affordances and constraints of CMC platforms. In the CALL-CMC literature, a great deal of task-based learning research is aimed at helping language teachers make rational pedagogical choices (e.g. Aston 1986; Lynch 1997; Robinson 2001; Foster 2009).

Much of this work is focused on identifying optimal conditions for language learning (for psycholinguistic conditions, see Bower and Kawaguchi 2011; for cognitive conditions, see Blake 2009; for sociocultural conditions, see Darhower 2000). Studies that help language teachers make rational choices share several pedagogical principles, including, but not limited to, the idea that learning is best accomplished by doing and that language input should be authentic and rich (see Doughty and Long 2003; Smith 2003).

Tasks should therefore reflect activities, situations, and communicative exchanges that students would likely experience outside of classrooms. For example, it is not uncommon for tasks to require students to ask for and give directions, order food, book a plane ticket, and provide directives. In CMC settings, tasks should also provide opportunities to use such language. In addition, tasks conducted online must be designed with technology in mind, as technological affordances and constraints will ultimately shape what students do when engaging in communicative activities.

An understanding of IC in CMSI can help language teachers and researchers address this latter issue. That is, the interactional competencies identified in the previous section can be used to design tasks that reflect the ways in which technological affordances and constraints influence online communication. Although the interactants of this study were not engaged in pedagogical tasks, their interactions shed light on what is and what is not interactionally possible in CMSI. In other words, whether students are casually conversing online or completing CMSI-based tasks, their interactions are shaped by the same online spoken competencies (e.g. managing turns at the turn constructional unit level). Therefore, interactional competencies can be used to make rational choices among the different technological choices that are available for task-based learning. The two technological choices discussed in this section are CMSI and text-based CMC.

When discussing the interactional competencies that are associated with CMSI- and text-based tasks, it is useful to draw on the turn-taking comparisons made in Chapter 6.

One of the most striking differences in CMSI and text-based CMC is the interactional competencies that are required to take turns in these two modes of online communication. Specifically, text-based CMC does not provide students with opportunities to manage turns at the turn constructional unit level, and should therefore not be used with tasks that aim to promote competencies in spoken communication. Although some research has shown that text-based tasks promote speaking skills (see, however, Chun 1994; Payne and Whitney 2002; Abrams 2003; Payne and Ross 2005; Blake 2009), this book has demonstrated that the interactional competencies that are required to manage spoken turns are fundamentally different than texting. This finding has implications for task designers.

For example, managing turns at the turn constructional unit level leads to a turn-taking system where students can, if they wish, provide opinions, interrupt, interject, and engage in other interactional practices that facilitate a dynamic exchange of opinions. Furthermore, when debating and providing opinions, it is important for students to be able to freely manage how turns are taken, which will then provide the necessary conditions for the development of oral fluency (Yanguas 2010). Therefore, teachers should not assume that debate and opinion-gap tasks administered in text-based CMC will allow students to manage, and thus develop, the skills necessary to freely manage how turns are taken.

However, if a teacher requires greater control over how students manage speaker-ship during, for example, debate and opinion-gap tasks (e.g. to prevent students from speaking before turn completion), then text-based tasks should be used because turn transitions only occur in one sequential location. For instance, a teacher may wish to use text-based tasks if students need additional time to articulate their opinions and/or organize their lines of argument. Students completing an opinion-gap task in text-based CMC may also benefit from the ability to edit (and re-edit) a message before it is sent. Conversely, pauses, hesitations, and self-corrections are audible in tasks conducted in CMSI platforms. These false starts and restarts can have a negative impact on how turn transitions are managed. Pauses can, for example, lead to overlapping utterances in CMSI.

The discussion of debate and opinion-gap tasks demonstrates that students must possess different interactional competencies when completing the same task in CMSI and text-based CMC. Other examples exist.

For instance, turn adjacency is another IC that has pedagogical and interactional consequences for task designers. Turn adjacency is particular important in tasks that require students to engage in long and/or complex utterances or messages. For example, persistent and substantial disjointedness in turn adjacency can occur when discussing human and ethical topics in text-based tasks. Because human and ethical topics require long and/or complex contributions (or at least comparatively more than objective/spatial topics), and given the fact that turn transitions always occur after turn completion in text-based CMC, the speed in which a student articulates a thought will partly affect whether, and the degree to which, a turn is delayed. This is especially true in multiparty text-based CMC (see Herring 1999).

In CMSI-based tasks, however, contributions to a discussion are less likely to be delayed because (1) turn disjointedness causes considerable incomprehensibility when speaking, and (2) the spoken medium allows students to manage turn adjacency as utterances unfold in real time. In other words, talk in CMSI is ephemeral—students are naturally inclined to minimize delay between turns in order to enhance comprehensibility. The turn-taking system in CMSI facilitates comprehension because the next turn is often related to the previous turn.

Despite the robustness of the turn-taking system in CMSI, minimizing delay between spoken turns requires a strong command of the target language. For this reason, low-proficiency students (beginners to low intermediates) may be better off using CMSI platforms for one-way information gap tasks or other communicative activities that limit how contributions are made and what can be said (see Ellis 2000).

Turn constructional units are also important to how tasks are completed in both modes of online communication. In CMSI-based tasks, students can listen to turn constructional units unfold in real time. Managing turns at the turn constructional unit level allows students to minimize gap and overlap. However, the turn-taking system in CMSI is likely to breakdown if students lack the proficiency to fluently project turn completion. In other words, talk in CMSI will be stilted if turn transitions only occur after turn completion. This is why platforms that support online spoken communication should only be used for two-way information gap tasks if all students involved possess the ability to make use of the turn-taking system of CMSI (e.g. possess the ability to monitor turn constructional units and take turns during transition relevant places).

In text-based tasks, students cannot see turn constructional units unfold in real time. Although text-based tasks do not afford students the ability to manage speakership at the turn constructional unit level (i.e. a message is only visible when a student presses the carriage return/enter key), messages can be constructed and reconstructed numerous times without other participants knowing that there may be a linguistic and/or interactional problem. This aspect of text-based CMC places less interactional pressure on students to contribute with little hesitation and self-correction. Therefore, the text medium may be more suitable for lower-proficiency students completing two-way information (and opinion) gap tasks.

Floor space and conversational floors are also managed differently in both types of online communication. In CMSI-based tasks, students can engage in overlapping talk and propose new topics, but the floor space does not afford them the ability to engage in two or more simultaneous conversations. Two explanations exist with regard to why this is the case. First, conversational schisms do not typically happen in CMSI because online spoken communication is ephemeral. The pedagogical implication of speaking online is that students use short-term memory to recall previous conversational exchanges. Consequently, students will often treat long stretches of simultaneous talk as problematic. The absence of nonverbal language further restricts the floor space in CMSI, as students cannot adjust body positions and/or gaze to manage talk that breaks into two or more conversations (see Egbert 1997). Second, in CMSI-based tasks, a student that takes a turn will often control the floor until the contribution is complete or near completion; thus, students are less likely to engage in multiple conversational floors.

A rigid floor space means that tasks will be completed with one conversational floor (i.e. one current speaker). With this in mind, CMSI may not be the best platform for teacher-fronted tasks and other multiparty interactions that require a communicative setting that supports multiple, sometimes overlapping and simultaneous, contributions. In CMSI, students working collaboratively in groups of three or more may find it difficult to identify each other and manage speakership in the absence of physical co-presence (see Sections 6.2.2 and 6.2.3).

In text-based tasks, students can type concurrently, but messages are transmitted one at a time. The permanency of text communication allows students to propose new topics and manage simultaneous conversations. Because students can scroll back to re-read messages, it is not uncommon to have two or more current speakers (i.e.

multiple conversational floors). Consequently, the floor space in text-based tasks is flexible. The pedagogical consequence is that text-based CMC platforms can be used for tasks that require sustained collaboration from large groups or an entire class-room (e.g. brainstorming and problem-solving tasks). It is indeed entirely possible for two or more groups to conduct different tasks in the same text-based chat room.

This section has applied an understanding of IC in CMSI to task design. The dis-cussion demonstrated that an understanding of interactional competencies allows teachers to make rational choices when designing and implementing tasks. This section has also established that CMSI- and text-based tasks possess different tech-nological affordances and constraints, and that these differences lead to dissimilar interactional and learning outcomes.

This section contributes to the scholarly work that has been conducted on the rela-tionship between task design and completion. For many decades, task-based research has helped language teachers optimize learning opportunities by identifying which task dimensions and variables provide the best conditions to acquire a language. This section has provided a small contribution to this body of work by identifying the interactional competencies that are used in CMSI and comparing them with text-based CMC. Much more work of this kind is needed, as few studies to date have attempted to provide a social-interaction perspective of language learning to CMSI- and text-based tasks.

Furthermore, in order to fully understand the interactional consequences of online communication technology, researchers must continue to utilize qualitative, dis-course analytic methods for the examination of CMC platforms. Studies that examine the micro details of texting and talking can equip teachers, as this section has dem-onstrated, with the necessary knowledge to make informed, pedagogical decisions.

Although this section has provided insights into how an understanding of IC in CMSI informs the design of task-based learning activities, the discussion has been limited to the "approach" level of Richards and Rodgers' (2001) task implementation model. This model suggests that there are three levels of task implementation: (1) approach, (2) design, and (3) procedure. The first level is concerned with understand-ing the optimal conditions for language learning (see Krashen 1985; Swain 1993; Long 1996). This level informs the decisions that are made when designing tasks. For example, the discussion in this section revealed that CMSI requires, and thus promotes, interactional competencies that cannot be acquired in text-based CMC. This discussion was then used to suggest that there are interactional and pedagogical implications for selecting a particular mode of online communication.

The first level informs the last two levels of task implementation: design and pro-cedure. That is, the last two levels of the task implementation model are concerned with implementing and evaluating tasks that were designed according to the infor-mation gleaned from the first level. Design and procedure were beyond the scope of the current discussion. Future research should, however, empirically test whether different interactional competencies are developed in CMSI- and text-based tasks. In other words, future research should examine the teaching practices involved in, the pedagogical challenges associated with, and the learning outcomes that result from, using CMSI- and text-based tasks.

## 8.3 DISCUSSION AND CONCLUSION

This chapter has applied the findings established in previous analytic chapters to two areas of investigation in the CALL-CMC literature: SLA and task-based learning. The discussion of SLA and task-based learning demonstrated that a purely qualitative, interaction-based account of CMSI has important pedagogical consequences. Namely, an investigation of CMSI is able to uncover the interactional competencies that are needed to converse in online spoken communication settings, and assist language teachers in making informed decisions with regard to task design.

Although SLA and task-based learning are important areas of investigation in the CALL-CMC literature, few studies to date have explored how the interactional features of online spoken communication can be used to inform teaching and learning practices. The review of the CALL-CMC literature in Chapter 3 revealed that spoken interaction is rarely treated as a complex phenomenon that requires a considerable amount of attention at the transcription and analytic levels of research. When spoken interaction is investigated, more often than not superficial observations are provided and/or deductive, reductionist approaches are adopted (e.g. coding and quantifying interactional features). That is to say, the features that make spoken interaction unique—for example, stress, intonation, pauses, and turn constructional units and transitions—are rarely transcribed and analyzed in CMSI studies (see Jepson 2005).

With this observation in mind, this chapter contributes to the CALL-CMC literature by providing an empirical basis for which future studies can explore the pedagogical implications of CMSI. This book has demonstrated that the turn-taking systems of text-based CMC and CMSI are different. This finding was then discussed in relation to pedagogical decisions and learning activities.

Despite the small advances made in this chapter, much more work in CMSI is needed. For example, in order to fully understand the pedagogical benefits of online spoken communication, researchers must examine how tandem learning is carried out in CMSI platforms. This type of research will shed light on how intercultural competence is developed in CMSI settings, and allow researchers to explore whether CMSI platforms provide different cultural learning opportunities than other modes of online communication. Other areas of pedagogy that can benefit from a social-interaction investigation of CMSI include distance education, informal learning, and language assessment and evaluation.

# 9

# SOCIAL AND CULTURAL ISSUES

## 9.1 INTRODUCTION

The Internet has enabled rapid communication across great geographical spaces and time zones, and this is especially true of platforms that support CMSI. Online communication technology has provided a number of different benefits to education, business, and the global society at large, including the ability to deliver distance education courses, carry out business meetings with geographically displaced colleagues, and stay in constant contact with family and friends while traveling abroad.

Many social and cultural issues have been investigated as a result of the mediating effects of technology on human conduct. Studies have investigated trust development (e.g. Bos *et al.* 2002), gender (e.g. Fox *et al.*), trolling behavior (Hardaker 2010), getting acquainted exchanges (e.g. Jenks 2009b), multilingualism (e.g. Kelly-Holmes 2006), social presence (e.g. Ko 2012), and ethnicity (e.g. Parker and Song 2006), to name a few.

Of the many issues and themes investigated in the literature, communities and identities are perhaps the two topics that have received the most attention (e.g. Sierpe 2005; Herring and Paolillo 2006; Rellstab 2007; Baek and Damarin 2008; Herring 2008). These two overlapping issues rank prominently in the literature because technological affordances and constraints have considerable influence over how meaning is co-constructed and human relations managed. Some of the facets of technology that have been shown to shape the co-construction and maintenance of identities and communities include anonymity (Hardaker 2010), mode of online communication (Fox *et al.* 2007), and the type of online communication technology used (Kim *et al.* 2007)

As topics of investigation, communities and identities belong to the sociality and culture empirical strand (see Chapter 3). As such, studies that investigate online communities and identities go beyond describing the interactional and linguistic features of CMC (cf. studies that fall within in the language and discourse empirical strand; see Chapters 5–7). For example, gender has been investigated by analyzing language use (Fox *et al.* 2007), the use of nicknames (Herring and Martinson 2004), genre (Herring and Paolillo 2006), turn allocation practices (Panyametheekul and Herring 2003), and conversational sequences (Rellstab 2007). For these types of study, the language and discourse of online communication is used as a way of understanding social phenomena rather than representing a topic of investigation in and of itself.

The main analytic aim in these studies is to examine how social and cultural issues are managed in, and through, CMC. This chapter carries on with this tradition by examining how English as a lingua franca (ELF) is used in second language chat rooms.

The issue of English, as it is used online and with people who do not share a common first language, is of great importance to both the sociality and culture and teaching and learning empirical strands. For the sociality and culture strand, the study of ELF in second language chat rooms contributes to the body of work that deals with how identities and communities are shaped and managed in online settings. For the teaching and learning empirical strand, the study of ELF in second language chat rooms provides an understanding of how interactional and linguistic norms and conventions are established, sheds light on whether speakers of English as an additional language see themselves as language learners or users, and informs how interactants from different parts of the world co-construct interculturality. These three pedagogical issues have generated much attention in the English language teaching literature (for a discussion of interactional and linguistic norms and conventions in ELF encounters, see House 2002; Jenks 2009b; for a study of language learner identities, see Virkkula and Nikula 2010; Jenks 2013a; 2013b; for an investigation of intercultural communication, see Brandt and Jenks 2011; Kaur 2011).

## 9.2 ENGLISH AS A LINGUA FRANCA

The Internet and other tools for online communication have had a profound impact on contemporary human society. In addition to facilitating the management of personal and professional relations, online communication has promoted the spread of some languages (e.g. English), though to the detriment of others (Kelly-Holmes 2006). English has become one of the dominant online languages for several reasons (see Graddol 2006), including perhaps most notably the need for geographically dispersed people who do not share a common first language to communicate (e.g. Durham 2003; Cassell and Tversky 2005). Therefore, it can be said that advances in, and increased dependency on, online communication technology is a key driving force in language choice and shift.

Globalization and hypermodernity has made it necessary for real time communication across many regions and nation states, and this, as alluded to above, has led to more ELF contexts and settings than ever before. For instance, it is not uncommon for a Japanese retailer to conduct a business call in English with a Brazilian manufacturer. Transnational business negotiations like these are conducted online and in lingua franca situations every day. It is equally common for language learners from different linguistic backgrounds to practice and learn English online with each other, as the interactants have done for this study.

Although English is one of several languages used as a lingua franca in online settings, it is certainly one of the most widely practiced. Current estimates indicate that speakers of English represent approximately a quarter of all Internet users (Internet World Stats 2011). This figure has a profound impact on the content that is created and consumed, as well as the types of speakers that make up online interactions. Consequently, speakers who are not proficient in English have limited choice with regard to what they can consume electronically and whom they can interact with. Accordingly, the study of ELF in online settings has important social and pedagogical implications, and represents an area of future growth for the sociality and culture and teaching and learning empirical strands (see Chapter 3).

While online communication technologies blur geographical boundaries and time zones, and provide opportunities for language learners to use English in situations that may not exist in their home countries, ELF encounters pose several social, interactional, linguistic, and cultural challenges, including determining what is right or wrong in terms of language norms and conventions. ELF encounters also create situations where the identities associated with being a part of a lingua franca community are negotiated alongside the local identities that speakers possess as English language learners/users. In the same vein, ELF interactions in online settings are transnational, and thus provide opportunities for speakers to discuss their cultural similarities and differences. The two sections that follow discuss how these issues manifest in, and as a result of, CMSI. That is, this chapter investigates the norms and convention that are established, and the identities that are co-constructed, in online ELF encounters.

## 9.2.1 NORMS AND CONVENTIONS

Communication in a chat room requires at least two interactants. As such, a chat room can be considered a group, a place where interaction takes place with people that share common interests, and/or possess similar sociocultural profiles. In this book, the interactants are online because they wish to engage in casual conversations with unacquainted people from diverse geographical locations. Furthermore, nearly all of the interactants speak English as an additional language and do not live in countries where English is widely spoken.

As with any group, communication in CMSI is a joint endeavor, one that requires a shared understanding of what is normatively right or wrong with regard to talk and interaction. CMSI participants may need to negotiate levels of formality, styles of speech, turn-taking rules, and communication etiquette, to name a few. This shared knowledge may require explicit negotiation on the fly, on a turn-by-turn basis, as interactants engage in communication. In other situations, little or no interactional work is involved in determining how online communication should be managed because interactants already possess and share this knowledge.

This shared knowledge represents the communicative norms and conventions of a chat room. The management of chat room norms and conventions is important to CMC studies for several reasons. Investigating how speakers co-construct norms and conventions provides insights into how technology is adopted and used for communicative purposes, reveals how interactants determine what is socially acceptable in terms of CMSI, establishes an understanding of how groups and communities are formed in online settings, and produces a basis for which researchers and practitioners can predict online communication behavior. More importantly, norms and conventions underpin all of the social and cultural order (and disorder) that occurs in human society.

Social norms or moral rules play an essential role in our existence within society. Following these rules helps ensure one's survival, happiness, and well-being as a societal member. Rules exist not only for the benefit of an individual, but extend to offer a collective benefit. This ensures that order exists within the culture so that individuals of different backgrounds and different facets of thinking can function together by knowing and following societal rules. (Pankoke-Babatz and Jeffrey 2002: 220)

These so-called rules are the building blocks of communities and social groups, including those formed by ELF speakers. Identifying the norms and conventions of groups allows researchers to better understand, and distinguish between, speech communities. In the ELF literature, for example, a great deal has been written on the types of social, interactional, and linguistic norms that exist when speakers of English as an additional language communicate in lingua franca settings. Research has shown that ELF speakers are normatively less concerned about grammatical construction and are readily cooperative and mutually supportive; research has also demonstrated that ELF speakers regularly drop third person present tense and omit definite articles (Seidlhofer 2004). The most notable finding with regard to ELF norms is Jenkins's (2002) observation of a phonological core for lingua franca settings, which includes "the aspiration of word initial voiceless stops, the presence of all sounds in word-initial clusters, maintenance of the contrast between long and short vowels; and placement of contrastive nuclear stress" (Elder and Davies 2006: 285).

According to these studies, norms and conventions show that there is a shared understanding among ELF speakers that talk and interaction ought to be produced and conducted in a certain way. Researchers have used these observations to state that there are ELF speech communities (see, however, House 2002, who questions the importance of group identity and culture in ELF interactions). Some scholars have even argued that the English spoken in lingua franca settings should be recognized as a linguistic variety in its own right (for an assessment of this belief, see Prodromou 2007), and thus speech communities from English-speaking countries should not determine, and/or be used as a model of, what is socially and linguistically right or wrong for ELF speakers.

Observations of ELF norms and conventions are not limited to the studies cited above. Many ELF studies are interested in discussing and comparing the linguistic and interactional norms and conventions of the English spoken in lingua franca settings with so-called native speaking norms (e.g. Seidlhofer 2011). These issues are indeed central to the future of ELF studies, as the number of speakers of English as an additional language is likely to increase for many years to come. Therefore, researchers must expand the current empirical database to include different communicative settings and participatory configurations. Because most studies to date have examine ELF in face-to-face settings among acquainted interactants, this section provides a unique look at lingua franca interaction by uncovering how unacquainted interactants in a chat room negotiate norms and conventions on the fly.

This is accomplished by examining how interactional and pragmatic norms and conventions are co-constructed at the micro-level. The aim here is not to devise a list of so-called ELF norms and conventions, but rather to show how technology is negotiated on a turn-by-turn basis, as interactants simultaneously interact and make sense of their communicative setting and determine what constitutes appropriate chat room participation. Therefore, this section is not so much about ELF features specifically, but rather how group norms are established in an online lingua franca setting. The analysis demonstrates that what is right or wrong is highly dependent on who is participating in a chat room, and that norms and conventions are created organically. This section is also concerned with showing how CMSI creates different interactional challenges than text-based CMC, and how these challenges manifest in, and through, online spoken communication.

The observations made in this section are based on three extracts taken from one chat room. The interaction in all of the extracts examined in this chapter can be characterized as lingua franca, as the CMSI participants do not share a common mother tongue nor do any of them speak English as their first language. The first of these three extracts begins shortly after the chat room opens for participation. In this extract, James proposes a "rule" for managing participation (i.e. performing some form of self-identification when attempting to participate in the chat room), as just prior to this extract some interactants expressed difficulty in determining the identity of various speakers.

```
(1)
1g—Skypecast
05:02—07:13
1     James:    June? (.) hello June?
2     June:     yes (0.4) yes↑ i'm↓ June↑
3               (0.2)
4     James:    hello yeah (.) hello my name's James so
5               okay? yeah
6     June:     yes
7     James:    i- think- that- you- are- host of this
8               group so i think that (0.6) you have
9               to c[ontrol
10    June:         [yeah
11    James:    some process you know (.) there are a
12              lot of (rules) and big echoes so we
13              should (.) i think that we- we can (.)
14              i- in my opinion we want to make some
15              kinda rule (0.5) if someone says
16              he↓llo:↑ (.) after that (.) we want to
17              have to say the↓ eye-dee name for
18              example me:: (.) hello my name's
19    June:     yes=
20    James:    =James after then we have to say (it)
21              you know (.) a lot of people say we- we
22              can't understand who is- who is
```

```
23              speaking an: so how can we:: answer the
24              some questions (.) so: and you are both
25              so↓ we are guests okay=
26    June:     =yeah
27    James:    (i said) uh:
28    Sky:      hello
29    James:    (it was) good- g- room or in skypecast
30              you will make a good- condition or
31              allow me so i hope so
32    June:     ye::s
33              (0.6)
34    James:    yeah
35    June:     yes
36              (0.7)
37    Sky:      <he:↓llo↑<
38    June:     and then sorry (0.5) because the- eh::
39              five minutes ago (0.8) there's some
40              problem in my computer so:: (.) i just
41              wonder (0.6) at the time it's okay
42              so::::
43    Sky:      yes
44    June:     we make(ness) of that. of our:: room.
45              how bout we talking about (0.8) uh:
46              <what is your problem< (0.5) >what is
47              your problem> (0.8) i think you have
48              a problem in your place in your work
49              (.) or when you studying, or anything
50              (0.9) yeah then i just think a kinda
51              gap (1.0) yeah (0.7) if you have a
52              problem just (2.5) just say it (.)
53              may::be↓ there is some people can solve
54              that problem (1.2) eh- uh actually:
55    James:    so y-
56    June:     actually::
57    James:    okay yeah yeah
58              (.)
59    June:     yes hehehe
60              (0.9)
61    James:    okay so
62    Sky:      [(you-)
63    James:    [yeah so yeah eh-em hello my names
64              James and June said that w- if we have
65              a big problem so (0.4) you can or some
66              other person solve the our problem
67              okay? (0.5) yeah (.) so=
```

```
68    Sky:         =you[r name's James?]
69    James:           [in my case ] yeah (0.9) >yup>
```

The extract begins with James making relevant the fact that June is the host (lines 7–9), and as such, must exercise some control over how interactants manage their participation in the chat room (lines 11–18). Moments later in the interaction, James expands his explanation and justification of the rule (lines 20–5 and 29–31).

During the proposal and explanation of the rule, James's co-interactants do not express disagreement, while June, the host, provides confirmation in several instances (lines 19, 27, 33). Somewhat interestingly, however, June does not adopt the rule when he later proposes a new topic of discussion in lines 44–54, though James subsequently does in lines 64–8.

In this first extract, an interactant attempts to address a challenge that many people face when communicating in CMSI-based chat rooms (i.e. matching screen names with voice). James takes control of the situation somewhat unilaterally, or at least shifts the responsibility to the host (lines 7–9), by proposing and implementing a strategy that he believes will provide better conditions for communication (lines 29–31). However, it is unclear whether James's co-interactants accept this proposal, as they neither agree with the rule nor adopt the strategy in their turns.

Given the difficulties these interactants were experiencing prior to Extract 1, self-identification seems to be a sensible rule. In text-based chat, for instance, screen names are automatically placed before messages—this built-in feature of text-based chat allows interactants to bypass the interactional work involved in identifying the "current speaker." However, in CMSI, screen names are not graphically displayed next to spoken utterances, nor are they illuminating whilst an interactant speaks.

The point to be taken in this discussion is that James's rule is not unusual in terms of what occurs in other CMC settings. It is commonly understood that interactants adjust their communication according to the affordances and constraints of technology (e.g. in text-based CMC, interactants identify message recipients by name in order to avoid confusion during turn transitions; see Herring 1999). Therefore, James's suggestion is just one example of an adjustment that can be made in order to maximize comprehension in the absence of physical co-presence. Such adjustments are a result of a shared understanding of a communicative context, and over time, lead to norms and conventions. This is true of the many normative practices that take place in CMC settings (e.g. text shorthand, engaging in overlapping talk in text-based chat, and using emoticons). Such norms do not simply happen, but begin as a process of negotiation. What is particularly noteworthy about Extract 1 is that it shows how the negotiation of a norm is initiated at a micro, turn-by-turn level.

In the next extract, James continues to employ the strategy of self-identification. The time lapse between Extracts 1 and 2 is approximately three minutes. During this time, James self-identifies in several turns. This strategy is never mentioned during this time period, and June and Sky—as well as other chat room participants—do not engage in any form of self-identification. Extract 2 begins with Sky talking about having a mental illness, an issue that is related to June's aforementioned topic of discussion (see Extract 1, lines 44–54).

```
(2)
1g—Skypecast
10:09—10:49
1       Sky:       you know how it feels to have a mental
2                  problem (0.8) it sucks man (0.4) i tell
3                  you it sucks (.) yeah (.) mmhm
4                  (0.3)
5       James:     yeah so=
6       Sky:       =yeah?
7       James:     i think that (.) hello my name is James
8                  so
9                  (0.9)
10      James:     hello?
11      Sky:       i know [your
12      James:            [yeah=
13      Sky        =names James we know (0.2) [you
14      James:                                [okay
15      Sky:       said i[t
16      James:           [yeah ye[ah
17      Sky:               [like (.) i do[n't
18      James:                             [yeah
19      Sky:       know how many times (.) maybe fifteen
20                 times (0.4) your names James (0.7) we
21                 memor(hh)ized yo(hh)ur n(hh)ame already
22                 hahahaha (.) haha you don't have to say
23                 it any[mo(hh)re
24      James:           [yeah=
25      Sky:       =hahaha [aha
26      James:              [yeah yeah okay (0.8) okay so i
27                 th[ink
28      Sky:         [haha
29                 ha[haha
30      James:       [that i hope that (goes to) (1.0) i
31                 want something that meanings uh: an::
32                 uh: (.) my friend live in U↑K
33                 (.) now in this room and uh: (0.4) she
34                 stayed in UK
```

In lines 1–3, Sky expresses his dissatisfaction with having a mental illness. As with Sky's previous verbal contributions to this chat room, he does not provide any form of self-identification before or after his turn. Although James is the only interactant that has thus far put the self-identification rule into practice, it is not clear whether his co-interactants disagree with this practice. Again, up until the beginning of Extract 2, Sky and June have not explicitly expressed disagreement or resistance to James's proposal.

In lines 7 and 8, James continues with the practice of self-identification in his response to Sky's admission. In line 9, a nearly one-second pause follows the self-identification. Although it is impossible to know whether James expects a response or acknowledgment token during this spate of silence, James treats the pause as noticeably absent. That is, rather than continue with his turn, James uses a "hello" greeting token to determine whether Sky is on the other end of the line (see Chapter 7).

Beginning in line 11, Sky responds to the greeting token by stating that he, and the chat room ("we know"), know James's name (line 13). Sky then exaggerates the number of times James completed a self-identification turn ("maybe fifteen times"), states that he and his fellow co-interactants have memorized James's name (lines 20 and 21), and informs James that he does not have to engage in this practice anymore (lines 22 and 23).

In so doing, Sky treats the self-identification rule as both redundant and problematic. The laughter tokens delivered throughout Sky's extended turn also serve to ridicule James's attempts to provide greater comprehension in the chat room. Although Sky is the only interactant to explicitly treat the practice of self-identification as problematic, his response to James establishes a competing (or different) interpretation of how turns should be designed in the chat room.

Extract 2 provides an example of how an attempt to make a communicative adjustment is later ridiculed by a fellow interactant. Unlike Extract 1, where no explicit agreement (or disagreement) was established with regard to the practice of self-identification, Sky in Extract 2 expresses his disapproval of James's proposed rule. The shared understanding that is established thus far in the interaction is that both interactants have different interpretations of the practice of self-identification.

For nearly nine minutes of interaction (where Extract 3 begins), James talks on several occasions, but does so without engaging in the practice of self-identification. During this time period, it could be said that James—at least momentarily—abandons his proposed rule. Extract 3 begins with James addressing Sky.

```
(3)
1g–Skypecast
18:51–19:23
1     Sky:     i don't eat pigs I've never seen pig in
2              real life i don't eat meat
3     June:    oh
4     James:   yeah yeah pig so (1.0) hel↑lo↓ Sky?
5              (0.6) hello↑
6     Sky:     hello? (0.6) hello=
7     James:   =yeah yeah (.) hello you know my names
8              James yeah
9              so i wonder you know:
10    Sky:     [[hehehe ((inaudible)) ]]
11    James:   [[there's a lotta ]] yeah [yeah
12    Sky:                               [hehehe
13    James:   you (think about) over fifteen minute
```

```
14              okay? (.) you know my name is so yeah
15              (0.4) i won[der
16    Sky:              [yeah
17    James:     you know in:: in this room there are a
18              lot of koreans so but i dont know where
19              you come from from
```

In line 4, James addresses Sky with a greeting token. This greeting token allows James to establish mutual orientation with Sky. Rather than assume that self-identification is necessary—as was the case with previous exchanges—James continues with his turn by stating that Sky already knows his name ("you know my names James"). This is particularly noteworthy, as James's turn explicitly builds on the shared understanding that both interactants established in Extract 2 (i.e. that Sky has memorized James's name). Somewhat interestingly, however, James's turn still reveals his name. For the remaining duration of this chat room, James does not—nor do any of his co-interactants—engage in the practice of self-identification.

Extracts 1–3 show how interactants build on each other's pragmatic understanding of chat rooms in order to make sense of what is normatively right and wrong with regard to CMSI. More importantly, the examples demonstrate that communicative norms and conventions do not simply exist, but require complex, collaborative interactional work. In these three extracts, James could not establish a shared understanding that self-identification is an appropriate way of participating in this chat room. In the end, James's proposed rule became the subject of laughter and ridicule.

The relevance of these observations to the ELF literature is two-fold. First, the observations in this section demonstrate that norms and conventions are co-constructed on a turn-by-turn basis. Again, they do not simply happen, but require interactants to negotiate an understanding of what are socially, linguistically, and interactionally acceptable forms of CMSI. Because norms and conventions are co-constructed, and can change (or be challenged) at any given point in interaction, linguistics and interactional features of ELF are neither stable nor static, but rather in a constant state of flux.

Take, for example, the observation that ELF interactants are normatively mutually supportive (see Seidlhofer 2001: 143). Many of the observations made regarding this norm come from business and academic settings. However, CMC researchers have observed that ELF interactants can be highly confrontational and reprehensive (Jenks 2012a), and indeed some scholars have reported that attention to form occurs in some business and academic contexts (see Firth 1996). Therefore, what can be said of the three extracts presented in this section is that the practice of self-identification is inappropriate, but this observation does not necessarily apply to all CMSI (and/or ELF) settings. Given the highly dynamic and fluid nature of lingua franca interaction, ELF researchers should spend more time examining how norms and conventions are established on turn-by-turn basis.

Second, this section shows that speakers in lingua franca settings are highly adaptive when talking with no visual access to body gestures and gaze. In many CMSI-based platforms, interactants must manage speakership by matching voices with screen names. This constraint is unique to CMSI, as interactants in other modes of online communication can easily see who is speaking/typing. Although Sky ridiculed the self-identification rule, James's proposal demonstrated a heightened pragmatic awareness of, and sensitivity to, technology and communication. The initiation, negotiation, and subsequent termination of the self-identification rule demonstrate that although technology mediates communication (see, for example, Chapter 7), interactants have a great deal of control over how talk and interaction is managed in online settings. For instance, the self-identification rule could be deemed useful by interactants in a different chat room. In other words, the shared understanding that James and Sky establish is limited to their chat room. This is, by and large, true of the norms and conventions established in most ELF encounters (Jenks 2012a).

### 9.2.2 LANGUAGE IDENTITIES

The formation and management of identities is a principal area of research in applied linguistics and CMC. This is because online communication technology has made it easier for people to communicate with speakers of languages that do not, in large numbers, reside in the same country (e.g. students of foreign languages engaging in language exchanges), and take part in communities that share similar interests (e.g. language teachers discussing best practices in an online forum). Such technologies blur national and social boundaries, leading to the formation of new group identities and transnational spaces (see Durham 2003). However, access to people from different parts of the world can also solidify national differences and stereotypical assumptions (Brandt and Jenks 2011).

Accordingly, online spoken communication provides opportunities for interactants to manage a number of different, interdependent, but sometimes competing, identities. For instance, the CMSI participants of this study possess English language identities that are relevant to their home country or nation state—the interactants may consider themselves learners of English as a foreign language (EFL), while other participants may call themselves expert users or bilingual speakers. Local identities vary within and across nation states, and reflect real, lived experiences—they are partly constructed by national norms, conventions, and policy, as well as societal perceptions of what constitutes a speaker of English (e.g. what they look like, how they speak, and whom they interact with).

Although CMSI participants possess identities that are relevant to their home country or nation state, the transnational nature of lingua franca interactions allows interactants to construct new online identities. For example, CMSI participants can construct global identities that reflect their participation in an online community of lingua franca speakers. Interactants may orient to their social status as ELF speakers when discussing and making relevant their English language identities (see Baker 2009a; 2009b; Virkkula and Nikula 2010), though this is an empirical question that deserves further scrutiny (see Jenks 2013b). The aim of this section is to examine what and how identities are made relevant during online ELF encounters.

It is important to examine what and how identities are made relevant when CMSI participants discuss their social status as English language speakers because the term ELF functions as a powerful descriptive tool and political device. ELF is a powerful descriptive tool in that researchers use this term to make characterizations of, and distinguish between, entire communities of English language speakers (Jenks 2013b). ELF is also used as a political device in that the term is used to dissuade researchers and language practitioners from adopting linguistic theories and models that are ethnocentric (see Jenkins 2006). While significant empirical and pedagogical contributions have been made as a result of lingua franca researchers, it is vital to continually assess whether and how ELF is used as a social category to construct English language identities.

The identity work that takes place in second language chat rooms often begins with an assessment based on a "hearing" of a previous turn (e.g. complimenting a participant's pronunciation). This is particularly interesting with regard to technological affordances and constraints, as it demonstrates that CMSI creates opportunities for interactants to use prosodic cues to manage English language identities. These "hearings," or language proficiency compliments, are embedded in much of the talk that is related to, and used for the co-construction of, English language identities.

For example, in Extract 4, China initiates the identity work in her chat room by providing a language proficiency compliment to Anne. In this extract, China is a new participant and Anne has been talking for some time. Moments before this extract, Anne compliments China on his attitude and patience, as seconds before a different interactant was disruptive.

```
(4)
1m—Skypecast
06:20—06:52
1                       (0.3)
2       China:    and your pronunciation and you[r accent
3       Anne:                                    [mmhm
4       China:    is very excellent
5                       (0.7)
6       China:    hh.heh
7       Anne:     oh!
8                       (0.2)
9       Anne:     hehehe $thank you very much$
10                      (0.5)
11      Anne:     hhhh=
12      China:    =you're wel[come
13      Anne:                [i try to speak very slowly
14                (.) slowly because this is English
15                practice room (.) so:::
16      China:    ye:s
17      Anne:     everyone should talk slowly hhh and
18      China:    o::ka[y
```

```
19    Anne:              [you'know we have to- (.) yeah we
20                       have to wait other people's eh::
21                       comment. end (0.5) okay (0.4) so
22                       Chin[a
23    China:                 [okay
24                       (0.6)
```

The exchange between China and Anne shows that language proficiency compliments create opportunities to co-construct English language identities. The identity work that takes place in this extract begins with China's compliment in lines 2 and 4; here he identifies two "assessable" features of Anne's language proficiency: pronunciation and accent. In so doing, China treats Anne's language proficiency as an issue that is open for evaluation (Pomerantz 1978). With regard to English language identities, this is particularly noteworthy because "open" or public linguistic evaluations occur in a limited number of contexts (e.g. language classrooms), and are generally given to a particular group of interactants (e.g. students). Students' language proficiencies are open to evaluation because they are actively engaging in language learning, and their status or identity as learners is part of the discourse of doing classroom language teaching (see Wong 2009).

However, examining China's compliment in isolation only reveals that his turn establishes an interactional frame where the discussion of identities is possible. In order to explore how identity manifests in the discourse of language proficiency compliments, Anne's response must be examined. Anne thanks China, thus providing the second-pair part of the compliment (line 9). In lines 13–15, Anne then provides the reason why her accent and pronunciation is worth praise (i.e. speaking slowly), and claims that she is speaking slowly because she believes the chat room should be used for practice.

By making relevant the action of practicing English, Anne treats the collective proficiency of the chat room as somewhat deficient. That is, practicing a language implies that mastery has not been achieved. Although Anne could respond to the compliment by stating that her pronunciation and accent are excellent because she is a competent (lingua franca) user of English, she responds to China by making relevant their social status as language learners.

Extract 4 has shown that language proficiency compliments are category-bound actions, as openly praising an interactant's linguistic competence may lead to the negotiation of English language identities. This extract has also demonstrated that CMSI affords interactants the ability to hear each other talk, which is crucial when engaging in any type of identification work. Furthermore, second language chat rooms are transnational in nature, and thus afford interactants the ability to create new identities related to their membership and participation in a group of lingua franca speakers. Despite this affordance, China and Anne do not make relevant their identity as competent lingua franca speakers of English, nor do they see themselves as members of an ELF community.

This is also the case in Extract 5, where Young and Sayed both explicitly orient to their identity as non-native speakers of English.

```
(5)
1d—Skypecast
19:50—20:45
1                       (1.2)
2       Young:          aren't you↓ supposed↑ to be at↓ school?
3                       (0.6) no?
4                       (1.4)
5       Sayed:          yeah i- i- yeah you're right but this
6                       semester i::
7                       (.) i didn't attend eh:: university
8                       (0.5) i go↓ back↑ the next semester.
9                       (0.8)
10      Young:          ah::: okay↓ (1.1) okay i↑ see↓=
11      Sayed:          =yeah (0.4) so. i'm. spending. my.
12                      time. on. skypecast.
13                      (0.4)
14      Young:          mmhm=
15      Sayed:          =improving my english
16                      (0.3)
17      Young:          >your english really good though> (.)
18                      <°i think.°<
19                      (1.8)
20      Sayed:          no- no s- s- som- somehow when i talk
21                      to (0.6) native speakers (0.2) i:::
22                      have↓ to, repeat↑ my sentences my- many
23                      times (0.5) they can't da- they- uh-
24                      they do not understand many of my words
25                      (0.8) my- i- i- i mean my pronunciation
26                      is not that good.
27                      (1.4)
28      Young:          but i can- o:h i can understand you
29                      maybe i'm not a native speaker maybe
30                      (0.2) i don't know.hhh (0.2) but uh-
31                      (.) your: english [is pretty good↓ i↑
32                      think↓
33      Sayed:                           [yes be- yeah because
34                      we have two foreigners
```

In lines 2 and 3, Young questions whether Sayed should be in school. In lines 5–8, Sayed states that he is not in school but will attend the following semester. Later in lines 11, 12, and 15, Sayed provides the reason why he is not in school (i.e. to improve his English). Sayed's reason for missing school makes relevant the issue of language proficiency, and initiates the identity work in this exchange. As with Extract 4, talk of language proficiency is embedded in the interactional work involved in negotiating English language identities.

For example, Young responds to the justification for missing school by positively evaluating Sayed's linguistic competence ("your English is really good though"). This response implies that practicing is for speakers that fall below the "good" marker. Young's language proficiency compliment is slightly hedged (cf. the slighter softer and slower delivery of "i think"), which may indicate that she is not fully confident in providing such an assessment. This is particularly noteworthy, as it demonstrates that openly evaluating a co-interactant's ability to speak is a delicate matter, especially in non-pedagogical settings.

Although Sayed could accept the language proficiency compliment, which is the preferred next action (Pomerantz 1978), he rejects Young's assessment. Sayed's rejection is based on his experience of not being able to effectively communicate with native speakers of English. His turn serves to treat his identity as different from native speakers of English ("they do not understand many of my words"). The identity work continues in Young's response to the rejection—here she provides a second language proficiency compliment. Specifically, Young states that although she is not a native speaker of English, she understands Sayed and believes his English is "pretty good." Sayed then explains that Young can understand him because they are both "foreigners" (line 31). While the social status of being a foreigner may be relevant to both interactants' local (national) context, it does not accurately reflect their identities as lingua franca speakers in this chat room.

Extract 5 shows how the native speaker construct is used to negotiate English language identities. For Sayed and Young, language proficiency is inextricably linked to their understanding of what it means to be an English speaker. Yet despite being a proficient speaker of English, Sayed does not use his linguistic competence to construct a more positive image of his identity, nor does he make relevant the fact that he and Young are highly capable lingua franca speakers.

The final extract in this section reveals how local professional norms are used to construct English language identities. The extract begins with Winnie complimenting Roci's voice.

```
(6)
1h—Skypecast
13:42—14:05
1     Winnie:     no you got a rea↑lly↓ be:autiful voice.
2                 you should be a dee↑[jay↓ sometime.
3     Roci:                          [yeah↓
4                 (1.0)
5     Roci:       u:h no↓ you know uh- i may- i- i- even
6                 tried to work at a call center here.
7                 (.) in the philippines but↑ you know↓
8                 (0.4) they think that my english is not
9                 yet too good so↓ i↑ was↓ not↑ hired↓
10    Winnie:     no it's pretty good t[o me.
11    Roci:                            [yeah
12                (1.0)
```

```
13    Roci:        alright thank you for that you↑ know↓
14                 because i have been practicing it here.
15                 i::n skype↓
```

In lines 1 and 2, Winnie states that Roci has "a really beautiful voice." Although this is not a language proficiency compliment (having a good voice or being a disc jockey is not limited to speakers of English), Roci uses the assessment as an opportunity to talk about his English language identity (lines 5–9). Specifically, Roci discusses how his language proficiency was used against him when looking for a job at a call center in his home country. In line 10, Winnie provides a language proficiency compliment by stating that Roci's English is "pretty good." In so doing, Roci's linguistic proficiency becomes procedurally consequential to the identity work in this exchange. Roci then accepts the compliment, and states that his English is commendable because he has been practicing it (lines 13 and 14). Roci uses his language proficiency to construct his identity as an English speaker. The identity that Roci constructs represents his experience in the physical world, where the issue of linguistic proficiency was used against him when seeking a job.

This section has uncovered how CMSI participants use the affordances of online spoken communication to engage in identity work. Much of the identity work that takes place in CMSI is related to how an interactant sounds. This demonstrates that prosodic cues are integral to CMSI participants' understanding of what it means to be an English speaker. The analysis demonstrated that sounding "good" is jointly constructed, and sometimes contested (cf. Extract 5). Language proficiency compliments were used to engage in much of the talk that is related to, and used for the co-construction of, English language identities.

Furthermore, all three extracts demonstrated that English language identities are important to talk in lingua franca encounters. Although the chat rooms examined here are prototypically lingua franca, CMSI participants often see themselves as language learners and/or non-native speakers when negotiating their English language identities. This creates a descriptive challenge for researchers working with lingua franca interactions. Namely, what are the best terms to describe speakers in lingua franca settings? While it is beyond the scope of this section to provide detailed suggestions and solutions (for a discussion of the ethical issues involved in using EFL and ELF, see Jenks 2013b), suffice it to say that the observations made in this section demonstrate that the term ELF may not be relevant for some participants of lingua franca interactions. Therefore, care should be taken when considering the utility and validity of using one term in lieu of another (e.g. using ELF instead of EFL because the former term provides a less ethnocentric interpretation of language proficiency).

## 9.3 DISCUSSION AND CONCLUSION

In the last two decades, there has been an attempt to move CMC research beyond the descriptive level. That is, in recent years, scholars have applied the findings from the language and discourse empirical strand to investigations of social conduct. This shift in research has been driven by societal changes in online media consumption and growing dependency on communication technologies. Although there is still much to be investigated with regard to the language and discourse of CMSI (see Chapter 3), this chapter has also moved beyond the descriptive level by applying an understanding of online spoken communication to two issues that are crucial to ELF studies in particular, and CMC studies in general: norms and conventions and language identities.

The section on group norms and conventions showed that what is deemed normatively right or wrong with regard to CMSI is based on a shared understanding of communication. The shared understanding that interactants possess is a result of complex, collaborative interactional work. In other words, norms and conventions do not simply happen, but require interactants to negotiate an understanding of what are socially, linguistically, and interactionally acceptable forms of CMSI. These findings highlight the highly fluid nature of norms and conventions in online lingua franca encounters.

The negotiation of norms and conventions also demonstrated that CMSI participants are aware of the mediating effects of technology on communication. However, while technology mediates communication and shapes what and how norms and convention are negotiated, the observations in this chapter have demonstrated that interactants have a great deal of control over how talk and interaction is managed in online settings.

The section on language identities showed how CMSI participants use the affordances of online spoken communication to engage in identity work. Specifically, the findings revealed that language proficiency compliments were used to engage in much of the identity work related to being an English speaker. Although chat rooms blur national and social boundaries, and thus provide opportunities for interactants to make relevant their membership of an online community of lingua franca speakers, CMSI participants often see themselves as language learners and/or non-native speakers.

Consequently, communicative settings are not the best indication of what identities are relevant to interactants. Participating in a lingua franca chat room does not mean that ELF is procedurally consequential to CMSI, nor does it determine how interactants construct their English language identities. For many of the interactants in this study, English language identities are shaped by local (national) perceptions of linguistic proficiency.

The findings made in this chapter contribute to the applied linguistics and CMC literature on identities and communities, though there are several areas of study that require further investigation. For example, this chapter has not examined how social and cultural issues are organized across different online communication platforms (e.g. Paltalk). This line of inquiry would provide much-needed insights into how online communication platforms shape the co-construction of norms and conventions. For example, are identities and communities constructed the same way in Skype and Paltalk? Future research should also investigate how trolling and bullying are managed in CMSI. Is trolling less likely to happen because CMSI participants are afforded less anonymity than interactants in text-based CMC? These questions demonstrate that there is still much to be investigated in CMSI. Knowledge of CMSI is not only important to the advancement of applied linguistics and CMC, but it also contributes—as this chapter has done with regard to ELF studies—to an understanding of social and cultural issues.

# DISCUSSION AND CONCLUSION

## 10.1 INTRODUCTION

This book has examined CMSI in second language chat rooms. By adopting a social-interaction perspective, this book has provided a unique look at how second language chat rooms are organized interactionally and socially. A social-interaction perspective of CMC is concerned fundamentally with how online interactions are organized and how this organization shapes social actions and practices. The utility in examining second language chat rooms from this perspective is that it treats online communication as both a site of investigation and an interactional space where human conduct is organized. A social-interaction perspective is equipped with powerful analytic tools that describe in great detail how human relations and conduct are managed in, and through, talk and interaction (see Richards and Seedhouse 2008; Antaki 2011).

Social-interaction perspectives have contributed much to the literature on CMC, though the methodologies that are associated with such perspectives have not been used in any comprehensive way to investigate the interactions that take place in second language chat rooms. Few studies have examined CMSI from a social-interaction perspective—and even fewer book-length publications have adopted a purely qualitative, transcript-based approach to the examination of CMSI. A notable exception is Hutchby's (2001) conversation analytic study of technology, though much of his analysis is based on telephone interactions.

A review of the CMC literature in Chapter 3 reveals that CMSI has been discussed in some detail in journal publications (see Ackerman *et al.* 1997; Aoki *et al.* 2003), though there is a tendency to superficially describe social interaction. Many CMC studies do not investigate CMSI as a highly complex and sequential phenomenon. CMSI research of this type is not based on detailed transcripts of spoken communication (see Hindus and Schmandt 1992; Dourish *et al.* 1996; France *et al.* 2001; Woodruff and Aoki 2004; Geerts 2006; Huang *et al.* 2009). While voice-only communication has been investigated from a social-interaction perspective, computers are not the analytic focus. For instance, conversation analytic studies have examined traditional telephones (Schegloff 1979; Mondada 2008), mobile phones (Arminen 2005; Hutchby 2005), and push-to-talk radios (Szymanski *et al.* 2006). When CMC studies examine online spoken communication from a social-interaction perspective, the technologies that are investigated are often experimental and unavailable for public use (see Aoki *et al.* 2003).

With these research gaps in mind, this book makes a significant contribution to the CMC literature in several ways. First, this book is one of only a few that has examined online spoken communication—and more specifically, CMSI-based second language chat rooms—from a social-interaction perspective. Second, the analyses were based on Skype, an online platform that is used by millions of people around the world (Skype Limited 2012). Therefore, the findings are of relevance to a wide range of academic disciplines and have practical implications for many users of communication technology, including language learners and teachers. Third, the sequential and interactional features that make CMSI unique were transcribed, presented, and analyzed in detail. At the time of writing, this is the only CMSI book that has done so. Fourth, the analyses uncovered the organization of multiparty voice-based chat, compared them with text-based chat, and discussed these findings in relation to several key areas of CMC research. That is to say, this book has not only provided a unique look at CMSI, but it has also situated and applied an understanding of online spoken communication in, and to, key themes and issues in the CMC literature.

The discussion and findings made in this book have been organized into three sections: survey, analysis, and application. In the survey section (Chapters 2–4), the state of CMC research was presented. Chapter 2 established what is included in a social-interaction study of second language chat rooms and discussed the importance of computer networks when conducting online spoken communication. In Chapter 3, three strands of CMC research were identified: teaching and learning, language and discourse, and sociality and culture. Chapter 4 identified what CMSI is, and how it was transcribed in this book. This chapter also introduced the data that were used to make the observations in subsequent analytic chapters.

The last two sections of the book (analysis and application) contributed to the three strands of CMC research in different ways. The analysis section (Chapters 5–7) contributed to the language and discourse strand by uncovering the interactional and sequential features of CMSI (Chapter 5), comparing these findings with text-based CMC (Chapter 6), and identifying five contextual variables that shape online spoken communication (Chapter 7). The application section (Chapters 8–10) contributed to the teaching and learning, and sociality and culture, strands by applying an understanding of online spoken communication to second language acquisition and task-based learning (Chapter 8), lingua franca communities and identities (Chapter 9), and research ethics and future directions (the present chapter).

Many noteworthy findings have been made in this book. For example, Chapter 5 revealed how the management of turn construction and transition in online spoken communication is dependent on the production and coordination of vocal cues, including micro changes in intonation. While turn construction and transition have been investigated in text-based CMC, very few, if any, studies have examined these interactional features in CMSI settings. Furthermore, the findings revealed how CMSI participants use pauses to deal with overlapping utterances, but also showed that prolonged spells of silence can lead to simultaneous talk. This finding demonstrates that pauses in CMSI act as both an affordance and a constraint.

Chapter 6 provided a unique look at CMSI and text-based CMC by juxtaposing the turn-taking practices in these two modes of online communication. Specifically, this comparative analysis chapter established that turn transitions occur in one sequential location in text-based CMC and in multiple locations in CMSI. Furthermore, turns are often adjacently placed in CMSI, but are typically disjointed in text-based CMC. In CMSI, turn constructional units unfold, and are monitored, in real time. In text-based CMC, messages are displayed after the carriage return/enter key is pressed. With regard to overlapping utterances, text-based CMC participants do not normatively orient to the one-speaker-at-a-time rule, as the floor space can handle multiple conversational floors. When overlap occurs in CMSI, at least one interactant will typically yield the conversational floor. Although similar comparisons have been made in the literature (see Huang *et al.* 2009), Chapter 6 uses detailed transcripts to uncover the differences in turn-taking practices between CMSI and text-based CMC. In other words, previous comparative studies of text and talk are not based on detailed transcripts of CMSI (e.g. Geerts 2006).

Chapter 7 revealed how background noises are interactionally consequential to the management of CMSI. Background noises stop ongoing conversations, compel interactants to check whether someone is on the other end of the line, and force interactants to re-establish mutual orientation. Other notable findings include the complex, collaborative work that takes place when CMSI participants determine who is in the chat room (e.g. using greeting tokens to establish who is talking), the ways in which pauses shape the management of CMSI (e.g. re-establishing mutual orientation after a prolonged pause), the interactional work that is accomplished to enter an ongoing conversation (e.g. knowing whom to address and when to speak), and how CMSI participants deal with the issue of audibility when speaking (e.g. using sound checks to determine whether a recipient can hear an utterance).

Chapter 8 provided an empirical basis from which future studies can explore the pedagogical implications of CMSI. This chapter established that a purely qualitative, interaction-based account of CMSI has important pedagogical consequences. For instance, the analysis uncovered the interactional competencies that are needed to converse in CMSI settings. In addition, the analytic observations demonstrated that the interactional resources that are used in CMSI are markedly different than those that are required to communicate in text-based CMC, and that these differences have consequences for task design.

Chapter 9 established that CMSI norms and conventions are established organically, and are therefore in a constant state of negotiation. CMSI participants do not necessarily follow pre-established communicative rules, but rather co-construct an understanding of what are socially, linguistically, and interactionally acceptable forms of online spoken communication. The analysis also revealed how CMSI participants use the affordances of online spoken communication to engage in identity work. Specifically, this chapter revealed that language proficiency compliments are used to engage in the identity work related to being an English speaker. Although second language chat rooms blur national and social boundaries, and thus provide opportunities for interactants to make relevant their membership of an online community of lingua franca speakers, CMSI participants often see themselves as language learners and/or non-native speakers.

The importance of these findings to the applied linguistics and CMC literature is clear. This book has expanded current understanding of online communication in general, and CMSI in particular. This book has uncovered the interactional features of CMSI and identified the contextual variables that shape online spoken communication. While this book has contributed much to the CMC literature, researchers must continue to examine CMSI settings (see Section 10.3 below). CMSI is important to the future of CMC research, not least because online spoken communication is installed on millions of computers and mobile devices, and many questions remain unanswered with regard to how these platforms are being used.

Furthermore, CMSI continues to grow in popularity because the platforms that enable this type of communication require less bandwidth than video-enabled CMC, create less social distance than text-based CMC, allow interactants to multitask without appearing inattentive, and now possess graphical communication tools that perform embodied actions (e.g. raising a hand to manage speakership), to name a few. However, efforts to investigate CMSI in these hyperconnected times require heightened awareness of, and sensitivity to, the ethics of collecting, transcribing, analyzing, and presenting online spoken communication data.

## 10.2 RESEARCH ETHICS

This section provides an overview of research ethics as it pertains to the collection, transcription, analysis, and presentation of online spoken communication data. The aim of this section is to raise awareness of the ethical issues involved in conducting CMSI research. However, this section does not attempt to establish a set of universal rules that all researchers must follow, as online communication varies too greatly and poses different investigatory challenges for researchers. Although some of the investigatory issues raised in this section are not new, nor do they apply exclusively to CMSI data, it is worth mentioning them here because the ethics of online communication research is not discussed enough in the CMC literature.

One challenge that researchers face is that technology advances at a much faster rate than the creation and modernization of legal structures and ethical guidelines as they pertain to the Internet as a site and tool for conducting research. Information needed to make informed decisions regarding the collection, analysis, and presentation of online data may not reflect current communicative settings and contexts. The potential disparity between ethical guidelines and empirical foci means researchers must be reflective of the ethical issues involved in conducting CMC research. It is important for researchers to possess an ethical philosophy because many methodological issues that are unique to engaging in CMC research have not been discussed extensively in publications. For example, it is helpful for CMC researchers to have a research stance on what is considered public information on the Internet, as many ethical guidelines do not address this issue.

Ethical issues that are not easily addressed and have often not been discussed extensively in research publications include the issue of whether researchers should use pseudonyms when collecting data, the difficulty in determining whether a communicative context is public or private, the challenge in identifying who is "involved" in a study, and the question of whether it is necessary to obtain informed consent from "lurkers." Although the ethics of conducting research in physical spaces is well documented, caution must be taken when applying ethical guidelines that pertain to face-to-face encounters. As mentioned above, online settings possess many unique ethical challenges when conducting research.

For example, the lack of physical co-presence between researcher and research participants presents several ethical challenges. Research participants should be informed that they are taking part in a study, but this may be difficult to do while maintaining the natural order of a setting. Researchers must also determine how and when informed consent will be requested. Informing research participants that a study is being conducted and requesting their consent to take part in the study is especially difficult to do because researchers generally have little control over who is involved in a research setting. For instance, interactants frequently enter and leave chat rooms. Should a researcher obtain informed consent from every participant or simply those that communicate more than others? If so, how does a researcher determine who participates enough to warrant informed consent?

Furthermore, in second language chat rooms, a researcher must weigh the benefits of verbally notifying participants that they are being recorded with requesting written consent. For the data collected in this book, a software program notified interactants via text and speech that they were being recorded and requested informed consent. These messages were sent out upon entering each chat room. Although these notifications created momentary disruptions, the research participants were able to quickly move on to the talk at hand.

Privacy is also a complicated issue when conducting CMSI research. All researchers have a general responsibility to protect the privacy of research participants. Disseminating sensitive information can potentially harm and/or embarrass research participants, so care should be taken when transcribing CMSI. Using pseudonyms for personal and place names is one way of ensuring anonymity (see Jenks 2011). To complicate matters further, CMSI platforms and websites have different privacy regulations, and the collection and dissemination of data from online sources may differ from country to country. Variation in, or a lack of, privacy regulations makes it difficult to distinguish between what data should be deemed public or private.

The issue of what is considered a public space can pose challenges when seeking informed consent from research participants. In many online settings, interactants are at least implicitly aware that what is said in a public forum will be heard or read by many undisclosed people. However, these interactants are likely unaware that what they say or write will be used for research purposes. Institutions and professional bodies have different policies with regard to whether and when informed consent is needed for research in public spaces. These sources are a good starting point for determining how to seek informed consent in CMSI settings.

## 10.3  FUTURE DIRECTIONS

This book has provided social-interaction observations of second language chat rooms. This was done by discussing what has been investigated in the applied linguistics and CMC literature, uncovering how second language chat room talk is sequentially organized and jointly produced, and applying an understanding of CMSI to the teaching and learning of languages and lingua franca interactions. Despite these contributions, there are several areas of research that have not been investigated in this book.

The first area that warrants close examination is multitasking. CMSI affords interactants the ability to multitask because their hands are free to send text messages, open, browse, and toggle between windows and applications, and engage in other activities in their physical space. Multitasking spreads out the attention that interactants can give to each activity (see Baron 2008b), and because of limitations in cognitive load (Best 1998), can also negatively affect message comprehension and group participation in CMSI settings. Research suggests that multitasking is a prevalent human behavior in online settings (Papper et al. 2004). It is therefore of paramount importance to understand how multitasking is managed during, and shapes, CMSI. However, multitasking presents researchers with several methodological challenges. Namely, collecting and presenting multitasking data requires screen-capturing technology, the use of camcorders to record physical movements, and unconventional transcription methods and media (see Jenks 2011).

While research aims and questions ultimately determine which data capturing and transcription tools will be used, the point to be taken here is that multitasking is an important but difficult phenomenon to investigate. For example, multitasking in CMSI settings requires careful consideration of how talk is transcribed and presented alongside the management of activities. Researchers must deal with the technical aspects of temporally aligning talk with electronic actions and determine how to sequentially represent the unfolding of multiple activities. Despite these challenges, it is necessary to understand multitasking in order for the field to move forward and reflect what people do with, and alongside, technology.

The second area of research that deserves further consideration is multimodality. Although a great deal of CMC is conducted primarily in one medium (see Herring 2007), CMC is inherently multimodal. Take, for example, CMSI. Most CMSI is managed in multimodal platforms that provide tools for sending and receiving text messages, sharing documents, and engaging in video chat. It is important to depict CMC (including CMSI) as inherently multimodal because it highlights the fact that despite a great deal of research conducted in online settings, many research gaps exist in the literature. For example, emails have spawned a plethora of research spanning many disciplines with different empirical foci. However, little is known about how audio and video are incorporated into, and shape, email communication. In the same vein, few studies have examined how interactants simultaneously manage different modes of communication within a single interface or software application. With regard to online spoken communication, it is important to investigate the multimodality of CMSI because it is likely to influence how talk and interaction is managed. Unfortunately, this is an empirical question that has yet to receive any substantial amount of attention in the literature (see, however, Sauro 2004; Naper 2011). As with multitasking, a multimodal study of CMSI presents researchers with several methodological challenges. These challenges are similar to capturing and transcribing multitasking (e.g. presenting multimodal data alongside talk and interaction).

The third area of research pertains to CMSI features. In this book, the analytic chapters examined several CMSI features and described how they were shaped by context. CMSI features that were not investigated in this book, and have not been investigated extensively using social-interaction approaches, include floor management, topic organization, backchannels, and repair organization. The interactional features that have not been investigated in this book demonstrate that there is still a great deal of descriptive-level work that is needed in order to fully understand CMSI.

The fourth area of research that warrants attention in the literature is asynchronous CMSI. At the time of writing, research has not examined how asynchronous CMSI is sequentially organized. A sequential understanding of asynchronous CMSI could be used to make linguistic and interactional comparisons with text-based discussion boards, design pedagogical activities, and provide the basis for which predications can be made with regard to using technology for specific communicative purposes.

The fifth and final area of research that deserves consideration is the examination and comparison of online platforms and CMC types. Communication tools vary across platforms, and this variation can potentially result in different human conduct. For example, France et al. (2001) examine audio conferencing meetings between business professionals, and show that the spoken medium amplifies inequalities in organizational status. It was observed that lower-status business professionals spoke less than they would in face-to-face meetings, as the absence of non-verbal cues hindered floor-taking opportunities for interactants with fewer organizational responsibilities. This finding is particularly interesting with regard to the mediating effects of technology because it contradicts the well-established notion that meetings conducted in text-based media provide greater distribution of communication and participatory rights than in face-to-face settings (see Kiesler and Sproull 1992).

This discussion highlights that examining and comparing different platforms and modes of online communication is important to the study of CMC because there is still much to be learned with regard to how technology mediates communication. While more work is clearly needed, this book has provided a small contribution to the study of CMC in general, and CMSI in particular.

# REFERENCES

Abrams, Z. I. (2001), "Computer-mediated communication and group journals: expanding the repertoire of participant roles," *System*, 29, 489–503.

Abrams, Z. I. (2003), "The effect of synchronous and asynchronous CMC on oral performance in German," *The Modern Language Journal*, 87 (2), 157–67.

Ackerman, M., D. Hindus, S. Mainwaring, and B. Starr (1997), "Hanging on the 'Wire: A field study of an audio-only media space," *ACM Transactions on Computer–Human Interaction*, 4 (1), 39–66.

Alastuey, M. C. B. (2010), "Synchronous-voice computer-mediated communication: Effects on pronunciation," *CALICO Journal*, 28 (1), 1–20.

Anderson, J. F., F. K. Beard, and J. B. Walther (2010), "Turn-taking and the local management of conversation in a highly simultaneous computer-mediated communication system," *Language@Internet*, 7, article 7, <http://www.languageatinternet.org/articles/2010/2804> (last accessed July 17, 2013).

Androutsopoulos, J. (2006a), "Introduction: Sociolinguistics and computer-mediated communication," *Journal of Sociolinguistics*, 10 (4), 419–38.

Androutsopoulos, J. (2006b), "Multilingualism, diaspora, and the internet: Codes and identities on German-based diaspora websites," *Journal of Sociolinguistics*, 10 (4), 520–47.

Antaki, C. (ed.) (2011), *Applied Conversation Analysis: Intervention and Change in Institutional Talk*, New York: Palgrave Macmillan.

Aoki, P. M., R. E. Grinter, A. Hurst, M. H. Szymanski, J. D. Thornton, and A. Woodruff (2002), "Sotto voce: Exploring the interplay of conversation and mobile audio spaces," *Proceedings of CHI 2002*, Minneapolis: ACM Press, pp. 431–8.

Aoki, P. M., M. Romaine, M. H. Szymanski, J. D. Thornton, D. Wilson, and A. Woodruff (2003), "The Mad Hatter's cocktail party: A social mobile audio space supporting multiple simultaneous conversations," *Proceedings of the ACM SIGCHI Conference on Human Factors in Computing Systems*, Fort Lauderdale: ACM Press, pp. 425–32.

Arminen, I. (2005), "Sequential order and sequence structure: The case of incommensurable studies on mobile phone calls," *Discourse Studies*, 7 (6), 649–62.

Arnold, N., and L. Ducate (eds.) (2006), *Calling on CALL: From Theory and Research to Directions in Foreign Language Teaching*, San Marcos, TX: CALICO.

Aston, G. (1986), "Trouble-shooting in interaction with learners: The more the merrier?" *Applied Linguistics*, 7 (2), 128–43.

Atkinson, J. M., and J. Heritage (1984), "Transcript notation," in J. M. Atkinson and J. Heritage (eds.), *Structures of Social Action: Studies in Conversation Analysis*, Cambridge: Cambridge University Press, pp. ix–xvi.

Baek, M., and S. K. Damarin (2008), "Computer-mediated communication as experienced by Korean women students in US higher education," *Language and Intercultural Communication*, 8 (3), 192–208.

Baker, C., M. Emmison, and A. Firth (eds.) (2005), *Calling for Help: Language and Social Interaction in Telephone Helplines*, Amsterdam: John Benjamins.

Baker, W. (2009a), "Language, culture and identity through English as a lingua franca in Asia: Notes from the field," *The Linguistics Journal*, Sept., 8–35.

Baker, W. (2009b), "The cultures of English as a lingua franca," *TESOL Quarterly*, 43(4), 567–92.

Baron, N. S. (2008a), *Always On: Language in an Online and Mobile World*, New York: Oxford University Press.

Baron, N. S. (2008b), "Adjusting the volume: Technology and multitasking in discourse control," in J. Katz (ed.), *Handbook of Mobile Communication Studies*, Cambridge, MA: MIT Press, pp. 177–93.

Baron, N. S. (2010), "Discourse Structures in Instant Messaging: The Case of Utterance Breaks," *Language@Internet*, 7, article 4, <http://www.languageatinternet.org/articles/2010/2651> (last accessed July 17, 2013).

Barraja-Rohan, A. (2011), "Using conversation analysis in the second language classroom to teach interactional competence," *Language Teaching Research*, 15 (4), 479–507.

Barrs, K. (2012), "Fostering computer-mediated L2 interaction beyond the classroom," *Language Learning and Technology*, 16 (1), 10–25.

Baym, N. K., Y. B. Zhang, and M. C. Lin (2004), "Social interactions across media," *New Media and Society*, 6 (3), 299–318.

Belz, J. A. (2003), "Linguistic perspectives on the development of intercultural competence in telecollaboration," *Language Learning and Technology*, 7 (2), 68–99.

Best, J. B. (1998), *Cognitive Psychology*, Malden, MA: Wiley-Blackwell.

Bjorge, A. K. (2007), "Power distance in English lingua franca email communication," *International Journal of Applied Linguistics*, 17 (1), 60–80.

Blake, C. (2009), "Potential of text-based Internet chats for improving oral fluency in a second language," *The Modern Language Journal*, 93 (2), 227–40

Blake, R. J. (2007), "New trends in using technology in the language curriculum," *Annual Review of Applied Linguistics*, 27, 76–97.

Bloch, J. (2004), "Second language cyber rhetoric: A study of Chinese L2 writers in an online USENET group," *Language Learning and Technology*, 8 (3), 66–82.

Block, D. (2003), *The Social Turn in Second Language Acquisition*, Edinburgh: Edinburgh University Press.

Bos, N., J. Olson, D. Gergle, G. Olson, and Z. Wright (2002), "Effects of four computer-mediated communication channels on trust development," *Proceedings of CHI 2002*, Minneapolis: ACM Press.

Bower, J., and S. Kawaguchi (2011), "Negotiation of meaning and corrective feedback in Japanese/English eTandem," *Language Learning and Technology*, 15 (1), 41–71.

Boyle, R. (2000), "Whatever happened to preference organisation?" *Journal of Pragmatics*, 32, 583–604.

Brandt, A., and C. J. Jenks (2011), "Is it okay to eat a dog in Korea . . . like China? Assumptions of national food-eating practices in intercultural interaction," *Language and Intercultural Communication*, 11 (1), 41–58.

Brouwer, C. E. (2003), "Word searches in NNS–NS interaction: Opportunities for language learning," *The Modern Language Journal*, 87 (4), 534–45

Brumfit, C. J. (1995), "Teacher professionalism and research," in G. Cook and B. Seidlhofer (eds.), *Principle and Practice in Applied Linguistics*, Oxford: Oxford University Press, pp. 27–41.

Buckingham D., and R. Willett (eds.) (2006), *Digital Generations: Children, Young People and New Media*, Mahwah, NJ: Lawrence Erlbaum Associates.

Calefato, P. (2004), "The 'public square' and the net: Polyphony, community, and communication," *Semiotica*, 148 (1/4), 175–85.

Cassell, J., and D. Tversky (2005), "The language of online intercultural community formation," *Journal of Computer Mediated Communication*, 10 (2), article 7.

Chapelle, C. A. (1997), "CALL in the year 2000: Still in search of research paradigms?" *Language Learning and Technology*, 1 (1), 19–43

Chapelle, C. A. (2001), *Computer Applications in Second Language Acquisition: Foundations for Teaching, Testing and Research*, Cambridge: Cambridge University Press.

Chapelle, C. A. (2007), "Technology and second language acquisition," *Annual Review of Applied Linguistics*, 27, 98–114.

Cherny, Lynn (1999), *Conversation and Community: Chat in a Virtual World*, Stanford: Center for the Study of Language and Information.

Cho, T. (2010), "Linguistic features of electronic mail in the workplace: A comparison with memoranda," *Language@Internet*, 7, article 3, <http://www.languageatinternet.org/articles/2010/2728> (last accessed July 17, 2013).

Chou, C. C. (2001), "Formative evaluation of synchronous CMC systems for a learner-centered online course," *Journal of Interactive Learning Research*, 12 (2/3), 169–88.

Chun, D. M. (1994) "Using computer networking to facilitate the acquisition of interactive competence," *System*, 22 (1), 17–31.

Chung, Y. G., B. Graves, M. Wesche, and M. Barfurth (2005), "Computer-mediated communication in Korean-English chat rooms: Tandem learning in an international languages program," *The Canadian Modern Language Review*, 62 (1), 49–86.

Ciekanski, M., and T. Chanier (2008), "Developing online multimodal verbal communication to enhance the writing process in an audio-graphic conferencing environment," *ReCALL*, 20 (2), 162–82.

Coleman, J. (1998), "Evolving intercultural perceptions among university language learners in Europe," in M. Byram and M. Fleming (eds.), *Language Learning in Intercultural Perspective*, Cambridge: Cambridge University Press, pp. 45–76.

Condon, S. L., and C. G. Cech (2001), "Profiling turns in interaction: Discourse structure and function," *Proceedings of the 34th Hawaii International Conference on System Science*, Los Alamitos, CA: IEEE Press.

Crystal, D. (2004), *A Glossary of Netspeak and Textspeak*, Edinburgh: Edinburgh University Press.

Crystal, D. (2006), *Language and the Internet*, 2nd edn, Cambridge: Cambridge University Press.

Crystal, D. (2011), *Internet Linguistics: A Student Guide*, New York: Routledge.

Danet, B., and S. C. Herring (eds.) (2007), *The Multilingual Internet: Language, Culture, and Communication Online*, Oxford: Oxford University Press.

Darhower, M. L. (2000), *Synchronous Computer-Mediated Communication in the Intermediate Foreign Language Class: A Sociocultural Case Study*, unpublished doctoral dissertation, University of Pittsburgh.

Debski, R. (2003), "Analysis of research in CALL (1980–2000) with a reflection on CALL as an academic discipline," *ReCALL*, 15 (2), 177–88.

Deutschmann, M., L. Panichi, and J. Molka-Danielsen (2009), "Designing oral participation in Second Life—a comparative study of two language proficiency courses," *ReCALL*, 21 (2), 206–26.

Doughty, C. J., and M. H. Long (2003), "Optimal psycholinguistic environments for distance foreign language learning," *Language Learning and Technology*, 7 (3), 50–80.

Dourish, P., A. Adler, V. Bellotti, and A. Henderson (1996), "Your place or mine? Learning from long-term use of audio-video communication," *Computer Supported Cooperative Work*, 5 (1), 33–62.

Dresner, E., and S. C. Herring (2010), "Functions of the nonverbal in CMC: Emoticons and illocutionary force," *Communication Theory*, 20, 249–68.

Drew, P. (1997), "'Open' class repair initiators in response to sequential sources of troubles in conversation," *Journal of Pragmatics*, 28, 69–101.

Durham, M. (2003), "Language choice on a Swiss mailing list," *Journal of Computer-Mediated Communication*, 9 (1), article 5.

Edelsky, C. (1981), "Who's got the floor?" *Language in Society*, 10 (3), 383–421.

Egbert, M. M. (1997), "Schisming: The collaborative transformation from a single conversation to multiple conversations," *Research on Language and Social Interaction*, 30 (1), 1–51.

Elder, C., and A. Davies (2006), "Assessing English as a lingua franca," *Annual Review of Applied Linguistics*, 26, 282–301.

Ellis, R. (2000), "Task-based research and language pedagogy," *Language Teaching Research*, 4 (3), 193–220.

Ellis, R. (2003), *Task-Based Language Learning and Teaching*, Oxford: Oxford University Press.

Ellis, R., and G. Barkhuizen (2005), *Analysing Learner Language*, Oxford: Oxford University Press.

Ferrara, K., H. Brunner, and G. Whittemore (1991), "Interactive written discourse as an emergent register," *Written Communication*, 8 (1), 8–34.

Firth, A. (1996), "The discursive accomplishment of normality: On conversation analysis and 'lingua franca' English," *Journal of Pragmatics*, 26, 237–59.

Fischer, G. (1998), *E-mail in Foreign Language Teaching: Towards the Creation of Virtual Classrooms*, Tubingen: Stauffenburg Medien.

Foster, P. (2009), "Task-based language learning research: Expecting too much or too little?" *International Journal of Applied Linguistics*, 19 (3), 247–63.

Fotos, S., and C. M. Browne (2004), *New Perspectives on CALL for Second Language Classrooms*, Mahwah, NJ: Lawrence Erlbaum Associates.

Fox, A. B., D. Bukatko, M. Hallahan, and M. Crawford (2007), "The medium makes a difference: Gender similarities and differences in instant messaging," *Journal of Language Social Psychology*, 26 (4), 389–97.

France, E. F., A. H. Anderson, and M. Gardner (2001), "The impact of status and audio conferencing technology on business meetings," *International Journal of Human–Computer Studies*, 54, 857–76.

Freiermuth, M. R. (2001), "Native speakers or non-native speakers: Who has the floor? Online and face-to-face interaction in culturally mixed small groups," *Computer Assisted Language Learning*, 14 (2), 169–99.

Freiermuth, M. R. (2011), "Debating in an online world: A comparative analysis of speaking, writing, and online chat," *Text and Talk*, 31 (2), 127–51.

Gao, L. (2001), "Digital age, digital English," *English Today*, 17 (3), 17–23.

Garcia, A. C., and J. B. Jacobs (1999), "The eyes of the beholder: Understanding the turn-taking system in quasi-synchronous computer-mediated communication," *Research on Language and Social Interaction*, 32 (4), 337–67.

Garfinkel, H. (1967), *Studies in Ethnomethodology*, Englewood Cliffs, NJ: Prentice-Hall.

Gass, S., A. Mackey, and L. Ross-Feldman (2005), "Task-based interactions in classroom and laboratory settings," *Language Learning*, 55 (4), 575–611.

Gass, S., and L. Selinker (2001), *Second Language Acquisition: An Introductory Course*, Mahwah, NJ: Lawrence Erlbaum Associates.

Geerts, D. (2006), "Comparing voice chat and text chat in a communication tool for interactive television," *Proceedings of the 4th Nordic Conference on Human–Computer Interaction: Changing Roles*, Oslo, Norway: ACM Press, pp. 461–4.

Georgakopoulou, A. (2006), "Postscript: Computer-mediated communication in sociolinguistics," *Journal of Sociolinguistics*, 10 (4), 548–57.

Godwin-Jones, R. (2005), "Skype and podcasting: Disruptive technologies for language learning," *Language Learning and Technology*, 9 (3), 9–12.

Gonzalez-Lloret, M. (2003), "Designing task-based CAAL to promote interaction: En Busca de Esmeraldas," *Language Learning and Technology*, 7 (1), 86–104.

Goodwin, C. (1981), *Conversational Organization: Interaction Between Speakers and Hearers*, New York: Academic Press.

Goodwin, C., and M. H. Goodwin (1990), "Interstitial argument," in A. Grimshaw (ed.), *Conflict Talk*, Cambridge: Cambridge University Press, pp. 85–117.

Graddol, D. (2006), *English Next: Why Global English May Mean the End of "English as a Foreign Language,"* London: British Council.

Gray, R., and G. Stockwell (1998), "Using computer mediated communication for language and culture acquisition," *On-CALL*, 12 (3), 2–9.

Guichon, N. (2010), "Preparatory study for the design of a desktop videoconferencing platform for synchronous language teaching," *Computer Assisted Language Learning*, 23 (2), 169–82.

Gülich, E. (2003), "Conversational techniques used in transferring knowledge between medical experts and non-experts," *Discourse Studies*, 5 (2), 235–63.

Hall, J. K., J. Hellermann, and S. Pekarek Doehler (eds.) (2011), *Interactional Competence and Development*, Clevedon: Multilingual Matters.

Hampel, R. (2003), "Theoretical perspectives and new practices in audio-graphic conferencing for language learning," *ReCALL*, 15 (1), 21–36.

Hampel, R. (2006), "Rethinking task design for the digital age: A framework for language teaching and learning in a synchronous online environment," *ReCALL*, 18 (1), 105–21.

Hampel, R., and M. Hauck (2004), "Towards an effective use of audio conferencing in distance language courses," *Language Learning and Technology*, 8 (1), 66–82.

Hardaker, C. (2010), "Trolling in asynchronous computer-mediated communication: From user discussions to academic definitions," *Journal of Politeness Research*, 6, 215–42.

Hassan, X., D. Hauger, G. Nye, and P. Smith (2005), *The Use and Effectiveness of Synchronous Audiographic Conferencing in Modern Language Teaching and Learning (Online Language Tuition): A Systematic Review of Available Research*, London: EPPI-Centre.

Heins, B., A. Duensing, U. Stickler, and C. Batstone (2007), "Spoken interaction in online and face-to-face language tutorials," *Computer Assisted Language Learning*, 20 (3), 279–95.

Herring, S. C. (1996), "Introduction," in S. C. Herring (ed.), *Computer-Mediated Communication: Linguistic, Social and Cross-Cultural Perspectives*, Amsterdam: John Benjamins.

Herring, S. C. (1999), "Interactional coherence in CMC," *Journal of Computer-Mediated Communication*, 4 (4), <jcmc.indiana.edu/vol4/issue4/herring.html> (last accessed July 17, 2013).

Herring, S. C. (2002), "Computer-mediated communication on the Internet," *Annual Review of Information Science and Technology*, 36, 109–68.

Herring, S. C. (2004), "Computer-mediated discourse analysis: An approach to researching online behavior," in S. A. Barab, R. Kling, and J. H. Gray (eds.), *Designing for Virtual Communities in the Service of Learning*, New York: Cambridge University Press, pp. 338–76.

Herring, S. C. (2007), "A faceted classification scheme for computer-mediated discourse," *Language@Internet*, 4, article 1, <http://www.languageatinternet.org/articles/2007> (last accessed July 17, 2013).

Herring, S. C. (2008), "Questioning the generational divide: Technological exoticism and adult construction of online youth identity," in D. Buckingham (ed.), *Youth, Identity, and Digital Media*, Cambridge, MA: MIT Press, pp. 71–94.

Herring, S. C. (2010), "Computer-mediated conversation: Introduction and overview," *Language@Internet*, 7, article 2, <http://www.languageatinternet.org/articles/2010/2801> (last accessed July 17, 2013).

Herring, S. C. (2011), "Commentary: Contextualizing digital discourse," in C. Thurlow and K. Mroczek (eds.), *Digital Discourse: Language in the New Media*, New York: Oxford University Press.

Herring, S. C., and A. Martinson (2004), "Assessing gender authenticity in computer-mediated language use: Evidence from an identity game," *Journal of Language and Social Psychology*, 23 (4), 424–46.

Herring, S. C., and J. C. Paolillo (2006), "Gender and genre variation in weblogs," *Journal of Sociolinguistics*, 10 (4), 439–59.

Hiltz, S. R., and M. Turoff (1978), *The Network Nation: Human Communication via Computer*, Cambridge, MA: MIT Press.

Hindus, D., M. S. Ackerman, S. Mainwaring, and B. Starr (1996), "Thunderwire: A field study of an audio-only media space," *Proceedings of the ACM Conference on Computer-Supported Cooperative Work*, Boston: ACM Press, pp. 238–57.

Hindus, D., and C. Schmandt (1992), "Ubiquitous audio: Capturing spontaneous collaboration," *Proceedings of the ACM Conference on Computer-Supported Cooperative Work*, New York: ACM Press, pp. 210–17.

Holt, E., and P. Drew (2005), "Figurative pivots: The use of figurative expressions in pivotal topic transitions," *Research on Language and Social Interaction*, 38 (1), 35–61.

House, J. (2002), "Developing pragmatic competence in English as a lingua franca," in K. Knapp and C. Meierkord (eds.), *Lingua Franca Communication*, Frankfurt am Main: Peter Lang, pp. 245–67.

Huang, E. M., G. Harboe, J. Tullio, A. Novak, N. Massey, C. J. Metcalf, and G. Romano (2009), "Of social television comes home: A field study of communication choices and practices in TV-based text and voice chat," *Proceedings of the 27th International Conference on Human Factors in Computing Systems*, Boston: ACM Press, pp. 585–94.

Hubbard, P. (ed.) (2009), *Computer Assisted Language Learning: Critical Concepts in Linguistics*, New York: Routledge.

Hubbard, P., and M. Levy (eds.) (2006), *Teacher Education in CALL*, Philadelphia: John Benjamins.

Hutchby, I. (1999), "Frame attunement and footing in the organisation of talk radio openings," *Journal of Sociolinguistics*, 3 (1), 41–63.

Hutchby, I. (2001), *Conversation and Technology: From the Telephone to the Internet*, Cambridge: Polity Press.

Hutchby, I. (2005), "'Incommensurable' studies of mobile phone conversation: a reply to Ilkka Arminen," *Discourse Studies*, 7 (6), 663–70.

Hutchby, I., and S. Barnett (2005), "Aspects of sequential organization of mobile phone conversation," *Discourse Studies*, 7 (2), 147–71.

Hutchby, I., and V. Tanna (2008), "Aspects of sequential organization in text messaging exchange," *Discourse and Communication*, 2 (2), 143–64.

Hutchby, I., and R. Wooffitt (2008), *Conversation Analysis*, Cambridge: Polity Press.

International Telecommunication Union (2010), *The World in 2010: Facts and Figures*, Geneva: International Telecommunication Union.

Internet World Stats (2011), *Internet World Users by Language*, <http://www.internetworldstats.com/> (last accessed July 17, 2013).

Isaacs, E. A., and J. C. Tang (1994), "What video can and can't do for collaboration: A case study," *Proceedings of the ACM Multimedia*, Anaheim, CA: ACM Press, pp. 199–206.

Ishida, M. (2009), "Development of interactional competence: Changes in the use of ne in L2 Japanese during study abroad," in H. Nguyen and G. Kasper (eds.), *Talk-in-Interaction: Multilingual Perspectives*, Honolulu: University of Hawaii, National Foreign Language Resource Center, pp. 351–85.

Jauregi, K., S. Canto, R. de Graaf, T. Koenraad, and M. Moonen (2011), "Verbal interaction in Second Life: towards a pedagogic framework for task design," *Computer Assisted Language Learning*, 24 (1), 77–101.

Jenkins, J. (2002), "A sociolinguistically based, empirically researched pronunciation syllabus for English as an International Language," *Applied Linguistics*, 23 (1), 83–103.

Jenkins, J. (2006), "Current perspectives on teaching world Englishes and English as a lingua franca," *TESOL Quarterly*, 40 (1), 157–81.

Jenks, C. J. (2009a), "When is it appropriate to talk? Managing overlapping talk in multi-participant voice-based chat rooms," *Computer Assisted Language Learning*, 22 (1), 19–30.

Jenks, C. J. (2009b), "Getting acquainted in Skypecasts: Aspects of social organization in online chat rooms," *International Journal of Applied Linguistics*, 19 (1), 26–46.

Jenks, C. J. (2009c), "Exchanging missing information in tasks: Old and new interpretations," *The Modern Language Journal*, 93 (2), 185–94.

Jenks, C. J. (2011), *Transcribing Talk and Interaction: Issues in the Representation of Communication Data*, Amsterdam: John Benjamins.

Jenks, C. J. (2012a), "Doing being reprehensive: Some interactional features of English as a lingua franca," *Applied Linguistics*, 33 (4), 386–405.

Jenks, C. J. (2012b), "Analysis of dialogue," in C. Chapelle (ed.), *The Encyclopedia of Applied Linguistics: Analysis of Discourse and Interaction*, Malden, MA: Wiley-Blackwell.

Jenks, C. J. (2013a), "'Your pronunciation and your accent is very excellent': Orientations of identity during compliment sequences in English as a lingua franca encounters," *Language and Intercultural Communication*, 13 (2), 165–81.

Jenks, C. J. (2013b), "Are you an ELF? The relevance of ELF as a social category in online intercultural communication," *Language and Intercultural Communication*, 13 (1), 95–108.

Jenks, C. J., and A. Brandt (2013), "Managing mutual orientation in the absence of physical co-presence: Multi-party voice-based chat room interaction," *Discourse Processes*, 50 (4), 227–48.

Jenks, C. J., and A. Firth (2013), "On the pragmatic and interactional character of multi-participant synchronous voice-based computer-mediated communication," in S. Herring, D. Stein, and T. Virtanen (eds.), *Handbook of the Pragmatics of Computer-Mediated Communication*, New York: Mouton de Gruyter, pp. 209–34.

Jepson, K. (2005), "Conversations—and negotiated interaction—n text and voice chat rooms," *Language Learning and Technology*, 9 (3), 79–98.

Kabata, K., and Y. Edasawa (2011), "Tandem language learning through a cross-cultural keypal project," *Language Learning and Technology*, 15 (1), 104–21.

Kalman, Y. M., and S. Rafaeli (2007), "Modulating synchronicity in computer mediated communication," paper presented at the International Communication Association, San Francisco.

Kasper, G. (2006), "Beyond repair: Conversation analysis as an approach to SLA," *AILA Review*, 19, 83–99.

Kaur, J. (2011), "Intercultural communication in English as a lingua franca: Some sources of misunderstanding," *Intercultural Pragmatics*, 8-1, 93–116.

Kelly-Holmes, H. (2006), "Multilingualism and commercial language practices on the Internet," *Journal of Sociolinguistics*, 10 (4), 507–19.

Kenning, M. (2010), "Differences that make the difference: A study of functionalities in synchronous CMC," *ReCALL*, 22 (1), 3–19.

Kiesler, S., and L. Sproull (1992), "Group decision making and communication technology," *Organizational Behavior and Human Decision Processes*, 52, 96–123.

Kim, H., G. J. Kim, H. W. Park, and R. E. Rice (2007), "Configurations of relationships in different media: FtF, email, instant messenger, mobile phone, and SMS," *Journal of Computer-Mediated Communication*, 12, 1183–207.

Kinginger, C., A. Gourvés-Hayward, and V. Simpson (1999), "A tele-collaborative course on French/American intercultural communication," *French Review*, 72 (5), 853–66.

Kitade, K. (2000), "L2 learners' discourse and SLA theories in CMC: Collaborative interaction in internet chat," *Computer Assisted Language Learning*, 13 (2), 143–66.

Ko, C. (2012), "A case study of language learners' social presence in synchronous CMC," *ReCALL*, 24 (1), 66–84.

Kramsch, C. (1986), "Language proficiency to interactional competence," *The Modern Language Journal*, 70 (4), 366–72.

Krashen, S. (1985), *The Input Hypothesis: Issues and Implications*, New York: Longman.

Lamy, M. (2004), "Oral conversations online: Redefining oral competence in synchronous environments," *ReCALL*, 16 (2), 520–38.

Lamy, M., and R. Hampel (2007), *Online Communication in Language Learning and Teaching*, New York: Palgrave Macmillan

LaRose, R., J. Gregg, and M. Eastin (1998), "Audiographic telecourses for the Web: An experiment," *Journal of Computer-Mediated Communication*, 4 (2), <jcmc.indiana.edu/vol4/issue2/larose.html> (last accessed July 17, 2013).

Larrue, J., and A. Trognon (1993), "Organization of turn-taking and mechanisms for turn-taking repairs in a chaired meeting," *Journal of Pragmatics*, 19, 177–96.

Lee, C. K. M. (2002), "Literacy practices in computer-mediated communication in Hong Kong," *The Reading Matrix*, 2 (2), 1–25.

Lee, Y. (2008), "Yes-no questions in the third-turn position: Pedagogical discourse processes," *Discourse Processes*, 45, 237–62.

Lerner, G. (1989), "Notes on overlap management in conversation: The case of delayed completion," *Western Journal of Speech Communication*, 53, 167–77.

Lerner, G. (2003), "Selecting next speaker: The context-sensitive operation of a context-free organization," *Language in Society*, 32, 177–201.

Levy, M. (2007), "Culture, culture learning and new technologies: Towards a pedagogical framework," *Language Learning and Technology*, 11 (2), 104–27.

Levy, M., and C. Kennedy (2004), "A task-recycling pedagogy using stimulated reflection and audio-conferencing in foreign language learning," *Language Learning and Technology*, 8 (2), 50–69.

Lewis, C. C., and J. F. George (2008), "Cross-cultural deception in social networking sites and face-to-face communication," *Computers in Human Behavior*, 24, 2945–64.

Li, L. (2000), "Email: A challenge to Standard English?" *English Today*, 16 (4), 23–9.

Liddicoat, A. J. (2011), *An Introduction to Conversation Analysis*, London: Continuum.

Liu, M., Z. Moore, L. Graham, and S. Lee (2002), "A look at the research on computer-based technology use in second language learning: A review of the literature from 1990–2000," *Journal of Research on Technology in Education*, 34 (3), 250–73.

Long, M. H. (1983), "Native speaker/non-native speaker conversation and the negotiation of comprehensible input," *Applied Linguistics*, 4, 126–41.

Long, M. H. (1996), "The role of the linguistic environment in second language acquisition," in W. C. Ritchie and T. K. Bahtia (eds.), *Handbook of Second Language Acquisition*, New York: Academic Press, pp. 413–68.

Lotherington, H., and Y. Xu (2004), "How to chat in English and Chinese: Emerging digital language conventions," *ReCALL*, 16 (2), 308–29.

Luff, P., and C. Heath (2002), "Broadcast talk: Initiating calls through a computer-mediated technology," *Research on Language and Social Interaction*, 35 (3), 337–66.

Lund, A. (2006), "The multiple contexts of online language teaching," *Language Teaching Research*, 10 (2), 181–204.

Lynch, T. (1997), "Nudge, nudge: Teacher interventions in task-based learner talk," *ELT Journal*, 51 (4), 317–25.

Mackey, A., and J. Philp (1998), "Conversation interaction and second language development," *The Modern Language Journal*, 82 (3), 338–56.

Marcoccia, M., H. Atifi, and N. Gauducheau (2008), "Text-centered versus multimodal analysis of instant messaging conversation," *Language@Internet*, 5, article 7, <http://www.languagea-tinternet.org/articles/2008/1621> (last accessed July 17, 2013).

Markman, K. M. (2009), "'So what shall we talk about': Openings and closings in chat-based virtual meetings," *Journal of Business Communication*, 46 (1), 150–70.

Marty, F. (1981), "Reflections on the use of computers in second language acquisition," *System*, 9 (2), 85–98.

McKinlay, A., R. Procter, O. Masting, and R. Woodburn (1993), "A study of turn-taking in a computer-supported group task," *Proceedings of Human–Computer Interaction: People and Computers*, Cambridge: Cambridge University Press, pp. 383–96.

Meager, M., and F. Castanos (1996), "Perceptions of American culture: The impact of an electronically-mediated cultural exchange program on Mexican high school students," in S. C. Herring (ed.), *Computer-Mediated Communication: Linguistic, Social and Cross-Cultural Perspectives*, Amsterdam: John Benjamins, pp. 187–201.

Meeker, M., S. Devitt, and L. Wu (2010), "Internet trends," paper presented at the 7th Annual Conversational Marketing Summit, New York.

Meskill, C., and N. Anthony (2005), "Foreign language learning with CMC: Forms of online instructional discourse in a hybrid Russian class," *System*, 33, 89–105.

Mitchell, R., and F. Myles (2004), *Second Language Learning Theories*, London: Arnold.

Mondada, L. (2008), "Using video for a sequential and multimodal analysis of social interaction: videotaping institutional telephone calls," *Forum: Qualitative Social Research*, 9 (3), article 39.

Montero-Fleta, B., A. Montesinos-Lopez, C. Perez-Sabater, and E. Turney (2009), "Computer mediated communication and informalization of discourse: The influence of culture and subject matter," *Journal of Pragmatics*, 41, 770–9.

Myers, G. (2006), "Where are you from? Identifying place in talk," *Journal of Sociolinguistics*, 10 (3), 320–43.

Naper, I. (2011), "Conversation in a multimodal 3D virtual environment," *Language@Internet*, 8, article 7, <http://www.languageatinternet.org/articles/2011/Naper> (last accessed July 17, 2013).

Negretti, R. (1999), "Web-based activities and SLA: A conversation analysis research approach," *Language Learning and Technology*, 3 (1), 75–87.

Nunan, D. (2004), *Task-Based Language Teaching*, Cambridge: Cambridge University Press.

O'Brien, M. G., and R. M. Levy (2008), "Exploration through virtual reality: Encounters with the target culture," *The Canadian Modern Language Review*, 64 (4), 663–91.

O'Conaill, B., S. Whittaker, and S. Wilbur (1993), "Conversations Over Video Conferences: An

Evaluation of the Spoken Aspects of Video-Mediated Communication," *Human–Computer Interaction*, 8, 389–428.

O'Dowd, R. (2003), "Understanding the 'other side': Intercultural learning in a Spanish–English e-mail exchange," *Language Learning and Technology*, 7 (2), 118–44.

O'Dowd, R. (2005), "Negotiating sociocultural and institutional contexts: The case of Spanish–American telecollaboration," *Language and Intercultural Communication*, 5 (1), 40–56.

O'Dowd, R. (ed.) (2007), *Online Intercultural Exchange: An Introduction for Foreign Language Teachers*, Clevedon: Multilingual Matters.

Otto, F. (1980), "Computer-assisted instruction (CAI) in language teaching and learning," *Annual Review of Applied Linguistics*, 1 (1), 58–69.

Pankoke-Babatz, U., and P. Jeffrey (2002), "Documented norms and conventions on the Internet," *International Journal of Human–Computer Interaction*, 14 (2), 219–35.

Panyametheekul, S., and S. C. Herring (2003), "Gender and turn allocation in a Thai chat room," *Journal of Computer-Mediated Communication*, 9 (1), <http://onlinelibrary.wiley.com/doi/10.1111/j.1083–6101.2003.tb00362.x/full> (last accessed July 17, 2013).

Paolillo, J. C. (2011), "'Conversational' codeswitching on usenet and Internet relay chat," *Language@Internet*, 8, article 3, <http://www.languageatinternet.org/articles/2011/Paolillo> (last accessed July 17, 2013).

Papper, R. A., M. E. Holmes, and M. N. Popovich (2004), "Middletown media studies: Media multitasking and how much people really use the media," *The International Digital Media and Arts Association Journal*, 1, 9–50.

Parker, D., and M. Song (2006), "New ethnicities online: Reflexive racialisation and the internet," *The Sociological Review*, 54 (3), 575–94.

Parsons, T. (1937), *The Structure of Social Action*, New York: The Free Press.

Payne, J. S., and B. M. Ross (2005), "Synchronous CMC, working memory, and L2 oral proficiency development," *Language Learning and Technology*, 9 (3), 35–54.

Payne, J. S., and P. J. Whitney (2002), Developing L2 oral proficiency through synchronous CMC: Output, working memory, and interlanguage development," *CALICO Journal*, 20 (1), 7–32.

Peterson, M. (2006), "Learner interaction management in an avatar and chat-based virtual world," *Computer Assisted Language Learning*, 19 (1), 79–103.

Peterson, M. (2009), "Learner interaction in synchronous CMC: A sociocultural perspective," *Computer Assisted Language Learning*, 22 (4), 303–21.

Pomerantz, A. (1978), "Compliment responses: Notes on the cooperation of multiple constraints," in J. N. Schenkein (ed.), *Studies in the Organisation of Conversational Interaction*, New York: Academic Press, pp. 79–112.

Postmes, T., R. Spears, and M. Lea (1998), "Breaching or building social boundaries? SIDE-effects of computer-mediated communication," *Communication Research*, 25, 689–715.

Prodromou, L. (2007), "Is ELF a variety of English?: A critical discussion of 'English as a lingua franca' (ELF) as both a novel phenomenon and in relation to ELT methodology," *English Today*, 23 (2), 47–53.

Provine, R. R., R. J. Spencer, and D. L. Mandell (2007), "Emotional expression online: Emoticons punctuate website text messages," *Journal of Language and Social Psychology*, 26 (3), 299–307.

Radicati Group (2012), *Email Statistics Report, 2012–2016*, <http://www.radicati.com> (last accessed July 17, 2013).

Randall, N. (2002), *Lingo Online: A Report on the Language of the Keyboard Generation*, MSN. CA, <http://www.arts.uwaterloo.ca/~nrandall/lingo-online.htm> (last accessed July 17, 2013).

Rellstab, D. H. (2007), "Staging gender online: Gender plays in Swiss internet relay chats," *Discourse and Society*, 18 (6), 765–87.

Richards, J. C., and T. S. Rodgers (2001), *Approaches and Methods in Language Teaching*, Cambridge: Cambridge University Press.

Richards, K., and P. Seedhouse (eds.) (2008), *Applying Conversation Analysis*, New York: Palgrave Macmillan.

Rintel, S. (2013), "Video calling in long-distance relationships: The opportunistic use of audio/video distortions as a relational resource," *The Electronic Journal of Communication/La Revue Electronic de Communication (EJC/REC)*, 22 (1),

Rintel, S., and J. Pittman (1997), "Strangers in a strange land: Interaction management on internet relay chat," *Human Communication Research*, 23 (4), 507–34.

Risager, K. (2005), "Languaculture as a key concept in language and culture teaching," in B. Preisler, A. Fabricius, H. Haberland, S. Kjaerbeck, and K. Risager (eds.), *The Consequences of Mobility*, Roskilde: Roskilde University, Department of Language and Culture, pp. 185–96.

Robinson, P. (2001), "Task complexity, task difficulty, and task production: Exploring interactions in a componential framework," *Applied Linguistics*, 22 (1), 27–57.

Robinson, P. (2005), "Cognitive complexity and task sequencing: Studies in a componential framework for second language task design," *IRAL*, 43, 1–32.

Rodenstein, R., and J. S. Donath (2000), "Talking in Circles: Designing a Spatially-Grounded Audioconferencing Environment," *Proceedings of CHI 2000*, Amsterdam: ACM Press, pp. 81–8.

Rosell-Aguilar, F. (2005), "Task design for audiographic conferencing: promoting beginner oral interaction in distance language learning," *Computer-Assisted Language Learning*, 18 (5), 417–42.

Rosen, L. D. (2010), *Rewired: Understanding the I-Generation and the Way They Learn*, New York: Palgrave Macmillan.

Rosenberg, J. (2010), "Social sharing 2.0: The rise of real-time," eComm 2010, San Francisco, April 19–21.

Ross, K. W. (2003), "Asynchronous voice: A personal account," *Visions and Views*, Washington, DC: IEEE Computer Society.

Sacks, H. (1995), *Lectures on Conversation*, Oxford: Blackwell Publishing.

Sacks, H., E. A. Schegloff, and G. Jefferson (1974), "A simplest systematics for the organization of turn-taking for conversation," *Language*, 50, 696–735.

Satar, H. M., and N. Özdener (2008), "The effects of synchronous CMC on speaking proficiency and anxiety: Text versus voice chat," *The Modern Language Journal*, 92, 595–613.

Sauro, S. (2004), "Cyberdiscursive tug-of-war: Learner repositioning in a multimodal CMC environment," *Working Papers in Educational Linguistics*, 19 (2), 55–72.

Sauro, S., and B. Smith (2010), "Investigating L2 performance in text chat," *Applied Linguistics*, 31 (4), 554–77.

Schegloff, E. A. (1979), "Identification and recognition in telephone conversation openings," in G. Psathas (ed.), *Everyday Language: Studies in Ethnomethodology*, New York: Irvington Publishers, pp. 23–78.

Schegloff, E. A. (1986), "The routine as achievement," *Human Studies*, 9, 111–51.

Schegloff, E. A. (1991), "Reflections on talk and social structure," in D. Boden and D. Zimmerman (eds.), *Talk and Social Structure*, Cambridge: Polity Press, pp. 44–70.

Schegloff, E. A. (2000), "Overlapping talk and the organization of turn-taking for conversation," *Language in Society*, 29, 1–63.

Schegloff, E. A. (2007), *Sequence Organization in Interaction: A Primer in Conversation Analysis*, Cambridge: Cambridge University Press.

Schiffrin, D., D. Tannen, and H. E. Hamilton (eds.) (2003), *The Handbook of Discourse Analysis*, Oxford: Blackwell Publishing.

Schmandt, C., J. Kim, K. Lee, G. Vallejo, and M. Ackerman (2002), "Mediated voice communication via mobile IP," *Proceedings of UIST 2002*, Paris: ACM Press, pp. 141–50.

Schönfeldt, J., and A. Golato (2003), "Repair in chats: A conversation analytic approach," *Research on Language and Social Interaction*, 36 (3), 241–84.

Searle, J. R. (1986), "Introductory essay: Notes on conversation," in D. Ellis and W. Donohue (eds.), *Contemporary Issues in Language and Discourse Processes*, Hillsdale, NJ: Lawrence Erlbaum Associates, pp. 7–19.

Searle, J. R., H. Parret, and J. Verschueren (1992), *(On) Searle on Conversation*, Amsterdam: John Benjamins.

Seedhouse, P. (2004), *The Interactional Architecture of the Language Classroom: A Conversation Analysis Perspective*, Malden, MA: Blackwell.

Seedhouse, P. (2005), "'Task' as research construct," *Language Learning*, 55 (3), 533–70.

Seedhouse, P. (2010), "The relationship between pedagogical focus and interaction in L2 lessons," in E. Macaro (ed.), *The Continuum Companion to Second Language Acquisition*, London: Continuum, pp. 220–46.

Seidlhofer, B. (2001), "Closing the conceptual gap: The case for a description of English as a lingua franca," *International Journal of Applied Linguistics*, 11 (2), 133–58.

Seidlhofer, B. (2004), "Research perspectives on teaching English as a lingua franca," *Annual Review of Applied Linguistics*, 24, 209–39.

Seidlhofer, B. (2011), *Understanding English as a Lingua Franca*, Oxford: Oxford University Press.

Sellen, A. J. (1995), "Remote conversations: The effects of mediating talk with technology," *Human–Computer Interaction*, 10, 401–44.

Selting, M. (2000), "The construction of units in conversational talk," *Language in Society*, 29 (4), 477–517.

Siebenhaar, B. (2006), "Code choice and code-switching in Swiss-German internet relay chat rooms," *Journal of Sociolinguistics*, 10 (4), 481–506.

Sierpe, E. (2005), "Gender distinctiveness, communicative competence, and the problem of gender judgments in computer-mediated communication," *Computers in Human Behavior*, 21, 127–45.

Simpson, J. (2005), "Conversational floors in synchronous text-based CMC discourse," *Discourse Studies*, 7 (3), 337–61.

Sindoni, M. G. (2011) "Online conversations: A sociolinguistic investigation into young adults' use of videochats," *Classroom Discourse*, 2 (2), 219–35.

Singer, A., D. Hindus, L. Stifelman, and S. White (1999), "Tangible progress: Less is more in Somewire audio spaces," *Proceedings of CHI 1999*, Pittsburgh: ACM Press, pp. 104–12.

Skehan, P. (2003), "Task-based instruction," *Language Teaching*, 36, 1–14.

Skype Limited (2012), <http://www.skype.com/> (last accessed July 17, 2013).

Smith, B. (2003), "Computer-mediated negotiated interaction: An expanded model," *The Modern Language Journal*, 87 (1), 38–57.

Smith, B. (2008), "Methodological hurdles in capturing CMC data: The case of the missing self-repair," *Language Learning and Technology*, 12 (1), 85–103.

Smith, B., M. J. Alvarez-Torres, and Y. Zhao (2003), "Features of CMC technologies and their impact on language learners' online interaction," *Computers in Human Behavior*, 19, 703–29.

Smith, B., and G. J. Gorsuch (2004), "Synchronous computer mediated communication captured by usability lab technologies: new interpretations," *System*, 32, 553–75.

Stickler, U., and M. Hauck (eds.) (2006), Special issue: "What does it take to teach online? Towards a pedagogy for online language teaching and learning," *CALICO Journal*, 23 (3), 463–642.

Stockwell, G., and M. Levy (2001), "Sustainability of e-mail interactions between native speakers and nonnative speakers," *Computer Assisted Language Learning*, 14 (5), 419–42.

Stokoe, E. H., and J. Smithson (2001), "Making gender relevant: Conversation analysis and gender categories in interaction," *Discourse and Society*, 12 (2), 217–44.

Stommel, W. (2008), "Conversation analysis and community of practice as approaches to studying online community," *Language@Internet*, 5, article 5, <http://www.languageatinternet.org/articles/2008/1537> (last accessed July 17, 2013).

Swain, M. (1993), "The output hypothesis: Just speaking and writing aren't enough," *The Canadian Modern Language Review*, 50, 158–64.

Sykes, J. M. (2005), "Synchronous CMC and pragmatic development: Effects of oral and written chat," *CALICO Journal*, 22 (3), 399–431.

Szymanski, M. H., E. Vinkhuyzen, P. M. Aoki, and A. Woodruff (2006), "Organizing a remote state of incipient talk: Push-to-talk mobile radio interaction," *Language in Society*, 35, 393–418.

Taran, P. A., and E. Geronimi (2003), *Globalization, Labor and Migration: Protection is Paramount*, Geneva: International Labour Organization.

ten Have, P. (2007), *Doing Conversation Analysis: A Practical Guide*, London: Sage.

Thorne, S. L., and R. W. Black (2007), "Language and literacy development in computer-mediated contexts and communities," *Annual Review of Applied Linguistics*, 27, 133–60.

Thurlow, C., L. Lengel, and A. Tomic (2004), *Computer-Mediated Communication: Social Interaction and the Internet*, London: Sage.

Tillema, T., M. Dijst, and T. Schwanen (2010), "Face-to-face and electronic communications in maintaining social networks: The influence of geographical and relational distance and of information content," *New Media and Society*, 12 (6), 965–83.

Toyoda, E., and R. Harrison (2002), "Categorization of text chat communication between learners and native speakers of Japanese," *Language Learning and Technology*, 6 (1), 82–99.

Trinder, L., A. Firth, and C. J. Jenks (2010), "So presumably things have moved on since then? The interactional management of risk allegations in child contact dispute resolution," *International Journal of Law, Policy and the Family*, 24 (1), 29–53.

Tudini, V. (2007), "Negotiation and intercultural learning in Italian native speaker chat rooms," *The Modern Language Journal*, 91 (4), 577–601.

Vetter, A., and T. Chanier (2006), "Supporting oral production for professional purposes in synchronous communication with heterogeneous learners," *ReCALL*, 18 (1), 5–23.

Vinagre, M., and B. Munoz (2011), "Computer-mediated corrective feedback and language accuracy in telecollaborative exchanges," *Language Learning and Technology*, 15 (1), 72–103.

Virkkula, T., and T. Nikula (2010), "Identity construction in ELF contexts: a case study of Finnish engineering students working in Germany," *International Journal of Applied Linguistics*, 20 (2), 251–73.

Volle, L. M. (2005), "Analyzing oral skills in voice e-mail and online interviews," *Language Learning and Technology*, 9 (3), 146–63.

Wadley, G., M. Gibbs, and P. Benda (2007), "Speaking in character: Using voice-over-IP to communicate within MMORPGs," *Proceedings of the Fourth Australasian Conference on Interactive Entertainment*, Melbourne, Australia.

Walther, J. B. (1997), "Group and interpersonal effects in international computer-mediated collaboration," *Human Communication Research*, 23 (3), 342–69.

Wang, S., and C. Vasquez (2012), "Web 2.0 and second language learning: What does the research tell us?" *CALICO Journal*, 29 (3), 412–30.

Wang, Y. (2004), "Supporting synchronous distance language learning with desktop videoconferencing," *Language Learning and Technology*, 8 (3), 90–121.

Wang, Y. (2006), "Negotiation of meaning in desktop videoconferencing-supported distance language learning," *ReCALL*, 18 (1), 122–46.

Wang, Y., N. Chen, and M. Levy (2010), "Teacher training in a synchronous cyber face-to-face classroom: characterizing and supporting the online teachers' learning process," *Computer Assisted Language Learning*, 23 (4), 277–93.

Ware, P. D., and C. Kramsch (2005), "Toward an intercultural stance: Teaching German and English through telecollaboration," *The Modern Language Journal*, 89 (2), 190–205.

Weisz, J. D., and S. Kiesler (2008), "How text and audio chat change the online video experience," *Proceedings of uxTV 2008*, Silicon Valley, CA: ACM Press, pp. 9–18.

Wilkins, H. (1991), "Computer talk: Long-distance conversations by computer," *Written Communication*, 8 (1), 56–78.

Williams, L., and R. A. van Compernolle (2009), "On versus tu and vous: Pronouns with indefinite reference in synchronous electronic French discourse," *Language Sciences*, 31, 409–27.

Wong, J. (2002), "'Applying' conversation analysis in applied linguistics: Evaluating dialogue in English as a second language textbooks," *International Review of Applied Linguistics*, 40, 37–60.

Wong, J. (2009), "'Very good' as a teacher response," *ELT Journal*, 63 (3), 195–203.

Woodruff, A., and P. M. Aoki (2004), "Push-to-talk social talk," *Computer Supported Cooperative Work*, 13, 409–41.

Wooffitt, R. (2005), *Conversation Analysis and Discourse Analysis: A Comparative and Critical Introduction*, London: Sage.

Wright, N., and M. Whitehead (1998), "Video-conferencing and GCSE oral practice," *Language Learning Journal*, 18, 47–9.

Yamada, M., and K. Akahori (2007), "Social presence in synchronous CMC-based language learning: How does it affect the productive performance and consciousness of learning objectives?" *Computer Assisted Language Learning*, 20, (1), 37–65.

Yang, Y. C., and L. Chang (2008), "No improvement—Reflections and suggestions on the use of Skype to enhance college students' oral English proficiency," *British Journal of Educational Technology*, 39, 721–5.

Yang, Y. F. (2011), "Learning interpretations of shared space in multilateral English blogging," *Language Learning and Technology*, 15 (1), 122–46.

Yanguas, I. (2010), "Oral computer-mediated interaction between L2 learners: It's about time!" *Language Learning and Technology*, 14 (3), 72–93.

Yanguas, I. (2012), "Task-based oral computer-mediated communication and L2 vocabulary acquisition," *CALICO Journal*, 29 (3), 507–31.

Yi, Y. (2009), "Adolescent literacy and identity construction among 1.5 generation students: From a transnational perspective," *Journal of Asian Pacific Communication*, 19 (1), 100–29.

Young, R. F. (2008), *Language and Interaction: An Advanced Resource Book*, New York: Routledge.

Young, R. F. and Miller, E. R. (2004), "Learning as changing participation: Discourse roles in ESL writing conferences," *The Modern Language Journal*, 88 (4), 519–35.

Zhou, L., J. K. Burgoon, D. Zhang, and J. F. Numamaker (2004), "Language dominance in interpersonal deception in computer-mediated communication," *Computers in Human Behavior*, 20, 381–402.

# INDEX

acquisition, 3, 20, 30, 32, 124, 155
affordances, 11, 18, 22–3, 29, 32, 42, 45, 60,
  63, 67, 74, 86, 106, 110, 126, 128, 131,
  134, 136, 142, 147, 151–2, 156
allocation, 3, 52, 59–60, 63, 74, 78, 82, 89–93,
  111, 130, 136
asynchronous, 16, 20, 25, 34–8, 78, 95–6, 160
audibility, 3, 96, 114–19, 156
audio, 13, 29, 33–4, 36–40, 47, 65, 75, 96,
  101, 125, 159

behavior, 11, 89, 136, 138, 159

capturing, 9, 42–44, 159
chat, 1–2, 7–18, 20, 22–6, 28, 30–3, 36–48,
  51–2, 54, 56, 58, 60–74, 76–119, 123–4,
  126–30, 132, 134, 137–40, 142–8,
  150–2, 154–6, 158–60
CMC, 1–3, 9–10, 12–14, 17–18, 20–9, 32–7,
  39, 42–7, 51–3, 55–6, 58–60, 64, 73–4,
  76–96, 100–1, 106, 110, 118, 123–8,
  131–8, 140, 142, 145–6, 151
CMSI, 2–3, 16, 18–22, 24–37, 39–47, 51–111,
  113–15, 117–19, 124–36, 138, 140, 142,
  145–8, 151–60
communities, 13, 26, 32–3, 136–9, 146–7,
  152, 155
competencies, 123–4, 126–32, 134–5, 156
computer, 1, 12–16, 18–20, 23, 25, 31, 36, 38,
  42, 44, 71, 73, 79, 88–9, 101–2, 106, 109,
  119, 141, 155; *see also* computers
computers, 14, 16–19, 32, 34, 36, 44, 66, 123,
  154, 157; *see also* computer
constraints, 11, 18, 22–3, 29, 32, 42, 45, 60,
  63, 67, 74, 83, 110, 126, 128, 131, 134,
  136, 142, 147
context, 8, 11, 22, 27, 35, 52, 79, 95–6,
  108–10, 126–7, 129–30, 142, 150, 157,
  160
conventions, 2–3, 12, 22, 24, 34, 43, 45–7,
  106, 110, 137–40, 142, 145–6, 152, 156
Crystal, 17, 24, 26, 36, 42, 96
culture, 2–3, 7, 18–19, 25–8, 32, 136–9, 155

electronic, 1, 14, 16, 36, 65–7, 74, 101–4, 109,
  119, 126, 159
ELF, 137–40, 145–8, 151–3
English, 1, 10, 24, 27–8, 40, 47, 103, 117,
  137–40, 146–52, 156
ethics, 132, 151, 157–8
experimental, 31–3, 87, 154

floors, 84, 86, 88, 90, 93, 98, 101, 133–4, 156
framework, 23, 30

Garcia, 23, 52, 78, 80, 89, 91, 95
gender, 7, 9, 19, 25, 28, 136
greeting, 48, 53–4, 62, 64–7, 69–70, 74, 84,
  90, 99–100, 102–5, 107–9, 111–16,
  118–19, 144–5, 156

Hampel, 20, 30, 123
HCI, 31–2
Herring, 1, 10, 14, 17, 23–8, 34, 36, 42, 52,
  56, 79, 81–3, 86, 89, 95–6, 127, 132, 136,
  142, 159
Hutchby, 7–9, 11–13, 26, 32–3, 64, 66–7,
  154

identification, 3, 24, 51, 66–74, 77, 130, 140,
  142–6, 148
identities, 3, 9, 12, 25–8, 32–3, 43, 136–8,
  146–52, 155; *see also* identity
identity, 7, 12, 19, 34, 139–40, 147–52, 156;
  *see also* identities
Internet, 13–18, 22, 24, 36–7, 44, 123, 136–7,
  157

learners, 21–2, 27, 124, 126–7, 129, 137–8,
  146, 148, 151–2, 155–6
learning, 2–3, 7, 10, 12–13, 18–22, 25–30,
  32–3, 47–8, 123–7, 129–31, 133–5,
  137–8, 148, 155, 159
lingua franca, 2–3, 13, 26, 137–40, 145–8,
  150–2, 155–6, 159
linguistics, 3, 17–19, 21, 23, 25, 27, 29, 31–3,
  125, 145–6, 152–3, 156, 158

media, 2, 17, 20, 22, 24, 26, 32, 35–6, 38, 43, 125, 152, 159
mediated, 1, 14, 16, 20, 24, 36, 119
methodological, 7–11, 20–1, 25, 28–9, 43–5, 55, 77, 96, 123–5, 157, 159
modes, 24, 28, 43, 56, 131, 133, 135, 146, 155, 159
multiparty, 14, 18, 37, 40, 56, 67, 76–7, 81, 93, 96, 100, 110, 127, 132–3, 155
multitasking, 44, 159

noise, 3, 44, 61, 72, 97–100, 107, 114
norms, 3, 7, 17, 28, 95, 106, 110, 123, 137–40, 142, 145–6, 150, 152, 156

openings, 13, 62, 64, 67–9, 73–4, 118
overlap, 26, 29, 56–7, 59–61, 83–8, 92–3, 114, 127–8, 133, 156; see also overlapping
overlapping, 2–3, 11, 18, 23–4, 28, 32, 45–6, 52, 55–9, 61, 74, 78, 82–90, 93, 106, 132–3, 136, 142, 155–6; see also overlap

pause, 45–6, 53, 56–60, 62, 84, 87, 90–2, 97–9, 106–11, 129, 144, 156; see also pauses
pauses, 3, 13, 29–30, 46, 56, 59, 74, 80, 84, 96, 100–1, 106–10, 119, 128–30, 132, 135, 155–6; see also pause
pedagogical, 9, 17–22, 26–30, 51, 77, 123–7, 130–5, 137–8, 147, 150, 156
physical, 3, 11, 13, 21, 33, 43–4, 52, 56, 58–9, 62–4, 66–7, 74, 76, 83, 95–6, 99, 101, 105–6, 109, 119, 127, 129–30, 133, 142, 151, 158–9
practice, 9, 21, 32, 47–8, 51, 60–1, 70, 73, 84, 102, 123, 137, 143–5, 147–8
pragmatic, 30, 123–4, 129, 139, 145–6
proficiency, 21, 30, 106, 118, 124–5, 132–3, 147–52, 156

qualitative, 29–30, 125–6, 134–5, 154, 156

resources, 9, 25, 45, 59, 63–4, 66–7, 71–4, 83, 86, 106, 110, 118, 124, 126–7, 129–30, 156

Sacks, 13, 23, 52, 56, 59–60, 62, 89
Schegloff, 7–9, 11–12, 56, 58–9, 64, 67–8, 83, 95, 109, 116, 154
sequence, 12, 57–8, 61, 64, 73, 95, 97–8, 114–16
sequential, 1, 9, 23, 29, 51–3, 59, 64, 66–8, 70, 74, 81, 89–90, 93, 95, 98–100, 106–7, 109, 114–15, 118–19, 126, 128–9, 132, 154–6
Simpson, 1, 23, 84, 86, 93, 95
Skype, 37–40, 42–3, 47, 118, 151–2, 155
Skypecast, 37, 39–42, 45, 53–8, 60–3, 65–6, 68–72, 80, 83, 85, 90–2, 98–9, 102–3, 105, 107–8, 111–13, 115–17, 128–9, 140–1, 143–4, 147, 149–50; see also Skypecasts
Skypecasts, 37, 39–40, 42, 45, 97; see also Skypecast
SLA, 20–1, 124–5, 135
sociality, 2–3, 7, 18–19, 25–6, 28, 32, 136–8, 155
sociolinguistics, 25–6
space, 36, 44, 51, 66, 77–8, 86–90, 93, 99, 104, 114, 133–4, 154, 156, 158–9; see also spaces
spaces, 13, 44, 127, 136, 146, 158; see also space
speakership, 42, 45, 53, 55–6, 58–9, 74, 79, 82–4, 90, 101–2, 106, 127–8, 132–3, 145, 157
structures, 7, 9, 11, 14, 23, 52, 157
students, 9, 21, 27–8, 30, 48, 110, 123–33, 146, 148
summons, 3, 64–8, 73–4, 77, 101, 105, 109, 119

talking, 40, 42, 51, 53, 55–7, 59, 61, 63, 65, 67–9, 71–3, 75–7, 79, 81, 83, 85–7, 89–91, 93, 96, 98–103, 106–7, 113, 115–16, 118, 129–30, 134, 141–2, 145, 147, 156
task, 3, 8–9, 12, 20–1, 25, 30, 43, 98, 109, 125, 130–2, 134–5, 156
technological, 2, 11–12, 17–19, 22–3, 29, 34, 36, 42, 44–5, 67, 74, 79, 86–7, 119, 130–1, 134, 136, 147
telephone, 12–13, 32–3, 36–8, 42, 45, 52, 60, 63–5, 67–8, 71, 73–5, 78, 126, 154
transcribing, 8–9, 12, 22, 25, 43–5, 157–9
turns, 7, 23, 52–55, 58–61, 63, 65–7, 70, 73–4, 77–9, 81–93, 95–6, 110–11, 118, 127–33, 142, 144, 156
typing, 77, 82–9, 91, 94, 96–100, 110, 146

units, 21–2, 52–5, 80–2, 93, 133, 135, 156
utterances, 3, 7, 11, 24, 34, 42–3, 45–7, 52, 55–9, 62, 74, 78–9, 82–4, 86–9, 93, 96, 106, 127, 132, 142, 155–6

verbal, 24, 28, 36, 66–7, 69, 71, 73, 96, 99, 101–6, 114, 128, 143
video, 13, 16, 28–9, 32, 34, 36–9, 88, 91, 106, 109, 125, 157, 159
voice, 1, 9, 11, 13, 18, 22, 29, 35–7, 43, 46, 48, 67, 71, 85, 87, 105, 110, 117–18, 128, 142, 150–1, 154–5
VoIP, 37–9, 44

writing, 24, 29–30, 36, 40, 82, 94, 155

Yanguas, 30, 76, 93, 118, 124–5, 132